DATE DUE

Aggressivity, Narcissism, and Self-Destructiveness in the Psychotherapeutic Relationship

Aggressivity, Narcissism, and Self-Destructiveness in the Psychotherapeutic Relationship

New Developments in the Psychopathology and Psychotherapy of Severe Personality Disorders

Otto F. Kernberg, M.D.

Yale University Press

New Haven and London

Set in Adobe Garamond type by The Composing Room of Michigan, Inc. Printed in the United States of America.

ISBN: 0-300-10180-5

A catalogue record for this book is available from the Library of Congress and the British Library.

The paper in this book meets the guidelines for permanence and durability of the Committee on Production Guidelines for Book Longevity of the Council on Library Resources.

10 9 8 7 6 5 4 3 2 1

To my children: Martin, Karen, and Adine

Contents

Preface

Significant advances have taken place in our present-day understanding of the etiology, psychopathology, and treatment of patients with severe personality disorders. The prevalence of severe personality disorders and their complications—disturbances in the capacity for work and intimate relationships, antisocial behvior, drug and alcohol dependency, and in particular suicidal and parasuicidal behavior—is a challenging concern in the treatment of emotional disorders. The etiology of personality disorders involves genetic and constitutional factors, especially the predisposition to the activation of excessive negative affect and affect dysregulation, expressed in temperamental disposition. To these causes have to be added the important influence of early attachment and its pathology, and the influence of psychic trauma—in particular, physical and sexual abuse, chronic family disorganization, and abandonment. The intricate mechanisms that link genetic and constitutional disposition with psychosocial environmental factors in the development of pathological behavior patterns that characterize personality disorders still are under investigation. Alternative theoretical approaches have proposed various mechanisms that link the influence of temperamental disposition with environmental influences.

The internalization of emotional relations with significant others—the central subject of psychoanalytic object relations theory—has emerged as one general frame that explains the linkage between the neurobiology of affects and the consolidation of the personality structure. This book, in fact, complements my earlier work in applying psychoanalytic object relations theory to the analysis of the relation between excessive negative affect—in particular, aggressive affect—and affective dysregulation related to inadequate cognitive control, on one hand, and the development of the syndrome of identity diffusion, on the other. I see the latter as a result of a pathological fixation at an early level of development in which the infant mind radically separates the memory traces of blissful and painful experiences. Identity diffusion, in turn, underlies a proposed classification of personality disorders that combines categorical differences and dimensional continuities and is relevant for the psychodynamic psychotherapy of these conditions.

This book starts out with a proposal for a general classification of personality disorders that includes such categorical and dimensional criteria. It then proceeds to analyze the vicissitudes of negative affect development, from the normal affect of rage to its complex characterological consequences in the psychopathology of hatred and envy and the characterological transformations of these emotions into chronic self-destructive behavior.

Probably up to one-third of all patients with severe personality disorder present significant narcissistic features, a specific combination of defensive mechanisms and pathological relations to self and significant others that, paradoxically, improves these patients' surface functioning at the cost of reducing their capacity for intimate and gratifying relationships with others and of an impoverishment of their experience of self. The relation of narcissistic conditions to the development of antisocial behavior, the diagnostic assessment of the severity and treatability of these conditions, and specific techniques in their treatment are explored and clinicallly illustrated. A particularly puzzling pathology in the sexual domain, perversion, or paraphilia, is then examined in the context of the analysis of the underlying personality disorders of these patients.

On the basis of the experience accumulated in twenty-five years' worth of collaborative work by a group of psychoanalysts and psychotherapists at the Personality Disorders Institute at the Weill Cornell Medical College, I start the second part of this volume with a clarification of the relation between psychoanalytic theory, on one hand, and the modalities derived from it—standard psycho-analysis, psychoanalytic psychotherapy, and supportive psychotherapy—on the other. In the process I specify their differential characteristics and the indications and contraindications for these treatments. A specific transference-focused psy-chotherapy (TFP) is proposed for a majority of patients with severe personality disorders, and this treatment is illustrated in its application to borderline, narcis-sistic, paranoid, and antisocial psychopathology, with a sharp focus on transfer-ence and countertransference developments in those treatments.

This overview is followed by exploration of particular complications in the treatment of severe personality disorders, beginning with the treatment of pathological narcissism with psychoanalysis proper and psychoanalytic psy-chotherapy. The diagnosis and psychotherapeutic management of acute and chronic countertransference reactions are then applied to the management of complications in the treatment situation. The last three chapters deal with the risk of suicide and severe parasuicidal behavior, the comorbidity with severe eating disorders, and the management of affect storms.

Alternative approaches to treatment of severe personality disorders, in par-ticular, psychopharmacological, cognitive-behavioral, and psychodynamically derived supportive psychotherapies, are currently under investigation. These approaches aim to modify therapeutically the direct manifestations of patho-logical character patterns and affect dysregulation of these patients, while the systematic elaboration and resolution of transference developments character-istic of psychoanalysis and psychoanalytic psychotherapy as described in this volume aim at modifying the underlying personality rather than directly oper-ating on specific symptoms. Preliminary evidence shows that all these treat-ments have indications and contraindications, successes and limitations. What inspires this book is a basic conviction that, given that we are able to bring about fundamental personality change in selected patients with transference-focused psychotherapy, the ongoing exploration of the treatment strategy de-veloped in this volume is a crucial task. The present effort to combine theoret-ical analysis and psychopathological studies with psychotherapeutic techniques in the context of the vicissitudes of treatment developments reflects my convic-tion that basic research, clinical research, and clinical observations in intense, long-term therapeutic encounters mutually deepen our knowledge and our ca-pacity to help our patients.

I am grateful to many colleagues and friends who, in our work together and in our discussions of all of these issues, helped me clarify my own thoughts and gain new understanding regarding many subjects touched on in this book. They include, in the United States, Doctors Martin Bergmann, Harold Blum, William Grossman, Paulina Kernberg, Robert Michels, Gertrude Ticho, Robert Tyson, and Robert Wallerstein. I am deeply grateful to Doctor André Green and the Borderline Research Group of the International Psychoanalytic Association, which he directs and of which I am a member, and to Doctors Peter Fonagy, Anne Marie Sandler, and the late Joseph Sandler in Great Britain. In France, in addition to the profound influence on my work exerted by André Green, I have been helped by discussions with Doctors Jeanine Chasseguet-Smirgel, Alain Gibeault, Jean Laplanche, Joyce McDougall, and Daniel Widlöcher. In Germany, I have benefited from stimulating interchange with Doctors Peter Buchheim, Horst Kaechele, Rainer Krause, and Ernst Lurssen.

I have already referred to the exciting stimulation I have received from colleagues at the Personality Disorders Institute at Cornell University, which I direct. I warmly thank the senior members of this institute, in particular, Doctors Ann Applebaum, who for many years has patiently edited my writings, including this book, Eve Caligor, Diana Diamond, Pamela Foelsh, James Hall, Catherine Haran, Paulina Kernberg, Sonia Kulchycky, Kenneth Levy, Armond Loranger, Michael Stone, and Frank Yeomans. In recent years, our collaboration with Doctors Mark Lenzenweger, Michael Posner, and David Silbersweig has opened new vistas to the relation between personality disorders and their genetic features, the influence of neurocognitive structures on affect control, and the exciting possibilities of magnetic imaging as a biological parameter for the study of brain functioning in borderline patients.

Above all, I express my profound gratitude to Doctor John Clarkin, co-director of the Personality Disorders Institute and the brain behind the transformation of our theoretical and clinical hypotheses into workable research designs, and to the Borderline Personality Disorders Research Foundation and its founder, Doctor Marco Stoffel, whose personal enthusiasm and confidence in our work have been instrumental in securing the foundation's enormous support of the institute, permitting a significant expansion of our studies that otherwise would not have been possible. I also thank Doctor Jack Barchas, professor and chair of the Department of Psychiatry of the Weill Cornell Medical College, for his warm encouragement and support for our research enterprise. Finally, I thank heartily the secretarial staff of the Personality Disorders Institute: Joanne Ciallella, who patiently typed many versions of the chapters of this book, Rosetta Davis, who organized the growing manuscript and was willing to take on additional chores with a friendly smile, and, in particular, my personal secretary, Louise Taitt, who for many years has been effectively taking care of the enormous amount of work and the responsibility for decisionmaking in many areas and who, with unerring judgment, tactfully but with strong determination did whatever was necessary to protect my time. She deserves my heart-felt gratitude.

Part One **Psychopathology**

Chapter 1 A Psychoanalytic Theory of Personality Disorders

Why is it important to attempt to formulate a psychoanalytic view of the etiology, structure, and mutual relations of the personality disorders? First, because of recent advances in the psychoanalytic understanding of particular types of personality disorders, and second, because of persistent controversies in psychological and psychiatric research concerning such issues as (1) whether categorical or dimensional criteria should be used for classifying these disorders, (2) the relative influence of genetic and constitutional, psychodynamic, and psychosocial determinants, and, most important, (3) the relation between descriptive or surface behavior and underlying biological and psychological structures.

An earlier version of this chapter was published in *Major Theories of Personality Disorders,* edited by John F. Clarkin and M. F. Lenzenweger. New York: Guilford Press, 1996.

CATEGORICAL VERSUS DIMENSIONAL MODELS

A major problem is the understanding of the psychopathology of these disorders—that is, how the various behavioral characteristics of any particular personality disorder (such as the borderline, the narcissistic, and the antisocial) relate to one another and to their predisposing and causative factors. Empirical researchers studying specific personality disorders have attempted to pinpoint the etiological factors but have repeatedly found that multiple factors appear to combine in the background of any particular disorder, without a clear answer as to how these factors relate to one another (Marziali 1992; Paris 1994a; Steinberg et al. 1994; Stone 1993a, 1993b).

Researchers using a dimensional model usually carry out complex factor analyses of a great number of behavioral traits in order to find a few overriding characteristics that, in combination, seem to apply to clinical descriptions of particular personality disorders (Benjamin 1992, 1993; Costa and Widiger 1994; Widiger and Frances 1994; Widiger et al. 1994). This approach links particular behaviors and lends itself to the establishment of a general theory in order to integrate the major dimensions arrived at by statistical analyses. So far, however, these dimensions seem to have been of little use for clinical purposes. (A notable exception may prove to be Benjamin's [1992, 1993] "structural analysis of social behavior," a model strongly influenced by contemporary psychoanalytic thinking.)

A currently popular dimensional model, the five-factor model, synthesizes numerous factor analyses into the proposal that neuroticism, extroversion, openness, agreeableness, and conscientiousness constitute basic factors that may describe all "officially" accepted personality disorders in DSM-IV (Costa and Widiger 1994; Widiger et al. 1994). But are these really fundamental determinants of the organization of the normal personality or even of the personality disorders? Factorial profiles developed for the various personality disorders on the basis of these five factors have a quality of unreality for the experienced clinician.

Researchers who maintain a categorical approach to personality disorders—usually clinical psychiatrists motivated to find specific disease entities—tend to study the clinically prevalent constellations of pathological personality traits, carry out empirical research regarding the validity and reliability of the corresponding clinical diagnoses, and attempt to achieve a clear differentiation among personality disorders, keeping in mind the clinical relevance of their approaches (Akhtar 1992; Stone 1993a). This approach, pursued in DSM-III and

DSM-IV, has helped to clarify—or at least to permit clinical psychiatrists to become better acquainted with—some frequently seen personality disorders. It has been plagued, however, by the high degree of comorbidity of the severe types of personality disorders and by the unfortunate politicization of decision-making, by committee, of which disorders to include and which to exclude in the official DSM system and under what labels (Jonas and Pope 1992; O. Kernberg 1992a; Oldham 1994). For this reason, a common personality disorder such as the hysterical personality has been excluded while the depressive-masochistic personality disorder, excluded from DSM-III, has reemerged as "depressive personality disorder" in the appendix of DSM-IV, shorn of the masochistic component previously "tolerated" in DSM-III-R under what was then the politically correct title of "self-defeating" personality disorder (O. Kernberg 1992a).

-)A major problem of both categorical and dimensional classification systems, in my view, has been the tendency to anchor empirical research too closely to surface behavior, which may serve very different functions according to the underlying personality structures. For example, what is seen as social timidity, social phobia, or inhibition and may contribute to a diagnosis of either a schizoid or an avoidant personality may in fact reflect the cautiousness of a deeply paranoid individual, the fear of exposure of a narcissistically grandiose individual, or a reaction formation against exhibitionistic tendencies in a hysterical individual. A related problem is that large-scale research efforts necessarily depend on standardized inquiries or questionnaires that tend to elicit responses reflecting, in part, the social values of particular personality traits. For example, excessive conscientiousness has a more desirable value than irresponsibility, generosity a higher value than envy, and so on. Our very diagnostic instruments need much more elaboration and may even have contributed to some of our problems.

It is far from my intention to suggest that a psychoanalytic exploration will resolve all existing problems. I cannot at this point present a satisfactory integrated psychoanalytic model of classification of personality disorders. For psychoanalytically oriented research has also been limited by the difficulty of assessing abnormal personality traits outside the clinical situation, the enormous difficulties inherent in carrying out research on the psychoanalytic situation itself, and the controversies that have developed within contemporary psychoanalysis regarding treatment approaches to some personality disorders—for example, the borderline and narcissistic personalities.

A psychoanalytic study of patients with personality disorders undergoing psychoanalytic treatment, however, allows us to observe(the relations between the patient's several pathological personality traits, between surface behavior and underlying psychic structure, between various constellations of pathological behavior patterns as they change in the course of treatment, and between motivation of behavior and psychic structure, as well as changes in the patient's behavior and shifts in dominant transference patterns.)In fact, the joint evaluation of a patient's motivation, intrapsychic structure, and therapeutic changes provides important information regarding the origins, functions, and mechanisms of these changes in patients with personality disorders.

In addition, the observation of infant-caregiver interactions from a psychoanalytic perspective, the study of the effects of early trauma on the development of psychological functioning, and efforts to link these observations with the study of early development from behavioral and biological perspectives should mutually enrich these fields. Perhaps more important, the psychoanalytic approach to personality disorders permits, I believe, the development of particular techniques to deal with the specific transferences of these disorders and to obtain significant characterological change as a consequence of shifts in transference patterns—a clinical observation that still needs to be grounded in empirical research. In this connection, some of the subtle aspects of the differential diagnosis of the personality disorders facilitated by a psychoanalytic approach permit us to establish prognostic indicators such as the differentiation between the narcissistic personality disorder, the malignant narcissism syndrome, and the antisocial personality proper (Bursten 1989; Hare 1986; P. Kernberg 1989; Stone 1990).

TEMPERAMENT, CHARACTER, AND THE
STRUCTURE OF THE NORMAL PERSONALITY

To begin, I shall refer to temperament and character as crucial aspects of personality. *Temperament* refers to the constitutionally given and largely genetically determined, inborn disposition to certain reactions to environmental stimuli, in particular, the intensity, rhythm, and thresholds of affective responses. I consider affective responses, especially under conditions of peak affect states, to be crucial determinants of the organization of the personality. Inborn thresholds for the activation of positive (pleasurable, rewarding) and negative (painful, aggressive) affects represent, I believe, the most important bridge between biological and psychological determinants of the personality (O. Kernberg 1994). Temperament also includes inborn dispositions to cognitive organization and to motor behavior such as the hormonal, and in particular, testosterone-derived differences in cognitive functions and aspects of gender role identity that differentiate male and female behavior patterns. Regarding the etiology of personality disorders, however, the affective aspects of temperament appear to be of fundamental importance.

Cloninger (Cloninger et al. 1993) related particular neurochemical systems to temperamental dispositions that he called "novelty seeking," "harm avoidance," "reward dependence," and "persistence." I question his direct translations of such dispositions into specific types of personality disorders in the DSM-IV classification system, however. Torgersen, on the basis of his twin studies of genetic and environmental influences on the development of personality disorders (1985, 1994), found genetic influences significant only for the schizotypal personality disorder; for practical purposes, they are significantly related to normal personality characteristics but have very little relation to specific personality disorders.

Another major component of personality, *character* refers to the dynamic organization of the behavior patterns that reflect the overall degree and level of organization of such patterns. Whereas academic psychology differentiates character and personality, the clinically relevant terms "character pathology," "character neurosis," and "neurotic character" refer to the same conditions (called personality trait and personality pattern disturbances in earlier DSM classifications and personality disorders in DSM-III and DSM-IV). From a psychoanalytic perspective, I propose that *character* be used to refer to the behavioral manifestations of ego identity: the subjective aspects of ego identity— that is, the integration of the self-concept and the concept of significant others—are the intrapsychic structures that determine the dynamic organization of character. Character also includes all the behavioral aspects of what in psychoanalytic terms are called ego functions and ego structures.

From a psychoanalytic viewpoint, the personality is determined by temperament and character; in addition, the superego value systems, the moral and ethical dimensions of the personality, and the integration of the various layers of the superego are important components of the total personality. Finally, the cognitive capacity of the individual, partly determined genetically but also culturally influenced, also constitutes an important part of the personality. Personality itself, then, may be considered to be the dynamic integration of all the behavior patterns derived from temperament, character, internalized value systems, and cognitive capacity (O. Kernberg 1976, 1980). In addition, the dynamic unconscious, or the id, constitutes the dominant and potentially con-

flictive motivational system of the personality. The extent to which sublimatory integration of id impulses into ego and superego functions has taken place
reflects the normally adaptive potential of the personality.

The psychoanalytic model for the classification of personality disorders that
I have proposed incorporates significant contributions by psychoanalytic researchers and theoreticians such as Salman Akhtar (1989, 1992), Rainer Krause
(Krause 1988; Krause and Lutolf 1988), Michael Stone (1980, 1990, 1993a), and
Vamik Volkan (1976, 1987). The normal personality is characterized, first of all,
by an integrated concept of the self and an integrated concept of significant
others. These structural characteristics, jointly called ego identity (Erikson
1956; Jacobson 1964), are reflected in an internal sense and an external appearance of self-coherence and form a fundamental precondition for normal self-
esteem, self-enjoyment, and zest for life. An integrated view of one's self assures
the capacity for a realization of one's desires, capacities, and long-range commitments. An integrated view of significant others guarantees the capacity for
an appropriate evaluation of others, empathy, and an emotional investment in
others that implies a capacity for mature dependency while maintaining a consistent sense of autonomy.

The second structural characteristic of the normal personality, largely derived from ego identity, is ego strength, particularly as reflected in a broad spectrum of affect dispositions, capacity for affect and impulse control, and capacity for sublimation in work and values (also contributed to in important ways
by superego integration). Consistency, persistence, and creativity in work as
well as in interpersonal relations are also largely derived from normal ego identity, as are the capacity for trust, reciprocity, and commitment to others, also
codetermined in significant ways by superego functions (O. Kernberg 1975).

The third aspect of the normal personality is an integrated and mature
superego, representing an internalization of value systems that is stable, deper-
sonified, abstract, individualized, and not excessively dependent on unconscious infantile prohibitions. Such a superego structure is reflected in a sense of
personal responsibility, a capacity for realistic self-criticism, integrity as well as
flexibility in dealing with the ethical aspects of decisionmaking, and a commitment to standards, values, and ideals, and it contributes to such aforemen-
tioned ego functions as reciprocity, trust, and investment in depth in relationships with others.

The fourth aspect of the normal personality is an appropriate and satisfactory management of libidinal and aggressive impulses. This involves the capacity for a full expression of sensual and sexual needs integrated with tenderness

and emotional commitment to a loved other and a normal degree of idealization of the other and the relationship. Here, clearly, freedom of sexual expression is integrated with ego identity and the ego ideal. A normal personality structure includes the capacity for sublimation of aggressive impulses in the form of self-assertion, for withstanding attacks without excessive reaction, and for reacting protectively and without turning aggression against the self. Again, ego and superego functions contribute to such an equilibrium.

Underlying these aspects of the normal personality—recently summarized by Wallerstein (1991) in a set of scales of psychological capacities—are significant structural and dynamic preconditions. These terms refer to the developmental processes by which the earliest internalization of interactions with significant others—that is, of object relations—leads to a series of steps that transform these internalized object relations into the normal ego identity. I am referring to the internalization of object relations into the early ego that starts with the "symbiotic phase" described by Mahler (Mahler and Furer 1968; Mahler et al. 1975)—in my view, the internalization of fused self-representations and object representations under the dominance of a positive or negative peak affect state that leads to "all-good" and "all-bad" fused self-representations and object representations. Such states of symbiotic fusion alternate with other states of internalization of differentiated self- and object representations under conditions of low affect activation; these provide ordinary internalized models of interaction between self and others, while the initially fused internalized object relations under conditions of peak affect states lead to the basic structures of the dynamic unconscious: the id. Rather than a "symbiotic phase," the temporary fusion of self- and object representations under conditions of peak affects constitutes a "symbiotic state." I define the id as the sum total of repressed, dissociated and projected, consciously unacceptable internalized object relations under conditions of peak affect states. Libido and aggression are the hierarchically supraordinate motivational systems representing the integration of, respectively, positive or rewarding and negative or aversive peak affect states (O. Kernberg 1992a, 1994).

At the second stage of ego development, again under conditions of peak affect states, a gradual differentiation occurs between self- and object representations under conditions of "all-good" and "all-bad" interactions, which lead to internal units constituted by self-representation and object-representation–dominant affect. In my view, these units make up the basic structures of the original ego-id matrix that characterizes the stage of separation-individuation described by Mahler.

Eventually, under normal conditions, in the third stage of development, "all-good" and "all-bad" representations of self are combined into an integrated concept that tolerates a realistic view of the self as potentially imbued with both loving and hating impulses. A parallel integration occurs in representations of others in combined all-good–all-bad images of the important persons in the child's life, mainly parental figures but also siblings. These developments determine the capacity for experiencing integrated, ambivalent relationships with others in contrast to splitting them into idealized and persecutory objects. This marks the stage of object constancy, or total internalized object relations, in contrast to the earlier stage of separation-individuation, in which mutually split-off, part object relations dominate psychic experience. Normal ego identity, as defined, constitutes the core of the integrated ego, now differentiated by repressive barriers from both superego and id.

This psychoanalytic model thus includes a developmental series of consecutive psychic structures, starting with the parallel development of realistic object relations under low affect activation and symbiotic object relations under conditions of peak affect activation, followed by the phase of separation-individuation, characterized by continuous growth of realistic relations under low affective conditions but significant splitting operations and related defensive mechanisms under activation of intense affect states, and, finally, by the phase of object constancy, in which a more realistic, integrated concept of self and of significant others evolves in the context of ego identity; at the same time, repression eliminates from consciousness the more extreme manifestations of sexual and aggressive impulses, which can no longer be tolerated under the effect of the integration of the normal superego.

This structural and developmental model also conceives of the superego as constituted by successive layers of internalized self- and object representations (Jacobson 1964; O. Kernberg 1984). The first layer, "all-bad," "persecutory" internalized object relations, reflects the demanding, prohibitive, primitive morality experienced by the child when environmental demands and prohibitions bar the expression of aggressive, dependent, and sexual impulses. A second layer of superego precursors is constituted by the ideal representations of self and others, reflecting early childhood ideals that promise love and dependency if the child lives up to them. The mutual toning down of the earliest persecutory level and the later idealizing level of superego functions and the corresponding decrease in the tendency to reproject these superego precursors bring about the capacity for internalizing more realistic, toned-down demands and prohibitions from the parental figures, leading to the third layer of the superego, corresponding to the ego's stage of object constancy. The integrative processes of the ego in fact facilitate this parallel development of the superego. An integrated superego, as we have seen, in turn strengthens the capacity for object relatedness as well as autonomy: An internalized value system makes the individual less dependent on external confirmation or behavior control while facilitating a deeper commitment to relationships with others. In short, autonomy and independence and a capacity for mature dependence go hand in hand.

THE MOTIVATIONAL ASPECTS OF PERSONALITY
ORGANIZATION: AFFECTS AND DRIVES

As I have written (O. Kernberg 1992a, 1994), I consider the drives of libido and aggression to be the hierarchically supraordinate integration of the corresponding pleasurable and rewarding or painful and aversive affect states. Affects are instinctive components of human behavior, that is, inborn dispositions common to all humans that emerge in the early stages of development and are gradually organized into drives as they are activated as part of early object relations. Gratifying, rewarding, pleasurable affects are integrated as libido; painful, aversive, negative affects are integrated as aggression. Affects as inborn, constitutionally and genetically determined modes of reaction are triggered first by physiological and bodily experiences and then gradually in the context of the development of object relations.

Rage represents the core affect of aggression as a drive, and the vicissitudes of rage explain the origins of hatred and envy—the dominant affects of severe personality disorders—as well as of normal anger and irritability. Similarly, sexual excitement constitutes the core affect of libido, which gradually crystallizes out of the primitive affect of elation. The early sensual responses to intimate bodily contact dominate the development of libido.

Krause (1988) has proposed that affects constitute a phylogenetically recent biological system evolved in mammals to signal the infant's emergency needs to its mother, corresponding to the mother's inborn capacity to read and respond to the infant's affective signals, thus protecting the early development of the dependent infant mammal. This instinctive system reaches increasing complexity and dominance in controlling the social behavior of higher mammals and, in particular, primates.

I propose that affectively driven development of object relations—that is, real and fantasied interpersonal interactions that are internalized as a complex world of self- and object representations in the context of affective interactions—constitutes the determinants of unconscious mental life and of the structure of the psychic apparatus. Affects, in short, not only are the building blocks of the drives but also signal the activation of drives in the context of the activation of a particular internalized object relation, as is typically expressed in the transference developments undergone during psychoanalysis and psychoanalytic psychotherapy.

In contrast to other contemporary psychoanalytic object relations theorists, I argue that we still need a theory of drives because a theory of motivation based on affects alone would fail to take into consideration the multiple positive and negative affects expressed toward the dominant objects of infancy and childhood. I believe that a theory of motivation based on drives as well as affects permits us to account for genetic and constitutional variations in the intensity of drives, as is reflected, for example, in the intensity, rhythm, and thresholds of affect activation commonly referred to collectively as temperament. This theory also permits us to consider how physical pain, psychic trauma, and severe disturbances in early object relations contribute to intensifying aggression as a drive by triggering intense negative affects. In short, I believe that the theory does justice to Freud's (1915) statement that drives occupy an intermediate realm between the physical and the psychic realms.

⟨Recent studies of alteration in neurotransmitter systems in severe personality disorders, particularly in the borderline personality disorder, although still tentative and open to varying interpretations, point to the possibility that neurotransmitters are related to specific distortions in affect activation (Stone 1993a, 1993b). Abnormalities in the adrenergic and cholinergic systems, for example, may be related to general affective instability; deficits in the dopaminergic system may be related to a disposition toward transient psychotic symptoms in borderline patients; impulsive, aggressive, self-destructive behavior may be facilitated by a lowered function of the serotonergic system (deVagvar et al. 1994; Steinberg et al. 1994; Stone 1993a, 1993b; van Reekum et al. 1994; Yehuda et al. 1994). In general, genetic dispositions toward temperamental variations in affect activation would seem to be mediated by alterations in neurotransmitter systems, providing a potential link between the biological determinants of affective response and the psychological triggers of specific affects.⟩

These aspects of inborn dispositions toward the activation of aggression mediated by the activation of aggressive affect states complement the now well-established findings that structured aggressive behavior in infants may derive from early, severe, chronic physical pain and that habitual aggressive teasing interactions with the mother are followed by similar behaviors of infants (Galenson 1986; Fraiberg 1983). Grossman's (1986, 1991) convincing arguments in favor of the direct transformation of chronic intense pain into aggression provide a theoretical context for earlier observations of the battered-child syndrome. The impressive findings concerning the prevalence of physical and sexual abuse in the history of borderline patients, confirmed by investigators both here and abroad (Marziali 1992; Perry and Herman 1993; van der Kolk et al. 1994), provide additional evidence of the influence of trauma on the development of severe manifestations of aggression.

I stress the importance of this model for our understanding of the pathology of aggression because the exploration of severe personality disorders consistently finds the predominance of pathologic aggression. (A key dynamic of the normal personality is the dominance of libidinal strivings over aggressive ones.) Drive neutralization, according to my formulation, implies the integration of the libidinally and aggressively invested, originally split idealized and persecutory internalized object relations, a process that leads from the state of separation-individuation to that of object constancy and culminates in integrated concepts of the self and of significant others and in the integration of affect states derived from the aggressive and libidinal series into the toned-down, discrete, elaborated, and complex affect disposition of the phase of object constancy.

Whereas a major motivational aspect of severe personality disorders—borderline personality organization—is the development of inordinate aggression and the related psychopathology of aggressive affect expression, the dominant pathology of the less severe personality disorders, which I have called neurotic personality organization (O. Kernberg 1975, 1976, 1980, 1984), is the pathology of libido, or sexuality. This field includes in particular the hysterical, obsessive-compulsive, and depressive-masochistic personalities, although it is most evident in the hysterical personality disorder (O. Kernberg 1984). Although all three are frequently found in outpatient practice, only the obsessive-compulsive personality is included in DSM-IV's (1994) main list. (As mentioned above, the depressive-masochistic personality disorder is included in part in the DSM-IV's appendix [1994], shorn of its masochistic components. The hysterical personality was included in DSM-II [1968], and one hopes that it will be rediscovered in DSM-V—institutional politics permitting. In these disorders— in the context of the achievement of object constancy, an integrated superego, a well-developed ego identity, and an advanced level of defensive operations centering around repression—the typical pathology of sexual inhibition, oedipalization of object relations, and acting out of unconscious guilt concerning infantile sexual impulses dominates the personality. In borderline personality organizations, by contrast, sexuality is usually "coopted" by aggression; that is, sexual behavior and interaction are intimately condensed with aggressive aims, and this severely limits or distorts sexual intimacy and love relations and fosters the abnormal development of paraphilias, with their heightened condensation of sexual and aggressive aims.

An early classification of personality disorders drawn up by Freud (1908, 1931) and Abraham (1920, 1921–1925) described oral, anal, and genital characters, a classification that has gradually been abandoned in practice because psychoanalytic exploration has found that severe personality disorders present pathological condensations of conflicts from all of these stages. The classification proposed by Freud and Abraham and their description of the relation between oral conflicts, pathological dependency, a tendency toward depression, and self-directed aggression still seem to be of value when limited to the less severe constellations of these disorders (O. Kernberg 1976) and is eminently relevant for personality disorders along the entire developmental spectrum, most specifically in the depressive-masochistic personality (O. Kernberg 1992a). This personality disorder, while reflecting an advanced level of neurotic personality organization, transports a constellation of oral conflicts into the oedipal realm in a relatively unmodified fashion. Similarly, anal conflicts are most clearly observable in the obsessive-compulsive personality disorder, which transports anal conflicts into the oedipal conflicts of object constancy. Yet anal conflicts are also relevant along the entire spectrum of personality disorders.

Fenichel (1945) attempted a psychoanalytic classification of character constellations into sublimatory and reactive types, the latter including avoidance (phobias) and opposition (reaction formations). He went on to classify personality disorders, or character pathologies, into pathological behavior toward the id (oral, anal, and phallic conflicts), toward the superego (moral masochism, psychopathy, and acting out), and toward external objects (pathological inhibitions, pathological jealousy, and pseudohypersexuality). This classification has also been abandoned in practice, mainly because it has become evident that all character pathology presents pathological behavior toward these psychic structures simultaneously.

A PSYCHOANALYTIC MODEL OF NOSOLOGY

My own classification of personality disorders centers on the dimension of severity (1976), ranging from psychotic personality organization to borderline personality organization to neurotic personality organization (fig. 1).

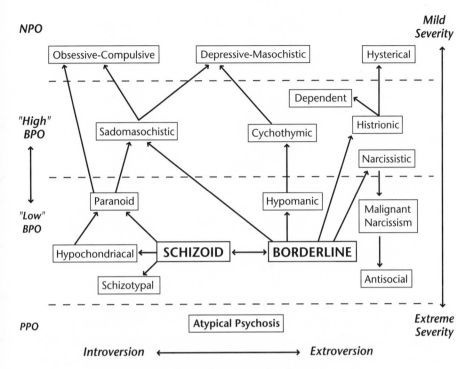

Figure 1. Personality Disorders: Their Mutual Relations

Psychotic personality organization is characterized by lack of integration of the concept of self and significant others (that is, identity diffusion), a predominance of primitive defensive operations centering around splitting, and loss of reality testing. The basic function of the defensive operations of splitting and its derivatives (projective identification, denial, primitive idealization, omnipotence, omnipotent control, devaluation) is to keep separate the idealized and persecutory internalized object relations in order to prevent the overwhelming control or destruction of ideal object relations by aggressively infiltrated ones and thus to protect the capacity to depend on good objects. This basic function of the primitive constellation of defensive operations, derived from the early developmental phases predating object constancy, actually dominates most clearly in the borderline personality organization. An additional function of these mechanisms, the most primitive, in the case of psychotic personality organization, is to compensate for the loss of reality testing in these patients.

Reality testing refers to the capacity to differentiate self from nonself and intrapsychic from external stimuli, and to maintain empathy with ordinary social criteria of reality, all of which capacities are typically lost in the psychoses and are manifested particularly in hallucinations and delusions (O. Kernberg 1976, 1984). The loss of reality testing reflects the lack of differentiation between self-representations and object representations under conditions of peak affect states, that is, a structural persistence of the symbiotic states of development—their pathological hypertrophy, so to speak. The primitive defenses centering around splitting attempt to protect these patients from the chaos in all object relations that stems from their loss of ego boundaries in intense relationships with others. All patients with psychotic personality organization represent atypical forms of psychosis. Therefore, in a clinical sense, psychotic personality organization represents an exclusion criterion for the personality disorders.

Borderline personality organization is also characterized by identity diffusion and the predominance of primitive defensive operations centering on splitting, but it is distinguished from the psychotic organization by the presence of good reality testing, reflecting the differentiation between self- and object representations in the idealized and persecutory sector characteristic of the separation-individuation phase (O. Kernberg 1975). Actually, this category includes all the severe personality disorders seen in clinical practice—typically the borderline, the schizoid and schizotypal, the paranoid, the hypomanic, the hypochondriacal (a syndrome that has many characteristics of a personality disorder proper), the narcissistic (including the malignant narcissism syndrome [O. Kernberg 1992a]), and the antisocial. These patients present identity diffusion, the manifestations of primitive defensive operations, and varying degrees of superego deterioration (antisocial behavior). A particular group of patients—namely, those with the narcissistic personality disorder, the malignant narcissism syndrome, and the antisocial personality disorder—typically suffer from significant disorganization of the superego.

> Because of identity diffusion, all those with personality disorders in the borderline spectrum present severe distortions in interpersonal relations, particularly in intimate relations with others, lack of a consistent commitment to work or profession, uncertainty and lack of direction in many other areas of their lives, and varying degrees of pathology in their sexual life. They often present an incapacity to integrate tender and sexual feelings, and they may show a chaotic sexual life with multiple polymorphous perverse infantile tendencies. The most severe cases may present with a generalized inhibition of all sexual responses as a consequence of an insufficient activation of sensuous responses in early relations with the caregiver and an overwhelming predominance of aggression, which interferes with sensuality rather than recruiting it for aggressive aims. These pa-

tients also evince nonspecific manifestations of ego weakness—that is, lack of anxiety tolerance, impulse control, and sublimatory functioning, expressed in an incapacity for consistency, persistence, and creativity in work. ⟵

Patients with a particular group of personality disorders present the characteristics of borderline personality organization but are able to maintain more satisfactory social adaptation and are usually more effective in attaining some degree of intimacy in object relations and in integrating sexual and tender impulses. Thus, in spite of presenting identity diffusion, they evince sufficiently nonconflictual development of some ego functions, superego integration, a benign cycle of intimate involvements, capacity for dependency gratification, and a better adaptation to work. This group, which constitutes what might be called a higher level of borderline personality organization or an intermediate level of personality disorder, includes the cyclothymic personality, the sado-masochistic personality, the infantile or histrionic personality, and the dependent personalities, as well as some better-functioning narcissistic personality disorders.

Neurotic personality organization is characterized by normal ego identity and the related capacity for object relations in depth, ego strength reflected in anxiety tolerance, impulse control, sublimatory functioning, effectiveness and creativity in work, and a capacity for sexual love and emotional intimacy disrupted only by unconscious guilt feelings reflected in specific pathological patterns of interaction in relation to sexual intimacy. This group includes the hysterical personality, the depressive-masochistic personality, the obsessive personality, and many so-called avoidant personality disorders—in other words, the "phobic characters" described in the psychoanalytic literature (which, in my view, remain problematic entities). Significant social inhibitions or phobias are found in several types of personality disorder; the underlying hysterical character structure that was considered typical for the phobic personality applies to only some cases.

DEVELOPMENTAL, STRUCTURAL, AND
MOTIVATIONAL CONTINUITIES

Having thus classified personality disorders in terms of their severity, I shall now examine particular continuities within this field that establish a psychopathologically linked network of personality disorders. The borderline and the schizoid may be described as the simplest forms of personality disorder, reflecting fixation at the level of separation-individuation and the "purest" expression of the general characteristics of borderline personality organization. Fairbairn (1954), in fact, described the schizoid personality as the prototype of all personality disorders and described the psychodynamics of these patients: the splitting operations separating "good" and "bad" internalized object relations, the self-representation and object representation dyads of the split-off object relations, the consequent impoverishment of interpersonal relations, and their replacement by a defensive hypertrophy of fantasy life. The borderline personality disorder presents similar dynamic characteristics—impulsive interactions in the interpersonal field—whereas they are expressed in the schizoid personality in the patient's fantasy life combined with social withdrawal (Akhtar 1992; Stone 1994).

In the course of psychoanalytic exploration, the apparent lack of affect display of the schizoid personality turns out to reflect severe splitting operations, to the extent of fragmentation of affective experience; this "empties out" the schizoid's interpersonal life, while his internalized object relations have split-off characteristics similar to those of the typical borderline patient (O. Kernberg 1975). In contrast, the intrapsychic life of the borderline personality disorder patient is enacted in his interpersonal patterns, very often replacing self-awareness with driven, repetitive behavior patterns. The borderline patient thus evinces the typical triad of identity diffusion, primitivity of affect display (affect storms), and lack of impulse control. It may well be that the descriptive differences between the schizoid and the borderline disorders reflect an important temperamental dimension—namely, that of extroversion and introversion—which emerges under different names in various models of classification.

The schizotypal personality represents the most severe form of schizoid personality disorder; the paranoid personality reflects an increase of aggression in comparison to the schizoid personality disorder, with the dominance of projective mechanisms and a defensive self-idealization related to efforts to control an external world of persecutory figures. If splitting per se dominates in the borderline and schizoid personality disorders, projective identification dominates in the paranoid. The hypochondriacal syndrome reflects a projection of persecutory objects onto the interior of the body; hypochondriacal personalities usually also show strong paranoid and schizoid characteristics.

The borderline personality proper presents intense affect activation and lack of affect control, which also suggest the presence of a temperamental factor, but the integration of aggressive and libidinal affects obtained in the course of treatment often brings about a remarkable modulation of affect response. The increase of impulse control and affect tolerance during treatment confirms that splitting mechanisms are central in the pathology. The hypomanic personality disorder, in contrast, appears to include a pathology of affect activation that points to temperamental predisposition; this probably also holds true for its milder form, the cyclothymic personality.

Borderline personality disorders presenting intense aggression may evolve into the sadomasochistic personality disorder. If a disposition to strong sadomasochism becomes incorporated into or controlled by a relatively healthy superego structure (which also incorporates a depressive potential into a disposition to guilt-laden responses), and ego identity is achieved, the conditions for a depressive-masochistic personality disorder are also present. This personality may be considered the highest level of two developmental lines that proceed from the borderline personality through the sadomasochistic to the depressive-masochistic, on one hand, and from the hypomanic through the cyclothymic to the depressive-masochistic personality disorders, on the other. This entire area of personality disorders thus reflects the internalization of object relations under conditions of abnormal affective development or affect control.

When a severe inborn disposition to aggressive reactions, early trauma, severe pathology of early object relations, physical illness, or sexual and physical abuse intensifies the dominance of aggression in the personality structure, a particular pathology of aggression may develop that includes, as we have seen, the paranoid personality, hypochondriasis, or sadomasochism and that may also characterize a subgroup of the narcissistic personality disorder.

The narcissistic personality disorder is of particular interest because in it, in contrast to all other personality disorders included in borderline personality organization, which clearly indicate identity diffusion, a lack of integration of the concept of significant others goes hand in hand with an integrated but pathological grandiose self. This pathological grandiose self replaces the underlying lack of integration of a normal self (Akhtar 1989; Plakun 1989; Ronningstam and Gunderson 1989). In the course of psychoanalytic treatment or psychoanalytic psychotherapy we may observe the dissolution of this pathological grandiose self and the reemergence of the typical identity diffusion of borderline personality organization before a new integration of normal ego identity can take place.

In the narcissistic personality, the pathological grandiose self absorbs both real and idealized self-representations and object representations into an unrealistically idealized concept of self, with a parallel impoverishment of idealized superego structures, a predominance of persecutory superego precursors, the reprojection of these persecutory superego precursors (as a protection against pathological excessive guilt), and a consequent weakening of the later, more integrated superego functions (O. Kernberg 1975, 1984, 1992a). The narcissistic personality therefore often presents some degree of antisocial behavior.

When intense pathology of aggression dominates in a narcissistic personality structure, the pathological grandiose self may become infiltrated by egosyntonic aggression, antisocial behavior, and paranoid tendencies, which translate into the syndrome of malignant narcissism. This syndrome is intermediate between the narcissistic personality disorder and the antisocial personality disorder proper, in which a total absence or deterioration of superego functioning has occurred (O. Kernberg 1992a). In psychoanalytic exploration, the antisocial personality disorder (Akhtar 1992; Bursten 1989; Hare 1986; O. Kernberg 1984) usually reveals severe underlying paranoid trends, together with a total incapacity for any nonexploitive investment in significant others. The absence of any capacity for guilt feelings or concern for self and others, the inability to identify with any moral or ethical value in self or others, and the incapacity to project a dimension of a personal future differentiate this disorder from the less severe syndrome of malignant narcissism, in which some commitment to others and a capacity for authentic guilt feelings are still present. The extent to which nonexploitive object relations are still present and the extent to which antisocial behaviors dominate are the most important prognostic indicators for any psychotherapeutic approach to these personality disorders (O. Kernberg 1975; Stone 1990).

At a higher level of development, the obsessive-compulsive personality may be conceived as one in which inordinate aggression has been neutralized by absorption into a well-integrated but excessively sadistic superego, leading to perfectionism, self-doubts, and the chronic need to control the environment as well as the self that is characteristic of this personality disorder. There are cases, however, in which this neutralization of aggression is incomplete; the severity of aggression determines the regressive features of this disorder, and transitional cases with mixed obsessive, paranoid, and schizoid features can be found that maintain a borderline personality organization in spite of significant obsessive-compulsive personality features.

Whereas the infantile or histrionic personality disorder is a relatively mild form of the borderline personality disorder, though still within the borderline spectrum, the hysterical represents a higher level of the infantile disorder within the neurotic spectrum of personality organization. In the hysterical personality the emotional lability, extroversion, and dependent and exhibitionistic traits of the histrionic personality are restricted to the sexual realm; these patients are able to have normally deep, mature, committed, and differentiated object relations in other areas. In addition, in contrast to the sexual "freedom" of the typical infantile personality, the hysterical personality often presents a combination of pseudohypersexuality and sexual inhibition, with a particular differentiation of relations to men and women that contrasts with the nonspecific orientation toward both genders of the infantile or histrionic personality (O. Kernberg 1992a).

The depressive-masochistic personality disorder (ibid.), the highest-level outcome of the pathology of depressive affect as well as that of sadomasochism, characteristic of a dominance of aggression in primitive object relations, presents not only a well-integrated superego (like all other personalities with neurotic personality organization) but an extremely punitive superego. This predisposes the patient to self-defeating behavior and reflects an unconscious need to suffer as expiation for guilt feelings or a precondition for sexual pleasure—a reflection of the oedipal dynamics characterizing this disorder. These patients' excessive dependency and easy sense of frustration go hand in hand with their "faulty metabolism" of aggression; depression ensues when an aggressive response would have been appropriate, and an excessively aggressive response to the frustration of their dependency needs may rapidly turn into a renewed depressive response as a consequence of excessive guilt feelings.

FURTHER IMPLICATIONS OF THIS CLASSIFICATION

Using the classification I have presented, which combines structural and developmental concepts of the psychic apparatus based on a theory of internalized object relations, we may differentiate personality disorders according to the severity of the pathology, the extent to which it is dominated by aggression, the extent to which pathological affective dispositions influence personality development, the effect of the development of a pathological grandiose structure of the self, and the potential influence of a temperamental disposition toward extroversion or introversion. In a combined analysis of the vicissitudes of instinctual conflicts between love and aggression and of the development of ego and superego structures, it permits us to differentiate as well as relate the different pathological personalities to one another.

This classification also demonstrates the advantages of combining categorical and dimensional criteria. Clearly, there are developmental factors relating several personality disorders to one another, particularly along an axis of severity. Figure 1 summarizes the relations among the various personality disorders outlined in what follows. Thus, a developmental line links the borderline, the hypomanic, the cyclothymic, and the depressive-masochistic personality disorders. Another developmental line links the borderline, the histrionic or infantile, the dependent, and the hysterical personality disorders. Still another developmental line links, in complex ways, the schizoid, the schizotypal, the paranoid, and the hypochondriacal personality disorders, and, at a higher developmental level, the obsessive-compulsive personality disorder. And finally, a developmental line links the antisocial personality, the malignant narcissism syndrome, and the narcissistic personality disorder (which, in turn, contains a broad spectrum of severity). Further relations of all prevalent personality disorders are indicated in figure 1.

The vicissitudes of internalized object relations and the development of affective responses emerge as basic components of a contemporary psychoanalytic approach to the personality disorders. Affects always include a cognitive component, a subjective experience of a highly pleasurable or unpleasurable nature, neurovegetative discharge phenomena, psychomotor activation, and, crucially, a distinctive pattern of facial expressions that originally serves a communicative function directed to the caregiver. The cognitive aspect of affective responses, in turn, always reflects the relation between a self-representation and an object representation, which facilitates the diagnosis of the activated object relation in each affect state that emerges in the therapeutic relationship.

A crucial advantage of the proposed classification of personality disorders is that the underlying structural concepts permit the immediate translation of the patient's affect states into the object relation activated in the transference and the "reading" of this transference in terms of the activation of a relation that typically alternates in the projection of self- and object representations. The more severe the patient's pathology, the more easily he may project either his self-representation or his object representation onto the therapist while enacting the reciprocal object or self-representation; this helps to clarify the nature of the relation in the midst of intense affect activation, and, by gradual interpretation of these developments in the transference, permits the integration of the patient's previously split-off representations of self and significant others. This conceptualization, therefore, has direct implications for the therapeutic approach to personality disorders. (The final section of this chapter describes a psychoanalytic psychotherapy derived from this conceptual framework.)

This classification also helps to clarify the vicissitudes of the development of the sexual and aggressive drives. From the initial response of rage as a basic affect develops the structured affect of hatred as the central affect state in severe personality disorders, and hatred, in turn, may take the forms of conscious or unconscious envy or of an inordinate need for revenge that will color the corresponding transference developments. Similarly, regarding the sexual response, the psychoanalytic understanding of the internalized object relations activated in sexual fantasy and experience facilitates the diagnosis and treatment of abnormal condensations of sexual excitement and hatred such as those found in the perversions or paraphilias and the inhibitions of sexuality and restrictions on sexual responsiveness derived from the absorption of sexuality into the patient's conflicts concerning internalized object relations.

The unconscious identification of the patient with the role of victim and victimizer in cases of severe trauma and physical and sexual abuse can also be better diagnosed, understood, and worked through in transference and countertransference in light of the theory of internalized object relations that underlies this classification. And the understanding of the structural determinants of pathological narcissism, particularly the psychopathology of the pathological grandiose self, permits us to apply therapeutic approaches to resolve the apparent incapacity of narcissistic patients to develop differentiated transference reactions, in parallel to their severe distortions of object relations in general.

Psychoanalytic exploration has been central in providing knowledge about the characteristics of the personality disorders. In addition to further refinements in the diagnosis of the personality disorders and in therapeutic approaches in particular, psychoanalysis has the important task of investigating the relations between the findings of psychoanalytic explorations and those of the related fields of developmental psychology, clinical psychiatry, affect theory, and neurobiology.

PSYCHOANALYSIS AND PSYCHOANALYTIC
PSYCHOTHERAPY OF PERSONALITY DISORDERS

In what follows I present an overview of the application of my ego psychology–object relations theory to the psychoanalysis and psychoanalytic psychotherapy of the personality disorders.

The analysis of the transference is a major concern in my general technical approach. Transference analysis consists in analyzing the reactivations of past internalized object relations in the here and now. At the same time, the component structures of ego and id and their intra- and interstructural conflicts are analyzed. I conceive of internalized object relations as reflecting a combination of realistic and fantasied—often highly distorted—internalizations of past object relations and defenses against them under the effects of instinctual drive derivatives. In other words, I see a dynamic tension between the here and now, which reflects intrapsychic structure, and the "there and then," unconscious psychogenetic determinants derived from the patient's developmental history.

The basic contribution of object relations theory to the analysis of the transference is to expand the frame of reference within which transference manifestations are explored so that the increasing complexities of transference regression in patients with deep levels of psychopathology may be understood and interpreted. The nature of transference interpretation depends on the nature of the patient's psychopathology. In practice, the transference of patients with a neurotic personality organization can be understood as the unconscious repetition in the here and now of pathogenic relations from the past—more concretely, the enactment of an aspect of the patient's unconscious infantile self in relating to (also unconscious) infantile representations of the parental objects.

Patients with neurotic personality organization present well-integrated superego, ego, and id structures. In the psychoanalytic situation, the analysis of resistances brings about the activation in the transference, first, of relatively global characteristics of these structures and, later, of the internalized object relations of which these are composed. The analysis of drive derivatives occurs in the context of the analysis of the relation of the patient's infantile self to significant parental objects as projected onto the therapist.

The fact that neurotic patients regress to a relatively integrated though repressed unconscious infantile self that relates to relatively integrated though unconscious representations of the parental objects makes such transferences fairly easy to understand and to interpret. The unconscious aspect of the infantile self carries with it a concrete wish reflecting a drive derivative directed to parental objects and a fantasied fear about the dangers involved in expressing this wish. What ego psychology–object relations theory stresses is that even in these comparatively "simple" transference enactments, the activation is always of basic dyadic units of a self-representation and an object representation linked by a certain affect, and these units reflect either the defensive or the impulsive aspects of the conflict. More precisely, an unconscious fantasy that reflects an impulse-defense organization is typically activated first in the form of the object relation representing the defensive side of the conflict and only later by the object relation reflecting the impulsive side of the conflict (O. Kernberg 1976, 1980, 1984).

What makes the analysis of internalized object relations in the transference of patients with severe personality disorders more complex (but also permits the clarification of such complexity) is the defensive primitive splitting of internalized object relations (O. Kernberg 1975, 1992a). In these patients, the tolerance of ambivalence characteristic of higher-level neurotic object relations is replaced by a defensive disintegration of the representations of self and objects into libidinally and aggressively invested part-object relations. The more realistic or more easily understandable past object relations of neurotic personality organization are replaced by highly unrealistic, sharply idealized, or sharply aggressivized or persecutory self- and object representations that canno̶ ̶t̶h̶e̶ ̶l̶i̶n̶k̶e̶d̶ immediately to actual or fantasied relations of the past.

⌊This process activates either highly idealized part-object relations under the impact of intense, diffuse, overwhelming affect states of an ecstatic nature, or equally intense but painful and frightening primitive affect states that signal the activation of aggressive or persecutory relations between self and object. We can recognize the nonintegrated nature of the internalized object relations by the patient's disposition toward rapid reversals of the enactment of the role of self- and object representations. The patient may simultaneously project a complementary self- or object representation onto the therapist; this, together with intense affect activation, leads to apparently chaotic transference developments. These rapid oscillations, as well as the sharp dissociation between loving and hating aspects of the relation to the same object, may be further complicated by defensive condensations of several object relations under the impact of the same primitive affect, so that, for example, combined father-mother images confusingly condense the aggressively perceived aspects of the father and the mother. Idealized or devalued aspects of the self similarly condense various levels of past experiences.⌋

An object relations frame of reference permits the therapist to understand and organize what looks like complete chaos so that he can clarify the various condensed part-object relations in the transference, bringing about an integration of self- and object representations, which leads to the more advanced neurotic type of transference.

⟨The general objectives of transference interpretation in the treatment of borderline personality organization include the following tasks (O. Kernberg 1984): (1) diagnosing the dominant object relation within the overall chaotic transference situation; (2) clarifying which is the self-representation and which the object representation of this internalized object relation and the dominant affect linking them; and (3) interpretively connecting this primitive dominant object relation with its split-off opposite.

A patient with borderline personality organization shows a predominance of preoedipal conflicts and psychic representations of preoedipal conflicts condensed with representations of the oedipal phase. Conflicts are not so much repressed as expressed in mutually dissociated ego states reflecting the primitive defense of splitting. The activation of primitive object relations that predate the consolidation of ego, superego, and id is manifest in the transference as apparently chaotic affect states; these, as noted above, have to be analyzed in sequential steps. Interpretation of the primitive transferences of borderline patients brings about a transformation of part-object relations into total object relations, of primitive transferences (largely reflecting stages of development that predate object constancy) into the advanced transferences of the oedipal phase.

At severe levels of psychopathology, splitting mechanisms permit the contradictory aspects of intrapsychic conflicts to remain at least partially conscious in the form of primitive transferences. Patients with neurotic personality organization, in contrast, present impulse-defense configurations that contain specific unconscious wishes reflecting sexual and aggressive drive derivatives embedded in unconscious fantasies relating to the oedipal objects. In these patients we find relatively less distortion of both the self-representations relating to these objects and the representations of the oedipal objects themselves. Therefore the difference between past pathogenic experiences and their transformation into currently structured unconscious dispositions is not as great as in the primitive transferences of patients with borderline personality organization.

I assume that in all cases the transference is dynamically unconscious in the sense that, because of either repression or splitting, the patient unconsciously distorts the current experience owing to his fixation to past pathogenic conflicts with a significant internalized object. The major task is to bring the unconscious transference's meanings in the here and now into full consciousness by means of interpretation. This is the first stage in analyzing the relation between the unconscious present and the unconscious past.

What is enacted in the transference is never a simple repetition of the patient's actual experiences. I agree with Melanie Klein's (1952) proposal that the transference derives from a combination of real and fantasied experiences of the past and defenses against both. This is another way of saying that the relation between psychic reality and objective reality always remains ambiguous: The more severe the patient's psychopathology and the more distorted his intrapsychic structural organization, the more indirect is the relation of current structure, genetic reconstruction, and developmental origins.

Chapter 2 Hatred as a Core
Affect of Aggression

THEORETICAL CONSIDERATIONS

There is little doubt today about the prevalence of aggression in the behavior, fantasies, and psychodynamics of patients with severe personality disorders. But clinicians, theoreticians, and researchers in this field continue to be troubled by the issue of whether aggression is inborn—an "instinct" or "drive"—or secondary to frustration and trauma. In short, is aggression the result of early experience or of constitution and genetics?

Studies have shown that early exposure to violence and to physical, psychological, and sexual abuse, particularly incest, is significantly more frequent in patients with severe personality disorders and in children at high risk for psychopathology than in patients with milder personality disorders and the population at large (Paris 1994a). At the same time, evidence is also increasing that abnormality of neuro-

An earlier version of this chapter was published in *The Birth of Hatred: Developmental, Clinical, and Technical Aspects of Intense Aggression,* edited by S. Akhtar, S. Kramer, and H. Parens. Northvale, N.H.: Jason Aronson, 1995.

chemical and neurohormonal systems may be related to significant aspects of personality pathology, particularly proneness to aggressive and reckless behavior, pointing to the importance of genetic and constitutional determinants of temperament (Stone 1993b)—the inborn disposition to a certain level of intensity, rhythm, and threshold for affective response. Temperament also includes genetically and constitutionally determined behavioral and cognitive patterns, such as some gender-role-specific traits. Accepting in theory the possibility that genetic and constitutional factors as well as environmental and psychodynamic factors may play a role, the question of how to conceptualize aggression and understand its involvement in the development of severe psychopathology remains.

Contemporary biological instinct theory has evolved into an integrated view of instinct and environment, conceptualizing inborn dispositions to behavior patterns that are activated under determinate environmental conditions, leading to the activation of a sequence of exploratory and consummatory behaviors. This chain of events leads to the overall organization of behavioral sequences that we designate as instinct. Thus inborn behavioral dispositions and environmental triggers jointly constitute the structural elements of instinctive behavior.

I have argued in earlier work (O. Kernberg 1992a) that this conception of instincts in biology may be applied to psychoanalytic theory, leading to a concept of drives as combined instinctive and environmental motivational systems—specifically, libido and aggression. Behind the distinction between these concepts lies Freud's corresponding differentiation. In fact, Freud distinguished between biological instincts as inborn, stable, and invariant behaviors common to all the individuals of a species, and what he designated as drives: highly individualized, developmentally consolidated motivations that constitute the unconscious determinants of psychic life and reveal themselves in mental representations and affects (Holder 1970).

I have proposed that affects are instinctive components of human behavior, inborn dispositions common to all individuals, and that they emerge in the earliest stages of development and are gradually organized, as part of early object relations, into gratifying, rewarding, pleasurable affects, or libido as an overarching drive, and painful, aversive, negative affects that, in turn, are organized into aggression as an overarching drive. In this conceptualization, affects are the inborn, constitutionally and genetically determined modes of reaction that are triggered first by various physiological and bodily experiences and then by the development of object relations from the beginning of life onward.

Rage, in this conceptualization, represents the basic affect of aggression as a drive, and the vicissitudes of rage explain, in my view, the origins of hatred and envy, as well as of anger and irritability as moods. Similarly, the affect of sexual excitement constitutes the core affect of libido, which slowly and gradually evolves out of the primitive affect of elation, produced initially by the infant's sensual responses to intimate bodily contact with the mother.

Unlike Fairbairn (1954) and Kohut (1971), who conceptualized aggression as secondary to frustation of the need for love, I believe that the capacities for both love and hatred are inborn and that both require activation and developments of the environment (objects, essentially). The most severe cases of borderline personality organization give evidence of a severe primary inhibition of the sexual response, derived from insufficient activation of bodily sensuality and the overriding development of aggressive reactions in the context of major disturbances in early object relations, particularly those of the mother-infant dyad.

As mentioned above, Krause (1988) has proposed that affects constitute a phylogenetically recent biological system evolved in mammals to signal the infant's needs to its mother, corresponding to the mother's inborn capacity to read and respond to the infant's affective signals. This instinctive system reaches increasing complexity and dominance in controlling the social behavior of higher mammals, particularly primates, culminating in the psychological development of affects in humans. I have proposed that the affectively driven development of object relations—that is, real and fantasied interpersonal interactions internalized as a complex world of self- and object representations in the context of affective interactions—constitutes the determinant of unconscious mental life and of the structure of the psychic apparatus. Affects are integrated into unconscious drives, and libido and aggression as overall supraordinate drives are represented in each enacted internalized object relation by the affect characteristic of that object relation. Affects, in short, are the building blocks of the drives and also serve as signals of the activation of drives in the context of particular internalized object relations.

This theoretical formulation helps clarify some apparent differences in the development and organization of libido and aggression as drives. I have proposed that it is the affect of elation—maximized with gratification of the baby at the breast and with intimate bodily contacts, particularly those involved in specialized sensuous zones—that activates, fosters, and structuralizes the development of sexual excitement in all its pregenital and genital aspects. The specific and core affect of sexual excitement, as well as the affective aspects of longing, tenderness, and concern, evolve from primitive elation.

By the same token, aggression as a drive develops from the primitive crying response that evolves first into the affect of rage and later into the crying response as part of sadness. Hatred, the core affect of aggression as a drive, is a later, structuralized aspect of rage, as is envy, a particular structural development of hatred.

The proposed reformulation of the relation between affects and drives in psychoanalytic theory conceptualizes the constitutionally given and genetically determined disposition toward intense activation of aggression expressed by means of temperament. In this connection, cognitive deficits, minimal brain dysfunctions that interfere with the organization of perceptive stimuli and facilitate the activation of anxiety under conditions of uncertainty, may also contribute to pathological affect activation. A limited capacity for time appraisal and spatial organization, for example, would increase an infant's sensitivity to separation from the mother. Most important, traumatic experiences such as intense and chronic pain, physical and sexual abuse, and severe pathology in early object relations would activate aggressive affects determining the predominance of overall aggression over libidinal striving, resulting in conditions of severe psychopathology. In short, the artificial separation of nature and nurture can be reconciled by a concept of drives that considers their constituent affect dispositions to be their structural underpinnings.

I have argued that libidinal development in the infant-mother relationship presupposes the infant's innate disposition toward attachment, which requires external stimulation to become activated, and that the same reasoning may be applied to the development of rage and angry protest when external circumstances frustrate the infant's needs or desires. In both cases an internal disposition toward a peak affect response is actualized by environmental stimuli—the caregiving object. At the center of each of these basic responses are primitive affects.

I assume that from the onset of object relations the experience of the self relating to an object during intense affect states generates an intrapsychic world of affectively invested objection relations of a gratifying or aversive quality. The basic psychic experiences that will constitute the dynamic unconscious are dyadic relations between self-representation and object representation in the context of extreme elation or rage. Symbiotic states of mind—that is, experiences of elation within which an unconscious fantasy of union or fusion between the self and object crystallizes—are easily associated with the psychic implications of the baby satisfied at the breast, the elation of the baby in visual contact with mother's smiling face. That states of intense rage also imply an experience of fusion between self and object under the control of such an intense affect is a conclusion derived from the transference analysis of patients suffering from severe psychopathology characterized by intense aggression.

Primitive affects are primary motivational systems that provide an integrative cognitive view of the total world of momentary experience in terms of the rewarding or aversive nature of that experience, with the implication of a desire to get closer to the source of pleasure or to escape from or destroy the source of unpleasure. Affects always include a cognitive component, a subjective experience of a highly pleasurable or unpleasurable nature, neurovegetative discharge phenomena, psychomotor activation, and, crucially, a distinctive pattern of facial expressions that serve a communicative function for the caregiver. From this viewpoint, affects, as the parts of a primary communicative system, serve a basic biological function that supersedes more primitive physiological regulation systems (Krause 1988). An inborn ability to "read" the affective implications of the caregiver's facial expression completes the infant's primitive system of communication, basic to attachment in the behavioral realm and to building up an internalized world of object relations in the intrapsychic realm. This capability complements the infant's inborn capacity for specific facial motor patterns expressing his varying affect states. This early communicative system has a crucial role in the organization of early affects. As Krause has shown, a discrepancy between the infant's subjective experience and the mother's affective expression may lead to the disorganization of early affect patterns that may end in the infant's inability to integrate his own subjective experience and affective expression, further disturbing early object relations.

In short, early affect activation initiates the infant's object relation with the mother; the nature of this relation may further contribute to organizing or disorganizing the affect, and early disorganization of affect states may in turn result in profound and early distortions of internalized object relations. Krause has demonstrated such disorganization of affects, for example, in the facial expression of affect states in schizophrenic patients and in the affective implications of stuttering.

Anger and rage, aversion and disgust, contempt and resentment are affects integrated into and serving to express particular aspects of aggression as an overall, hierarchically supraordinate drive. If we accept a modified version of Mahler's developmental schemata stating that very early differentiation during low-level affect states alternates with states of mind reflecting the development of the symbiotic phase under conditions of peak affect states, my view fits comfortably with Mahler's contributions to the understanding of normal and pathological symbiosis development (Mahler et al. 1975). I believe that ego maturation and development under conditions of low-level affect states and the gradual construction of the dynamic unconscious during peak affect states permit us to integrate infant observation with our growing understanding of the structural characteristics of the dynamic unconscious derived from psychoanalytic exploration.

Aggressively invested undifferentiated self- and object representations, built up separately from libidinally invested undifferentiated self- and object representations, characterize the basic layer of the dynamic unconscious and reflect early symbiosis. The subsequent differentiation of self- and object representations within the libidinal and the aggressive domains establishes the structural characteristics of separation-individuation and the psychopathology of borderline personality organization. I believe that there is an indissoluble connection between the internalization of early object relations and affect states, the dyad of self-representation and object representation and its affective context.

Drive neutralization, according to this concept, implies the integration of originally split idealized and persecutory internalized object relations, leading to an integrated concept of the self and of significant others and the integration of derivative affect states from the aggressive and libidinal series into the toned-down, discrete, elaborated, and complex affect disposition of the phase of object constancy.

PSYCHOPATHOLOGY

Under certain conditions the aggressive drive dominates the early development of the psychic apparatus so powerfully that it leads to the psychopathological structures we observe in psychosis, borderline personality organization, the severe types of perversion, and some psychosomatic disorders. The most central clinical observation in such conditions is the activation of intense, pervasive rage in the transference. From mild, chronic irritation and irritability to acutely focused and intense expressions of anger, the patient easily shifts into the basic affect of rage, which, when its unconscious fantasy elements are explored, eventually reveals the structural characteristics of hatred.

The earliest function of rage is the effort to eliminate a source of irritation or pain. Rage is thus always secondary to frustration or pain, although the intensity of the rage response may depend on temperamental features. The second function of rage is to eliminate an obstacle or barrier to a fantasied or real source of gratification. This is the prototype for a higher-level function of rage: to eliminate a bad object—that is, a supposedly willful source of frustration—standing between the self and gratification of a need.

Kleinian theory (Klein 1940, 1946) postulates the immediate transformation of very early states of severe frustration, such as the absence of the mother, into the fantasied image of a bad mother, the original bad inner and external object. I agree with Laplanche (1992), however, that later traumatic experiences may retrospectively transform earlier experiences into secondarily traumatic ones and that, therefore, the point at which the rage-related internalized object relation crystallizes is not as important as the fact that it does so.

At a more advanced developmental level, the wish is no longer to destroy the bad object but to make it suffer; here, we are definitely in the complex developmental area in which pleasure and pain combine, sadism expresses a condensation of agression with pleasure, and the original affect of rage appears transformed into hatred with new, stable structural characteristics. At a still higher level of development, the wish to make the bad object suffer changes into the wish to dominate and control the bad object in order to avoid feared persecution by it; now obsessive mechanisms of control may psychopathologically regulate the suppression or repression of agression. Finally, in sublimatory aspects of the aggressive response, the search for autonomy and self-affirmation, for freedom from external control, reflects characteristics of the original self-affirmative implications of rage.

Hatred, I propose, is a compex, structured derivative of the affect of rage that expresses a wish to destroy a bad object, to make it suffer, or to control it. In contrast to the acute, transitory, and disruptive quality of rage, it is a chronic, stable, usually characterologically anchored or structured affect. The object relation framing this affect concretely expresses the desire to destroy or dominate the object. An almost unavoidable consequence of hatred is its justification as revenge against the frustrating object; the wish for revenge is typical of hatred. Paranoid fears of retaliation also usually accompany intense hatred, so that paranoid features, the wish for revenge, and sadism go hand in hand.

One complication of hatred derives from the fact that very early frustration and gratification are experienced as stemming from the same source. This brings us to the psychopathology of envy, which Klein (1957) explained as a major manifestation of human aggression. Very early frustration—in Klein's terms, the absence of the good breast—is experienced by the baby as if the breast withheld itself, with an underlying projection onto the breast of the baby's aggressive reaction to that frustration. The baby's aggression takes the form of greedy wishes to incorporate the frustrating breast, experienced as greedily withholding itself. The breast that aggressively withholds itself is, in turn, hated, and its fantasied contents are spoiled and destroyed. A vicious circle may ensue in which the destroyed and destructive breast is experienced in a persecutory way, thus exaggerating and prolonging the experience of frustration and rage. Here lies the origin of envy, the need to spoil and destroy the object that is also needed for survival and that in the end is the object of love. The introjection of the image of a spoiled, destroyed breast leads to a sense of internal emptiness and destruction, which may damage the previous introjection of the good breast that was lost, so that the effects of envy and the related development of greed corrode both the good external and the good internal object.

The clinical study of patients with narcissistic personality disorder regularly reveals envy (unconscious and conscious) as a major affective expression of aggression. As we move from the better-functioning narcissistic pathology to severe narcissistic personality disorders with overt borderline functioning, that is, with generalized lack of impulse control, anxiety tolerance, and sublimatory channeling, the intensity of aggression mounts, reaching its height in the syndrome of malignant narcissism. At times, hatred is so intense that it results in a primitive destruction of all awareness of the affect, a transformation of aggressive affects into action or acting out. In addition to defending against subjective awareness of the affect, this action obliterates ordinary cognitive functioning. These developments characterize the syndrome that Bion (1957) described as constituted by arrogance, curiosity, and pseudostupidity; here envy and hatred become almost indistinguishable.

Most patients with severe histrionic or borderline personality disorder and severe self-destructive, self-mutilating, suicidal, or antisocial trends evince strong elements of envy in the context of the intense activation of hatred. On the other hand, what might be called the purest manifestation of hatred—with the relative absence of envy per se—may be seen in patients who have been physically traumatized and in some victims of sexual abuse or incest.

What is striking in this context is that the greater the envy, the more the envied person is perceived as one who possesses highly desirable or "good" qualities. In other words, the object of hatred is experienced as in some ways possessing the goodness that the patient misses and desires for himself. This is not the case when pure hatred is directed at an object perceived as a dangerous, sadistic enemy. Hatred aims at the destruction of a source of frustration perceived as sadistically attacking the self; envy is a form of hatred of another who is perceived as sadistically or teasingly withholding something highly desirable. Typically, but not always, patients with severe narcissistic pathology have a history of a relationship with a parental figure who seemed to be operating as a good-enough parent but had an underlying indifference toward the patient and a tendency to narcissistically exploit the patient. For example, the parent may have used the patient as a source of admiration while fostering in the patient the gratification of being an admired object.

CLINICAL APPROACH

Hatred thus emerges as the more primitive, more direct derivative of rage in response to the experience of suffering, pain, or aggression; envy emerges as a special form of hatred under conditions of a relationship in which highly desirable and teasingly withheld aspects of the object complicate the experience of rageful frustration. Clinically, clarification of the subtle differences between these affects and their impact in the transference is a crucial aspect of psychoanalytic and psychotherapeutic work with severe personality disorders.

The first step in such an approach is to help the patient become aware of the intensity of his hatred or envy. This, in turn, will challenge the therapist's countertransference disposition. His capacity of emotional "holding" and cognitive "containing" of the hatred that the patient must express in action or somatization rather than tolerate as psychic experience converges with the therapist's creative use of his countertransference awareness. In the second therapeutic step, the patient will require help to acknowledge the intense, painful, and at times humiliating aspects of hatred or envy and also to acknowledge the sadistic pleasure that acting out hatred and envy provides (which may be a fundamental source of the repetition compulsion of such behavior). In the third step, the patient will eventually have to learn to tolerate the feelings of guilt derived from his recogition that his attack on the "bad" object is at the same time an attack on the potentially good and helpful object.

Sometimes the patient's relentless attack on the therapist corresponds to an unconscious hope that behind the projected bad object an ideal good object will eventually emerge and defuse the situation. It is extremely difficult for the patient to recognize that his behavior consistently interferes with gratification of his deepest wishes; the ascendance of "depressive" transferences after successful working through of antisocial and paranoid transferences is a very painful yet essential aspect of treatment (O. Kernberg 1992a).

Envy, the most typical manifestation of aggression in the transference of narcissistic personalities, is expressed as unconscious envy of the analyst experienced as a good object and as greedy incorporation of what the analyst has to offer, both leading to a sense of emptiness and frustration. Unconscious envy in the analytic situation is a significant source of the negative therapeutic reaction, more primitive and severe than unconscious guilt, which expresses more advanced superego pressures and conflicts. Unconscious envy projected onto the analyst and reintrojected into superego functions may lead to unconscious envy directed against the self.

Another consequence of the structural fixation of rage in the form of hatred is an unconscious identification with the hated object. Insofar as the internalized object relation of hatred is that of a frustrated, impoverished, pained self relating to a powerful, withholding, teasing, sadistic object, unconscious identification with both victim and victimizer intensifies the actual relation with the frustrating object, bringing about increased dependency in reality on the hated object in order to influence, control, or punish it or to transform it into a good object. At the same time, it leads to the unconscious tendency to repeat the relation with the hated object with role reversals, becoming the dominating, teasing, frustrating object mistreating another object, onto which the self-representation has been projected. The children described by Fraiberg (1983) and Galenson (1986) illustrate this basic mechanism of identification with the aggressor by their teasing behavior.

Trauma as the actual experience of sadistic behavior on the part of a needed, inescapable object instantaneously shapes the rage reaction into hatred of the sadistic object. The prevalence of physical abuse, sexual abuse, and the witnessing of violence in patients with severe psychopathology has been reported in this country and abroad (Grossman 1986, 1991; Marziali 1992; Paris 1994a; Perry and Herman 1993). Even given the distortion of statistical analyses under the impact of the current ideologically motivated stress on incest and sexual abuse, the evidence of such abuse as a significant etiological factor in severe personality disorders is convincing. The underlying mechanism, I suggest, is the establishment of an internalized object relation under the control of structured rage—that is, hatred.

When hatred overwhelmingly dominates an unconscious world of internalized object relations, primitive splitting operations persist, resulting in a borderline personality organization characterized by an internal world of idealized and persecutory object relations, with a dominance of the latter. Corollary to this are paranoid tendencies, characterologically structured egosyntonic hatred, sadism, and vengefulness; dissociated efforts are made to escape from a persecutory world by means of illusory and dissociated idealizations. Under traumatic conditions, then, the basic mechanisms would include the immediate transformation of pain into rage and of rage into hatred; hatred consolidates the unconscious identification with victim and victimizer.

The most important clinical manifestation of the dominance of hatred in the transference is the patient's attribution to the therapist of an intense, relentless degree of hatred. By means of projective identification, the internal world of torturer and tortured, tyrant and slave is enacted; the therapist is assigned the role of the sadistic tyrant, and the patient makes unconscious efforts to provoke him into such a role by inducing conditions in the countertransference that eventually tend to activate whatever role responsiveness the therapist possesses in order to fulfill the patient's fearful expectations and to control him in order to limit his dangerousness.

Under extreme circumstances, typically seen in schizophrenic panic and rage attacks but also with transference regression in borderline patients, the patient's fear of his own hatred and of the hatred projected onto the therapist is such that reality itself becomes intolerable. If, under conditions of symbiotic regression in the tranference or even intense activation of projective identification in nonsymbiotic conditions, the entire world is a sea of hatred, blocking out the awareness of reality is the most primitive and dominant mechanism for dealing with this situation. This may lead to psychotic confusional states or, in nonpsychotic patients, to a malignant transformation of the therapist-patient dyad in which all honest communication is suppressed and what I have called psychopathic transferences prevail: The patient is deceptive and expects the therapist to be deceptive, all communication takes on a quality of pseudocommunication, and violent affect storms are expressed in dissociated forms.

Under less extreme conditions, such as those one may see in malignant narcissism, the patient may manifest intense curiosity about the therapist, to the extent of actively spying on the therapist's life; the patient shows consistent arrogance toward and contempt for the therapist and an incapacity to conduct cognitive communication that may amount to a form of pseudostupidity (Bion 1957). I have described in earlier work (1992) how the gradual working through of such conditions in the transference may eventually lead the patient to tolerate his hatred rather than having to project it. Conscious tolerance of hatred may then be expressed as joyful attacks, insults, depreciation, and teasing of the therapist that may be gradually traced to its origins in traumatic situations from the past and to intense envy of the therapist as an individual not controlled by the same terrifying world as the patient is.

Another manifestation of primitive hatred that the patient cannot tolerate in conscious awareness is the transformation of hatred into somatization in the form of primitive self-mutilation. Such patients chronically mutilate themselves by picking at their skin or mucosas and present other patterns of primitive sadomasochistic behavior. Characterologically anchored suicidal tendencies in borderline patients are another expression of self-directed hatred.

The antisocial personality proper may be conceived as a personality structure so dominated by hatred that primitive, split-off idealizations are no longer possible; the world is populated exclusively by hated, hateful, sadistic persecutors. One can triumph in such a terrifying world only by becoming a persecutor, the sole alternative to destruction and suicide. Under milder conditions, unconscious identification with the hated object and its characterological translation into antisocial tendencies, cruelty, contempt, and sadism may be present in many forms. A restricted, encapsulated sadistic perversion may represent one outcome of these conflicts. As Stoller (1985) pointed out, sexual excitement always includes an element of aggression, and an organized perversion typically expresses the need to undo in fantasy an experienced trauma or humiliation from the past in the sexual realm.

In still less severe characterological forms of hatred, the sadistic implications of certain obsessive-compulsive personality structures contain this dynamic, as may certain personality structures with reaction formations against dependency that express the unconscious fear that all dependent relationships imply submission to a sadistic object. Masochistic reaction formations against identification with a hateful object internalized in the superego reflect less severe outcomes of these dynamics. More frequently, the internalization of a hated, sadistic object in the superego may be manifest as sadistic moralism—the tendency toward "justified indignation" and moralistic cruelty.

At a sublimatory level of transformation of hatred, self-assertion, courage, independent judgment, moral integrity, even the capacity for self-sacrifice may include, on analytic exploration, traces of the dynamics we are exploring.

SEXUAL AND PHYSICAL ABUSE

Incest as trauma has received much recent attention, and psychoanalytic study of its victims indeed illustrates the basic dynamic of internalization of an object relation dominated by hatred. In exploring these psychodynamics we have to keep in mind that the sadomasochistic component of sexual excitement permits the recruitment of aggression in the service of love. But this is a response that, when a sexual response is overwhelmed by rage and hatred, may be transformed into sexual sadomasochism in which love is recruited in the service of aggression. That is, sexual intercourse may become a symbolic gratification of sadomasochistic tendencies, replicating in the sexual area the interactions I have described in relationships dominated by hatred.

Not all sexual abuse is experienced as aggressive; unconscious infantile sexuality, the excitement, gratification, and triumph resulting from breaking oedipal barriers, and the guilt such triumph produces, complicate the psychological effects of sexual abuse. Nevertheless, the distortion of superego structures brought about when cross-generational (in particular, parent-child) incest occurs destroys the potential for integrating sadistic parental images into the superego. The conflict between sexual excitement and guilt is thus transformed into one between frail idealization and overwhelming aggression, creating a truly traumatic situation in which libidinal and aggressive strivings can no longer be differentiated. The unconscious identification with the victimizer and the victim may become confused. The repetition compulsion of incest victims who transform their later sexual life into a chain of traumatophilic experiences often makes it difficult to determine whether the patient was the victim or the victimizer.

In the clinical situation, such incest victims reactivate the identification with the victim-victimizer dyad and unconsciously attempt to reproduce the traumatic situation in order to undo it and to recover the ideal object behind the persecutor. In addition, the repetition compulsion expresses the desire for revenge, the rationalization of hatred of the seducer, and the potential sexualization of the hatred in the form of efforts to seduce the seducer. The psychoanalytic treatment of incest victims who have had sexual experiences with former therapists sometimes repeats these experiences with uncanny clarity. Unconscious envy of the current therapist, not involved in the chaotic mixture of hatred and sexuality in which the patient experiences himself as hopelessly mired, is another source of negative therapeutic reactions.

Recent research by Paris (1994b) confirms the importance of a history of sexual abuse in patients with borderline personality disorder as well as their tendency toward dissociative reactions. Paris also points out that a predisposition to dissociative reactions does not seem to be secondary to sexual trauma. In clinical practice, both types of problems are seen together with some frequency. Some borderline patients present dissociative reactions in the form of amnesias, depersonalization states, and even multiple personalities, of which the patients are cognitively aware but which are affectively split.

What is often striking in such dissociative states is the patient's remarkable indifference to what seems to be a dramatic psychopathological phenomenon: Indeed, some patients present an almost defiant affirmation of the "autonomy" of their split-off personalities while refusing to consider any personal responsibility for these phenomena. Often, the mutual dissociation of alternate personality states raises the question of why some apparently not incongruous personality states appear to be split from each other.

In my experience, when the clinician asks how the patient's central personality, her sense of awareness, concern, and responsibility, relates to these split-off personality states, this immediately triggers a new development in the transference. Many patients develop a paranoid reaction to such inquiry; this evolves into a specific transference disposition in which the therapist appears as a persecutory figure in contrast to other persons in the patient's life, including other therapists, who are idealized as helpful, tolerant, nonquestioning, admiring, and supportive. The patient's alternate personality states take on more specific meanings in relation to such split object representations, permitting a clarification of the function of such split states in the transference. In short, approaching the patient from the position of an assumed observing, central, "categorical" self illuminates hidden splits in the transference and permits exploration of the unconscious dynamics involved in the split personality state that are obscured by the usual, apparently untroubled enactment of such states.

The patient now may be tempted to angrily accuse the therapist of not believing in the existence of his multiple personalities. The therapist's concerned and neutral stand—being interested in the patient's experience, not questioning its authenticity, but at the same time evaluating the implications for the patient's central self-experience—gradually permits the patient to increase his self-observing function in contrast to the previous defensive denial of concern and what might be called blind enactment of dissociative states.

In severe personality disorders, the approach I have just outlined transforms what appears to be a dreamlike, often apparently affectless dramatization into a concrete object relation in which intense rage and hatred emerge, split off from other idealized object relations. Once the emergence of mutually split-off peak affect states in the context of split-off primitive object relations becomes evident in the transference, the intepretive integration of these developments may proceed.

This approach contrasts with a tendency on the part of some therapists to explore each dissociated personality state while respecting its split-off condition, bypassing the defensive denial of concern about this condition. I believe that such an approach tends to prolong the dissociative condition itself unnecessarily and may aggravate it.

When such dissociative reactions occur in the context of real or fantasied past incest or sexual abuse, a similar defensive denial of concern for the nature of the dissociative process may often be observed. Such a development contrasts markedly with cases in which, under psychoanalytic exploration, repressed memories of past sexual abuse, including incest, are uncovered, leading to a traumatic emotional reaction that colors the psychotherapeutic relationship for perhaps several months and is gradually worked through. In this latter case, characteristics of a post-traumatic stress syndrome may emerge in the psychotherapeutic relationship; the patient shows great concern for himself, intense ambivalence in relation to the abuser, and ambivalence regarding his own past and present sexuality. The elaboration of such a traumatic recovery of memory contrasts sharply with the long-term repetitive evocation of past traumatic sexual experiences in the context of a present-day expression of hatred, disgust, and revulsion linked to the patient's sexual life in general or to all persons of the gender of the traumatizing agent.

In such cases, particularly when traumatic sexual memories appear repeatedly in the context of dissociative ego states, a characteristic lack of concern, denial, or dramatic indifference toward the dissociative process may also be present. The patient may insist on engaging the therapist as a "witness" or support figure in the struggle against a hated and feared sexual object. In the transference, the therapist may be identified with either the abusing object or a conspiratorial helper (for example, the "innocent bystander" mother, who, in subtle or not-so-subtle ways, protected an incestuous father).

Here again, the world seems to be split between those who side with the traumatizing object and those who support the patient's wishes for a vengeful campaign against that object. Because of the current cultural concerns about sexual abuse, the patient's split world of object relations may be rationalized in a conventional ideology that confirms and maintains his condition as a victim.

I have found it very helpful to ask the patient what keeps the hatred alive in his life and what its functions are in his current conflicts. When the fact of past sexual abuse is unclear, even in the patient's mind, the patient may insistently demand the therapist's confirmation of his suspicions. The therapist's stance— that the patient's experiences are real in their present quality and that the patient himself will eventually be able to clarify and gain understanding of and control over the internal past—often raises the same intensity of suspicion and rage in the transference as do attempts to clarify the relation between the patient's central self-experience and a dissociative state. In other words, the patient may not be able to tolerate the therapist's concerned but neutral position, which runs counter to the overriding need to divide the world into allies and enemies. The therapist's consistent interpretation of the patient's need to maintain such split relations will eventually, under optimal conditions, permit more specific focus on the enactment of the relationship between victimizer and victim, with frequent role reversals, in the transference. This permits analysis of the patient's unconscious identification with the victimizer as well as with the victim role as the major dynamic that maintains the characterologically anchored hatred.

A positive consequence of such a therapeutic approach is the gradual liberation of the patient's sexual life from its infiltration by unrecognized, unmetabolized hatred. The revulsion against sexuality in victims of early sexual abuse has many roots: The invasion of their psychic and physical boundaries is experienced as a violent attack; the transformation of a person in a parental function into a sexual abuser is experienced as sadistic treason, in addition to disorganizing the early buildup of an integrated if primitive superego. The reprojection of early persecutory superego precursors in the form of paranoid tendencies intensifies yet more the aggressive implications of a sexual attack and weakens the capacity for any trusting relationship.

Unconscious guilt arising from the activation of the patient's own sexual impulses in the context of sexual seduction and abuse increases this revulsion against all sexuality and the temptation to reproject such guilt feelings, thus reinforcing the patient's paranoid approach to sexual objects and repression of sexual wishes, fantasies, and experiences. If traumatized victims of concentration camps or torture have to reencounter awareness of their own sadistic tendencies as they discover their unconscious identification with both victim and victimizer, the victims of sexual abuse have to reencounter an awareness of their own sexuality in unconscious identification with both the self and the object of the traumatic experience. The treatment cannot be completed if such a reencounter has not been achieved. Stoller's (1985) understanding of the nature of erotic excitement as an early fusion of sensuous experience and unconscious identification with an aggressive object—in other words, the erotic roots of polymorphous perverse sadomasochism—is relevant in this connection. At some point, a toned-down, tolerable sadomasochistic tendency should become available for retranslation into a language of erotic fantasies, opening up the polymorphous perverse component of adult genital sexuality.

FURTHER COMMENTS ON TREATMENT

In the treatment of patients whose transferences are dominated by hatred, it is important, first of all, to establish a rigorous, flexible, and yet firm frame for the therapeutic relationship; this step controls life- and treatment-threatening acting out. The therapist has to experience himself as safe in order to be able to analyze the deep regression in the transference. Setting a contract for patients who are suicidal or engaged in dangerous sexual behavior or other types of destructiveness and self-destructiveness encourages the expression of hatred in the transference rather than through the alternative channels of somatization or acting out. As Green (1986) has pointed out, it is extremely important to facilitate the transformation of somatization and acting out into psychic experience in the transference.

When distortion of verbal communication exists, psychopathic transferences should be resolved first; that is, deceptiveness in the communication must be reduced sufficiently for the underlying paranoid tendencies in the transference to emerge more clearly and make it possible to work through them. The therapist should remain alert to the activation of a victim-victimizer paradigm, analyzing this dyadic relation in the transference as it is repeated, again and again, with role reversals. This requires the therapist to be extremely alert to the countertransference: Painful experiences of himself as victim and the temptation to act out strong aggressive countertransference reactions as victimizer may alternate.

The tendency to avoid analyzing the patient's identification with the aggressor must be especially guarded against in the treatment of victims of abuse. To treat the patient consistently as a victim is to facilitate the projection of the aggressor role outside the transference. This perpetuates an idealized transference situation dissociated from the basic dyad controlled by hatred, thus perpetuating the patient's psychopathology.

I have found the analysis of unconscious envy as a specific manifestation of characterological hatred particularly relevant under certain clinical conditions: first, in connection with pervasive defenses against dependency and regression in the transference, typical of the narcissistic personality; second, in the presence of strong negative therapeutic reactions not based on an unconscious sense of guilt; third, in cases showing an apparent dependency on and greedy incorporation of what comes from the analyst, together with a surprising inability to learn from the experience and a persistent sense of emptiness in the analytic situation; fourth, when inordinate ambition and the search for power appear in combination with conscious and unconscious self-devaluation and depression easily triggered by lack of gratification of expectations; fifth, in the face of habitual inhibitions of creative pursuits; sixth, when unconscious conflicts involving fears of humiliation and shame are combined with paranoid fears of potentially envious and persecutory attitudes from the surrounding world; and finally, when patients continue to lack the capacity to let ideas and feelings grow as a consequence of the psychoanalytic interchange, do not trust the survival of goodness in their heart, and are not able, symbolically speaking, to "mother themselves."

The tolerance of envy, its elaboration and working through as part of emotional growth, the sense of internal richness and wealth that derives from the capacity for gratitude and appreciation of others, and the enjoyment of others' success—these are fundamental objectives and consequences of analytic work. The resolution of conflicts involving unconscious envy permits the growth of the capacity for gratitude and derived reparatory and sublimatory potential.

There are limits, I believe, to the treatment of conditions derived from the kind of hatred I have been describing. The most fundamental one, in my experience, is the deterioration or absence of superego functions that we find in antisocial personalities. Patients with a syndrome of malignant narcissism currently define the boundary of what I believe can be reached with analytically oriented approaches.

When egosyntonic expression of hatred translates into a sadistic enjoyment of attacks on the therapist, the importance of emotional "holding" as well as cognitive "containing" cannot be overstressed. The therapist's consistent work with countertransference developments, often outside the treatment sessions, may become important at such times. When the denial of hatred takes more complex forms, such as dissociative reactions or efforts to seduce the therapist into an enactment of hateful revenge, the interpretive approach to such developments may temporarily increase aggression in the transference, but it does permit the full analysis of the involved internalized object relation. Finally, chronic sadomasochistic developments in the transference have to be explored most carefully in terms of their value for information and working-through, in contrast to a repetitive acting out that does not advance the therapeutic task but may simply reinforce or even create a new channel for acting out aggression.

Chapter 3 Pathological Narcissism and Narcissistic Personality Disorder: Theoretical Background and Diagnostic Classification

Clarification of the concept of narcissism is complicated by the existence of two parallel and complementary levels of definition. In the psychoanalytical theory of metapsychology (that is, a consideration of structural, dynamic, economic, adaptive, and genetic principles of mental functioning), narcissism is defined as the libidinal investment of the self. In the ego-psychology frame of reference, the self is regarded as a substructure of the system ego reflecting the integration of all the component self-images or self-representations that develop throughout the individual's interactions with other human beings (objects). The investment of libido in such objects and their psychic representations (object representations) constitutes object libido. Object libido is in a dynamic relation with narcissistic libido invested in the self.

The second level of conceptualizing of narcissism has to do with the

An earlier version of this chapter appeared in *Narcissism: Diagnostic, Clinical, and Empirical Clinical Implications,* edited by Elsa F. Ronningstam. Washington, D.C.: American Psychiatric Press, 1997, 29–51. www.appi.org.

clinical syndromes that characterize patients with abnormal self-esteem regulation. Self-esteem, or self-regard, usually fluctuates according to whether one's relationships with others are gratifying or frustrating and according to one's evaluation of the distance between one's goals or aspirations and one's achievements. Beyond these commonsense observations are complex relations between self-esteem, predominant affects or moods, the extent to which various self-representations are integrated or dissociated, and the vicissitudes of internalized object relations (the reciprocal relations between self-representations and object representations).

The first conceptualization, which is more difficult, provides us with models of unconscious psychic functioning that explain the clinical phenomena we observe. Metapsychological analysis postulates that self-esteem regulation is dependent on, among other factors, the pressures the superego exerts on the ego: The more excessive the infantile morality (unconscious demands for perfections and prohibitions), the lower self-esteem may be. Such a lowering of self-esteem would reflect a predominance of self-directed aggression (stemming from the superego) over the libidinal investment of the self.

Lowered self-esteem also may be caused by the lack of gratification of instinctual needs of both a libidinal and an aggressive nature (reflected in dependent, sexual, and aggressive strivings). In other words, unconscious ego defenses that repress the awareness and expression of instinctual needs would impoverish the ego (self) of gratifying experiences and thus deplete libidinal ego (self) investments and diminish self-esteem.

In addition, the internalization of libidinally invested objects in the form of libidinally invested object representations greatly reinforces the libidinal investment of the self; that is, the presence in the mind of the images of those we love and by whom we feel loved strengthens our self-love. As a song by the French composer-poet George Brassens has it, "There are friends in the forest of my heart." In contrast, when excessive conflicts involving aggression weaken our libidinal investments in others and corresponding object representations, the libidinal investment of the self and self-love also suffer.

HISTORY

The term *narcissism,* first used in a psychiatric sense by Ellis (1898) and used by Näcke (1899) to describe a sexual perversion, entered the psychoanalytical lexicon because of the work of Sadger (1908). After mentioning narcissism briefly in various papers, in 1914 Freud published one of his major contributions to psychoanalytical theory. In "On Narcissism: An Introduction" Freud describes narcissism as a form of sexual perversion as well as a characteristic of all perversions, as a stage in libidinal development, as an underlying characteristic of schizophrenia because of the withdrawal of libido from the external world, and with reference to a type of object choice in which the object is selected because it represents what the subject was, is, or would like to be.

These multiple applications have facilitated significant psychoanalytic investigations but have also resulted in considerable confusion about the definition of narcissism. Gradually, however, narcissism as a concept in psychoanalytical theory became distinguished from the clinical use of the term, which has come to refer to the normal and pathological regulation of self-esteem. Descriptions of the narcissistic personality disorder (NPD) gradually evolved from this second context; the diagnostic category resulted from observation of a particular constellation of resistances in the psychoanalytic treatment of certain patients corresponding to a particular type of character pathology manifest in the daily lives of these patients.

Jones (1955) wrote the first description of pathological narcissistic character traits. Abraham (1919) was the first to describe the transference resistances of patients with these traits; he pointed to the need for consistent interpretation of their tendencies to look down on the analyst and to use the analyst as an audience for their independent "analytic" work, and he drew attention to the link between narcissism and envy. Riviere (1936) observed that narcissistic resistances were an important source of negative therapeutic reactions; these patients cannot tolerate the idea of improvement because that would mean the need to acknowledge help received from somebody else. These patients cannot tolerate receiving something good from the analyst because of their intolerable guilt concerning their own basic aggression.

Elaborating on Klein's book *Envy and Gratitude* (1957), Rosenfeld (1964, 1971, 1975, 1978) wrote the first detailed description of the psychostructural characteristics of narcissistic personalities and their transference developments in the course of psychoanalysis.

Important contributors to an understanding of the phenomenology and psychopathology of narcissistic personalities include Reich (1953, 1960), Jacobson (1971a, 1971b), van der Waals (1965), and Tartakoff (1966). On the basis of Jacobson's formulations, and in an effort to integrate the American and British contributions to the diagnosis and treatment of the narcissistic personality within an ego-psychology frame of reference, I (O. Kernberg 1970, 1974, 1975, 1976, 1980) proposed an alternative theoretical and clinical frame to the one suggested by Rosenfeld. At the same time, Kohut (1968, 1971, 1972, 1977, 1979) proposed a completely different theoretical frame, clinical explanations, and therapeutic procedure.

The proliferation of contributions relating to narcissism from Great Britain and the United States had a parallel in France. Grunberger (1979), whose work was first published in the 1950s and 1960s, focused on the wider clinical and metapsychological aspects of narcissism as observed in the psychoanalytical treatment of a broad range of pathologies.

Pulver (1970) clarified this bewildering expansion of the concept of narcissism. More recent contributions to the study of the narcissistic personality and the psychoanalytic treatment of these patients have come from Modell (1976), Volkan (1973, 1979), and Bach (1977a, 1977b). Akhtar and Thomson (1982) provided a broadly based analysis of NPD and its relation to the definition of this disorder in DSM-III. A volume concerning NPD that I edited (O. Kernberg 1989a) includes updated descriptions of NPD by Akhtar, Cooper, Horowitz, Ronningstam and Gundeson, and P. F. Kernberg and exploration of the relation between NPD and antisocial personality disorder by Stone, McGlashan and Heinssen, and Bursten, as well as myself. In the same volume, Plakun, Stone, and Rinsley report on clinical observations and empirical research on etiology as well as a differential diagnosis and follow-up study of patients with NPD. Psychoanalytic approaches to the treatment of these patients are summarized by Chasseguet-Smirgel, Goldberg, Steiner, and myself. Further contributions are presented in a book edited by Plakun (1990).

One major subject related to narcissism that, for all practical purposes, Freud (1914) did not touch on is narcissism as character pathology. He referred to only one type of character pathology linked to narcissism: Male homosexual patients, he said, may select another man as their object choice, one who stands for themselves while they identify with their own mother; they then love this man as they would have wanted to be loved by her.

In 1984 I proposed the classification of narcissism along a dimension of severity from normal to pathological. I described the following major categories (pp. 192–96):

• Normal adult narcissism is characterized by normal self-esteem regulation. It is dependent on a normal self-structure related to normally integrated or "total" internalized object representations; an integrated, largely individualized, and abstracted superego; and the gratification of instinctual needs within the context of stable object relations and value systems.

- Normal infantile narcissism is important because fixation at or regression to infantile narcissistic goals (infantile mechanisms of self-esteem regulation) is an important characteristic of all character pathology. Normal infantile narcissism consists of the regulation of self-esteem by age-appropriate gratifications that include or imply normal infantile "value systems," demands, or prohibitions.
- Three types of pathological narcissism can be described: (1) Regression to infantile self-esteem regulations, reflecting the mildest type of narcissistic character pathology, involves precisely the fixation at or regression to this level of normal infantile narcissism. This type is represented by the frequent cases of personality or character disorders in which the regulation of self-esteem seems to be overly dependent on the expression of or defenses against childish gratifications that are normally abandoned in adulthood. Here the problem is that the ego ideal is controlled by infantile aspirations, values, and prohibitions. One might say that, in fact, when Freud (1916) described the neurotic lowering of self-esteem related to excessive repression of the sexual drive, he was implicitly describing what would later be formulated as the structural characteristics of psychoneurosis and neurotic character pathology. This is a common and—in light of current knowledge of more severe narcissistic pathology—relatively mild disturbance that is usually resolved in the course of ordinary psychoanalytic treatment. (2) A second, more severe, but relatively infrequent type of pathological narcissism is what Freud (1914) described as an illustration of narcissistic object choice. In this type the patient's self is identified with an object while the representation of the patient's infantile self is projected onto that object, thus creating a libidinal relation in which the functions of self and object have been interchanged. This condition, indeed, is found among some people who love another as they wish to be loved. (3) The third and most severe type of pathological narcissism is the narcissistic personality disorder proper, one of the most challenging syndromes in clinical psychiatry. Because of the intense study of its psychopathology and the psychoanalytic technique optimally geared to resolve it, it has now become one of the standard indications for psychoanalytic treatment. It is also a frequent indication, in its more severe forms, for psychoanalytic psychotherapy.

CLINICAL CHARACTERISTICS OF NPD

The essential pathological character traits of those with NPD center on pathological self-love, pathological object love, and pathological superego.

Pathological self-love is expressed in excessive self-reference and self-centeredness. These patients also manifest grandiosity, reflected in exhibitionistic tendencies, a sense of superiority, recklessness, and ambitions that are inordinate in view of what they can actually achieve. Their grandiosity is frequently expressed in infantile values—physical attractiveness, power, wealth, clothing, manners, and the like. Those who are highly intelligent may use this endowment as the basis for intellectual pretentiousness.

Further expressions of self-love include an overdependence on admiration from others without an accompanying sense of gratitude—admiration is taken for granted rather than appreciated. These patients are emotionally shallow, especially in relation to others. Feelings of grandiosity alternate with feelings of insecurity or inferiority, conveying the impression that these patients feel either superior or totally worthless. What they fear most is being "average" or "mediocre." Of all these indicators, grandiosity is the most characteristic of pathological self-love.

Pathological object love is manifest by excessive—at times, overwhelming—envy, both conscious and unconscious (the latter reflected in conscious attempts to avoid or deny its existence). Such patients also use devaluation, consciously or not, in an effort to defend themselves against potential feelings of envy. Consciously, pathological object love is manifest as a lack of interest in others and their work or activities and as contempt. Unconsciously, it is manifest as a "spoiling" maneuver consisting of simultaneously incorporating what comes from others and devaluing what has been incorporated. These patients may also defend themselves against envy by means of exploitativeness. Excessive greed results in a wish to steal or appropriate what others have. A sense of entitlement is also often present.

Another manifestation of pathological object love is an inability to depend on others. A temporary idealization of others may quickly change to devaluation; the patients unconsciously seem to experience those around them first as idols, then as enemies or fools. As might be expected, these patients are unable to empathize with or make substantive commitments to others.

A pathological superego is less decisive in establishing the diagnosis but is very important in establishing the prognosis for psychotherapeutic treatment. These character patterns and affective disturbances include the incapacity to experience differentiated forms of self-critique or mild depression (such as remorse, sadness, and critical self-reflection) in contrast to the presence of severe mood swings, often sparked by a failure to succeed in grandiose efforts or obtain admiration from others or following criticism that shatters grandiosity.

Self-esteem is regulated by shame rather than guilt. The patients show little interest in ethical, aesthetic, or intellectual values; their values are childish, aimed at protecting self-esteem and pride. Their inordinate dependency on external admiration indirectly reflects their immature superego functioning. Some narcissistic patients with particularly severe superego pathology present the syndrome that I call malignant narcissism, described in previous chapters and summarized below.

Patients with NPD typically feel a sense of emptiness or of being alone. The patients are usually incapable of learning from others, have intense stimulus hunger, and feel that life is meaningless. They characteristically feel bored when their need for admiration and success is not being gratified.

The functioning of narcissistic persons depends on the severity of their pathology, ranging from almost "normal" personalities to overtly borderline functioning. For borderline patients, a differential diagnosis with psychotic illness may have to be entertained.

Those functioning at the highest level (that is, having the least severe pathology) do not have neurotic symptoms and seem to be adapting to social reality. They have little awareness of emotional illness except for a chronic sense of emptiness or boredom and an inordinate need for approval and success. They also have a remarkable incapacity for empathy and emotional investment in others. Few of them seek treatment, but they subsequently tend to develop complications secondary to their narcissistic pathology that may bring them to treatment. The middle range of severe NPD presents the typical symptoms already described.

At the lowest level of the continuum (the most severe pathology) are patients who, despite the defensive functions provided by the pathological grandiose self in social interactions, show overt borderline characteristics—that is, lack of impulse control, lack of anxiety tolerance, severe crippling of their sublimatory capacities, and a disposition to explosive or chronic rage reactions or severe paranoid distortions.

ETIOLOGY OF NARCISSISTIC PERSONALITY DISORDER

The clinical description of NPD derives mainly from the study of patients in the course of psychoanalytic or psychoanalytically oriented psychotherapeutic treatment. The theories proposed by Rosenfeld (1964, 1971, 1975, 1978), by Kohut (1971, 1972, 1977, 1979), and by me (1975, 1976, 1980, 1984) all point to the essentially psychodynamic etiology of these disorders and the pathology of self-esteem regulation as the key pathogenic issue in addition to postulating the presence of an abnormal self-structure. The three approaches disagree, how-ever, regarding the origin of this pathological self-structure, and, as a conse-quence, they propose significantly different psychotherapeutic techniques.

Rosenfeld (1964), a Kleinian psychoanalyst, proposed that narcissistic pa-tients identify themselves with an omnipotently introjected, all-good, primi-tive "part object," thus denying any distinction between self and object. This identification permits the patients to deny any need for dependency on an orig-inally good external object. Dependency would imply the need for such a loved (and potentially frustrating) object who is also intensely hated, with the hatred taking the form of extreme envy. Envy, Rosenfeld assumes, following Klein (1957), is a primary intrapsychic expression of the death instinct, the earliest manifestation of aggression in the realm of object relations. Narcissistic object relations permit the subject to avoid aggressive feelings caused by frustration and any awareness of envy. Rosenfeld (1971) also described the complication arising in these personality structures when self-idealization is contaminated by idealization of the aggressive parts of the self. The infiltration of the pathologi-cal "mad" self by primitive aggression results in violent self-destructiveness. In extreme cases, such patients feel secure and triumphant only when they have destroyed everyone else and particularly when they have frustrated the efforts of those who love them. Rosenfeld (1975) thought this need was responsible for the most severe forms of negative therapeutic reaction. The pathological grandiose self of these patients reflects a more primitive and intractable resis-tance to treatment than do the unconscious guilt feelings, stemming from a sadistic superego, characteristic of milder forms of negative therapeutic reac-tion.

Kohut (1971, 1977) argued that there is a group of patients whose psy-chopathology is intermediary between the psychoses and borderline condi-tions, on one hand, and the psychoneuroses and milder character disorders, on the other. This group of NPDs, whom Kohut considered analyzable, can be differentiated primarily by transference manifestations, not by clinical descrip-tive criteria. Kohut diagnosed NPD within the psychoanalytical situation by recognizing the development of two types of transference: idealizing and mir-roring. He proposed that these represent the activation in the psychoanalytic situation of an arrested stage of development—an archaic grandiose self. The fragility of that archaic self requires an empathic mother as "self-object" whose love, ministrations, and mirroring acceptance of the infant permit the development of the archaic self into more mature forms of self-esteem and self-confidence. At the same time, optimal empathic relations with the mirroring self-object facilitate the idealization of the self-object that stands for the original perfection of the grandiose self, now practically preserved in the relation with such an idealized self-object. This idealization culminates eventually in what Kohut called the "transmuting internalization" of the idealized self-object into an intrapsychic structure that will originate the ego ideal and provide the idealizing qualities to the superego, thus preserving the now-internalized regulation of self-esteem.

Narcissistic psychopathology, according to Kohut, derives from the traumatic failure of the mother's empathic function and the failure of the undisturbed development of idealization processes. These traumatic failures bring about a developmental arrest at the level of the archaic infantile grandiose self and an endless search for the idealized self-object needed to complete structure formation—all of which are reflected in the narcissistic transferences already mentioned.

In short, in Kohut's view, narcissistic psychopathology reflects the psychopathology of the stage of development that begins with the cohesion of the archaic grandiose self and ends with the transmuting internalization of the ego ideal. This stage centers on the gradual buildup of what Kohut called the "bipolar self." He suggested that one pole, the bulk of nuclear grandiosity of the self, consolidates into nuclear ambitions in early childhood; the other pole, pertaining to the nuclear idealized goal structures of the self, is acquired somewhat later. These two poles of the self derive, respectively, from the mother's mirroring acceptance (which confirms nuclear grandiosity) and her holding or caring (which allows experiences of merger with the self-object's idealized omnipotence). Nuclear ambitions and nuclear ideals are linked by an intermediary area of basic talents and skills. Kohut considered these component structures of the bipolar self as reflecting both the origin and the seed of narcissistic psychopathology, in contrast to the drives- and conflict-derived psychopathology of the tripartite structure of the mind, which characterizes the later oedipal period. For Kohut, then, the etiology of NPDs resides in an arrested stage of development of the normal self.

I have proposed (O. Kernberg 1975, 1980, 1984) that the specific character features of patients with NPD reflect a pathological narcissism that differs from both ordinary adult narcissism and fixation at or regression to normal infantile narcissism in that it reflects libidinal investment not in a normal, integrated self-structure but in a pathological self-structure. The pathological grandiose self contains real self-representations, ideal self-representations, and ideal object representations. Devalued or aggressively determined self- and object representations are split off or dissociated, repressed or projected. The psychoanalytic resolution of the grandiose self as part of the systematic analysis of narcissistic character resistances regularly brings to the surface—that is, activates in the transference—primitive object relations, conflicts, and defensive operations characteristic of developmental stages that predate object constancy. These transferences, however, are always condensed with oedipally derived conflicts, so that they are strikingly similar to those of patients with borderline personality organization.

The psychic development of NPD does not proceed smoothly through the early stages of development described by Jacobson (1964) and Mahler (Mahler and Furer 1968; Mahler et al. 1975). Their description of the early stages of separation-individuation and object constancy underlies my theoretical model, but I believe that sometime between ages three and five, the narcissistic personality, instead of integrating positive and negative representations of self and of objects—"on the road to object constancy" (Mahler et al. 1975)—puts together all the positive representations of self and objects. This results in an extremely unrealistic and idealized pathological grandiose self. Fostering the development of such a self are parents who are cold and rejecting, yet admiring. Narcissistic individuals devalue the real objects, having incorporated the aspects of the real objects that they want for themselves. They dissociate from themselves and repress or project onto others all the negative aspects of themselves and others.

The ideal self-object representations that would normally become part of the superego are incorporated into the pathological grandiose self. This leads to a superego containing only the aggressively determined components (the early prohibiting and threatening aspects of the parental images distorted under the impact of the projection of the child's own aggressive impulses). This successfully harsh superego also tends to be dissociated and projected, which leads to further development of "persecutory" external objects and to the loss of the normal functions of the superego in regulating self-esteem, such as monitoring and approval.

The devaluation of others, the emptying out of the internal world of object representations, is a major contributing cause of the narcissistic individual's lack of normal self-esteem and also determines his remarkable inability to empathize with others. The sense of an internal void can be compensated for only by endless admiration from others and by efforts to control others so as to avoid the envy that would otherwise be caused by the autonomous functioning, enjoyment of life, and creativity that others enjoy.

DIFFERENTIATING NPD AND ANTISOCIAL PERSONALITY DISORDER

The virtually total absence of the capacity for nonexploitative object relations and of any moral dimension in personality functioning is the key element differentiating the antisocial personality proper from the less severe syndromes of malignant narcissism and NPD. The antisocial features in NPD may range from minor dishonesty to a full-fledged antisocial personality disorder, suggesting that the antisocial personality may be considered a narcissistic personality with additional superego pathology.

What follows is a classification, according to severity, of personality disorders in which antisocial features are prominent.

Antisocial Personality Disorder

In all patients with antisocial behavior, it is helpful first to rule out the diagnosis of an antisocial personality proper. For this reason, the potential presence of antisocial behavior in all patients with NPD is systematically investigated.

Patients with antisocial personality disorder typically present with an NPD with symptoms described above. Antisocial personality disorder proper involves even more serious superego pathology than does NPD, including such behaviors as lying, stealing, forgery, swindling, and prostitution, all of which are characteristic of a predominantly "passive-parasitic" type; assault, murder, and armed robbery are characteristic of the "aggressive" type (Henderson 1939; Henderson and Gillespie 1969). In other words, the behaviorally aggressive, sadistic, and usually paranoid orientation of some patients with antisocial personality disorder can be differentiated clinically from the passive, exploitative, parasitic behavior of others.

Passive and aggressive antisocial behavior as part of an NPD are differentiated from an antisocial personality disorder proper by the capacity to feel guilt and remorse. Even after being confronted with the consequences of their behavior, and in spite of their profuse protestations of regret, persons with antisocial personality disorder do not change their behavior toward those they have attacked or exploited or show any spontaneous concern about this failure to change.

Although differential diagnosis of the capacity for experiencing guilt and concern requires the inferential step of evaluating a patient's reaction to confrontation and the breakdown of omnipotence, other characteristics reflecting this incapacity for guilt and concern may become directly evident in the interviews, for example, in the inability to imagine an ethical quality in others. The inability to invest in nonexploitative relationships with others may be reflected in transient, superficial, indifferent relationships, the inability to invest emotionally even in pets, and the absence of any internalized moral values, let alone the capacity to empathize with such values in others. The deterioration of these patients' affective experience is expressed in their inability to tolerate any increase in anxiety without developing additional symptoms or pathological behaviors, their inability to experience depression with reflective sorrow, and their inability to fall in love or experience any tenderness in their sexual relations.

Patients with antisocial personality disorder have no sense of the passage of time, of planning for the future, or of contrasting present experience and behavior with aspired-to ideal ones; they can plan only to improve present discomforts and reduce tension by achieving immediately desired goals. Their failure to learn from experience is an expression of the same incapacity to conceive of their lives beyond the immediate moment. Their manipulativeness, pathological lying, and flimsy rationalizations are well known. The term "holographic men" was coined by P. F. Kernberg (personal communication, December 1981) to refer to patients who create a vague, ethereal image of themselves in diagnostic sessions that seems strangely disconnected from their current reality or their actual past. This image changes from moment to moment in the light of different angles of inquiry and leaves the diagnostician with a disturbing sense of unreality.

Again, once the diagnosis of a narcissistic personality structure is obvious, the crucial diagnostic task is to evaluate the severity of any presenting antisocial features, their history and childhood origins, and the patient's remaining capacity for object relations and superego functioning.

Malignant Narcissism Syndrome

If antisocial personality disorder proper can be ruled out, the next diagnostic category to be considered is an NPD with the syndrome of malignant narcissism.

In contrast to those with antisocial personality disorder proper, these patients—characterized by a typical NPD, antisocial behavior, egosyntonic sadism or characterologically anchored aggression, and a paranoid orientation—still have the capacity for loyalty to and concern for others and for feeling guilty. They are able to conceive of other people as having moral concerns and convictions, and they may have a realistic attitude toward their own past and in planning for the future.

Their egosyntonic sadism may be expressed in a conscious "ideology" of aggressive self-affirmation but also quite frequently in chronic, egosyntonic suicidal tendencies. These tendencies emerge not as part of a depressive syndrome but rather in emotional crises or even out of the blue, with the underlying (conscious or unconscious) fantasy that to be able to take one's life reflects superiority and triumph over the usual fear of pain and death. To commit suicide, in these patients' fantasies, is to exercise sadistic control over others or to walk out of a world they feel they cannot control.

The paranoid orientation of these patients (which psychodynamically reflects the projection onto others of unintegrated sadistic superego precursors) is manifest in their experience of others as idols, enemies, or fools in an exaggerated way. These patients have a propensity to regress into paranoid micropsychotic episodes in the course of intensive psychotherapy; thus, they illustrate most dramatically the complementary functions of paranoid and antisocial interactions in the interpersonal realm (Jacobson 1971b; O. Kernberg 1984). Some of them may present rationalized antisocial behavior, for example, as leaders of sadistic gangs or terrorist groups. An idealized self-image and an egosyntonic sadistic, self-starving ideology rationalize the antisocial behavior and may coexist with the capacity for loyalty to their own comrades.

Narcissistic Personality Disorders with Antisocial Behavior

Patients with NPD may present a variety of antisocial behaviors, mainly of the passive-parasitic type, and show remnants of autonomous moral behavior in some areas and ruthless exploitativeness in others. They do not evince the egosyntonic sadism, self-directed aggression, or overt paranoid orientation typical of malignant narcissism. They have a capacity to experience guilt, concern, and loyalty to others. They have an appropriate perception of their past, and they may realistically conceive of and plan for the future. In some cases, what appears to be antisocial behavior is simply a manifestation of an incapacity for commitment in depth to long-range relationships. Narcissistic types of sexual promiscuity, irresponsibility in work, and emotional or financial exploitation of others are prevalent in such cases, although these patients are still able to care for others in some areas and to maintain ordinary social responsibility in more distant interpersonal interactions.

Antisocial Behavior in Other Personality Disorders

The next level of pathology, with fewer negative prognostic and therapeutic implications, is antisocial behavior in personality disorders other than NPD. These are patients with borderline personality organization and nonpathological narcissism. Typical examples are the infantile, histrionic, hysteroid, and Zetzel type 3 and 4 personality disorders (not to be confused with hysterical personality proper), and the paranoid personality disorder. In the infantile personality, pseudologia fantastica is not uncommon; the "paranoid urge to betray" (Jacobson 1971a) illustrates treacherousness in a paranoid context. In my experience, most patients with factitious disorder with psychological or physical symptoms, pathological gambling, kleptomania, pyromania, or malingering who do not have a typical NPD have one of these personality disorders with antisocial features.

Neurotic Personality Disorders with Antisocial Features

Patients in this category, such as Freud's (1914) criminals with an unconscious sense of guilt, are of great clinical interest. Their sometimes dramatic antisocial behavior occurs in the context of a neurotic personality organization and has an excellent prognosis for psychotherapeutic and psychoanalytic treatment.

Antisocial Behavior as Part of a Symptomatic Neurosis

Antisocial behavior as part of a symptomatic neurosis refers to occasional antisocial behavior as part of adolescent rebelliousness, in adjustment disorders, or in the presence of a social environment that fosters channeling psychic conflicts into antisocial behavior.

Dissocial Reaction

A clinically relatively rare syndrome, dissocial reaction refers to the normal or neurotic adjustment to an abnormal social environment or subgroup. In clinical practice, most patients with this syndrome present some type of personality disorder that facilitates their uncritical adaptation to a social subgroup with antisocial behaviors.

CONCLUSION

Pathological narcissism constitutes a dimension within the field of personality disorders that includes, in order of progressive severity, narcissistic personality disorder, malignant narcissism, and antisocial personality disorder. The clinical importance of this continuum resides in the prognostic implications of antisocial behavior for all psychotherapeutic approaches to these conditions. Without antisocial behavior NPD has a good prognosis; that prognosis worsens with significant antisocial behavior. Malignant narcissism syndrome has a reserved prognosis. And antisocial personality disorder has a grave outlook for all currently used psychotherapeutic measures.

Given the high prevalence of narcissistic pathology, the advances in clinical and psychopathological knowledge of these conditions represent an important contribution to the evolving understanding of the entire field of personality disorders.

Chapter 4 The Diagnosis of
Narcissistic Pathology in
Adolescents

The most important task for the psychiatrist examining a troubled adolescent is to establish a reliable diagnosis regarding the severity of the psychopathology, differentiating manifestations of emotional turmoil as part of a neurosis or an adjustment reaction from more severe character pathology that makes its first appearance in adolescence. Varying degrees of anxiety and depression, emotional outbursts and temper tantrums, excessive rebelliousness or dependency, sexual inhibition, and polymorphous perverse sexual impulses and activities may present in adolescents without severe character pathology and in those with very severe characterological disturbances.

Published in *Annals of the American Society for Adolescent Psychiatry,* edited by A. H. Esman, I. T. Flaherty, and H. A. Horowitz. Hillsdale, N.J.: Analytic Press, 1998, 22:169–186.

THE DIAGNOSIS OF IDENTITY DIFFUSION AND
REALITY TESTING

The narcissistic personality disorder, as we have seen, is one of the most prevalent of the severe personality disorders, presenting the syndrome of identity diffusion typical of borderline personality organization. Therefore, the diagnosis of identity diffusion is an essential aspect of the diagnosis of pathological narcissism. It is the first step in evaluating the severity of any character pathology in an adolescent.

The key anchoring point of the differential diagnosis of milder types of character pathology and neurotic personality organization, on one hand, and severe character pathology and borderline personality organization, on the other, is the presence of normal identity integration as opposed to the syndrome of identity diffusion. This differential diagnosis should not present many difficulties to the experienced clinician. Normal identity crises in adolescence reflect the impact of the relatively rapid physical and psychological changes that emerge with puberty, the adolescent's internal sense of confusion regarding the emergence of strong sexual impulses and the contradictory pressures regarding how to deal with them, and the widening gap between the perception of the adolescent by his traditional family environment and his self-perception. *Adolescent identity crisis,* in short, refers to the significant discrepancy between the adolescent's rapidly shifting self-concept and his experience of others' perceptions of him (Erikson 1956a). *Identity diffusion,* in contrast, refers to a severe lack of integration of the concepts of the self and of significant others; it usually has its roots in early childhood and is related to a failure of normal resolution of the stage of separation-individuation (Mahler et al. 1975). The syndrome of identity diffusion may make its appearance throughout childhood, but, given the protective functions of the ordinary structured environment of childhood, the symptoms usually become evident only when the structure of the parental home environment decreases in the course of adolescent development.

Adolescents with the symptoms of identity diffusion may present a completely chaotic and contradictory view of themselves without awareness of the nature of the description of the self that they convey, or else a rigid adherence to social norms—an overidentification with either traditional norms or adolescent group formations—reflected in what has been called the "quiet borderline patient" who impresses the therapist as a relatively affectless, indecisive, undefined, pseudosubmissive youngster (Sherwood and Cohen 1994). In response to a request to describe himself briefly, providing a picture of himself that would differentiate him from others, he gives a self-description that, in the case of adolescent identity diffusion, is usually contradictory and chaotic, except when flatness and an overly compliant attitude toward family demands and cultural clichés predominate. In contrast, an adolescent with normal identity integration may offer a rich and highly personalized image of himself. In addition, the adolescent with identity diffusion describes himself in ways that present sharp discrepancies from interactions in the diagnostic interviews.

The integration of the representations of significant others is an even more important aspect of ego identity than the integration of the self because, in the special case of the narcissistic personality, examined below, whereas a pathological grandiose self contributes to a kind of integration of the self-concept, integration of the concept of significant others remains glaringly absent.

In this regard, an adolescent with a neurotic personality organization, severe conflicts at home or at school, and a rebellious and affectively unstable style of interpersonal interaction may be highly critical of the adults who surround him, in particular, parents and teachers, involved in tense conflicts of loyalties and group formation, and yet able to describe with remarkable depth the personalities of those involved with whom he has intense personal conflicts. In contrast, the adolescent with identity diffusion shows a remarkable incapacity to convey a lively picture of those who are closest to him and with whom conflicts, dependency, submission, and rebellion are most intense. Therefore, a consistent request that the adolescent describe the persons who are most important in his life, regardless of whether he likes or dislikes them, provides crucial information regarding his capacity to integrate the concept of significant others. In cases where the personalities of significant others are objectively chaotic and contradictory, the adolescent with normal identity formation should be able to describe such chaos but to do so critically, accompanied by an internal need and an active attempt to sort out these contradictions in significant others.

Although the combination of a lack of integration of the self-concept and a lack of integration of the concept of significant others defines identity diffusion and, by itself, determines the diagnosis of borderline personality organization, the certainty of this diagnosis can be reinforced by evaluation of an adolescent's superego functioning. A major consequence of normal ego identity integration is the facilitation of the integration of the superego, that is, completion of the process of integrating the earliest layer of persecutory superego precursors, the later layer of idealized superego precursors, the still later layer of realistic superego precursors of the oedipal period, and the final processes of depersonification, abstraction, and individualization of the superego. The absence of normal identity integration in the ego interferes with this integration of the superego and results in various degrees of lack of maturation of the superego.

In fact, the extent of superego integration is one of the two most crucial prognostic factors for all types of psychotherapeutic intervention; the other factor is the quality of the adolescent's object relations, his capacity to invest in values beyond narrow self-interests and direct narcissistic gratification: his interest in work, art, and culture, his commitments to ideology, and the maturity of the value judgments he makes with regard to such investments. Obviously, the adolescent's cultural background will crucially codetermine his orientation toward value systems, but within any particular socioeconomic and cultural background, adolescents with normal identity integration have the capacity to invest in such values as commitment to friends, loyalty, honesty, interest in sports or music, politics, the success of a group to which they belong, or the history of their particular social group. Under conditions of identity diffusion there is a remarkable poverty of such investment in value systems, even in the absence of antisocial behavior. Naturally, the more severe the lack of maturation of the superego, the more prevalent antisocial behavior may be. Antisocial behavior, in turn, has to be evaluated in terms of adaptation to a particular social subgroup as opposed to individualized antisocial behavior.

An additional indicator of a normally integrated superego is the capacity for romantic idealization and falling in love. Although not falling in love in early or middle adolescence may not yet be diagnosable as a symptom of superego pathology, intense love experiences are positive indicators of good superego integration; this capacity normally emerges very fully after the latency years. Its importance in early childhood development has been conventionally underestimated (P. Kernberg and A. K. Richards 1994).

In contrast to these key signs of ego identity and the derived maturation of the superego, the following characteristics, which usually indicate severe character pathology in adults, are less meaningful in adolescents. To begin, the presence or dominance of primitive defensive operations, typical of borderline personality organization in adults, has much less diagnostic meaning in adolescents. Given the significant regression in the youngster's early adaptation to the upsurge of sexual impulses, his efforts to reduce his dependency on the parental home and to transfer early conflicts at home to school, social group formation, and relations with authorities outside the home, and given, in particular, the normal reactivation of intense oedipal conflicts and preoedipal defenses against them, a broad spectrum of defensive operations—from mature ones centering around repression to primitive ones centering around splitting—may be activated in the adolescent patient's interpersonal interactions. Splitting, primitive idealization, devaluation, projection and projective identification, denial, omnipotence, and omnipotent control may coexist with an increased tendency toward repression, reaction formations, displacement, intellectualization, and various inhibitions, all of which manifest themselves in the early diagnostic interviews.

Typically, however, in adolescents with neurotic personality organization, once the initial anxiety in the diagnostic interviews decreases, primitive defensive operations tend to decrease as well, although they may continue unabated in the current areas of conflict outside the treatment situation. By the same token, severe neurotic symptoms, affective crises, polymorphous perverse activities, or sexual inhibitions do not, in themselves, indicate severe pathology, except in the case of a consolidated perversion with significant and dangerous sadistic and masochistic components. In these cases, the extent to which superego controls protect against excessive activation of aggression becomes an important aspect of the diagnostic assessment.

All the criteria examined so far serve to differentiate neurotic from borderline personality organization. The criterion of reality testing, in contrast, permits the differentiation of borderline personality organization from psychotic personality organization, or the most severe character pathologies from incipient or atypical psychotic developments. The diagnosis of present or absent reality testing is therefore crucial. Reality testing, as I have pointed out in earlier work (O. Kernberg 1975, 1984), consists in the capacity to differentiate self from nonself and intrapsychic from external origins of stimuli, and the capacity to maintain empathy with ordinary social criteria of reality.

In practice, the adolescent's reality testing may be tested, first, by exploring whether he presents hallucinations or delusions, that is, "productive symptoms" of psychosis. Obviously, the presence of psychotic symptoms (hallucinations or delusions) indicates the loss of reality testing. In cases in which there is no overt evidence of such symptoms but in which abnormal sensory perceptions or ideations are present (for example, pseudohallucinations, hallucinosis, illusions, or overvalued ideas), it is very helpful to assess the adolescent's evaluation of his symptom and his capacity to empathize with the therapist's view.

More generally, a helpful method of clarifying the patient's reality testing is to evaluate what in his behavior, affect, thought content, or formal organization of thought processes impresses the diagnostician as strange, bizarre, peculiar, or inappropriate. At some point in the interview, the diagnostician should tactfully confront the patient with what seems most inappropriate in order to evaluate his ability to empathize with the diagnostician's subjective opinion. When the patient's response indicates that he is able to resonate with the reality testing of the therapist, his reality testing is considered to be maintained. When, in contrast, the adolescent patient seems to disorganize further under the impact of this confrontation, reality testing is probably lost. This is a relatively simple procedure in the hands of an experienced clinician, and it is of enormous value in the differential diagnosis of atypical psychosis.

For example, one adolescent became depressed because, after having been the best student in mathematics throughout elementary school and high school, he came out second on a math test in his senior year of high school. Asked why this had produced such a depressive reaction, the adolescent insisted that he was convinced that he was "the best mathematician of the world," and this was an unforgivable failure. On tactful inquiry, however—how could he be sure that he was the best mathematician of the world if, for example, another young man of his age in some other country might be even better—the patient became very angry. He told the examining psychiatrist that he was "completely idiotic" and then exploded in rage. Subsequent exploration of this breakdown in communication confirmed the impression that this young man's grandiose idea had delusional qualities and was not part of a pathological grandiose self—that is, a narcissistic personality structure. The diagnosis of a schizophrenic illness was confirmed by later developments.

The diagnosis of reality testing by the method described above usually solves the problem of the differential diagnosis of borderline personality organization and psychotic personality organization in one or two interviews. Some conditions, however, make this diagnosis particularly difficult. First, where, even without any pathological sensory perception or delusion formation, severe social withdrawal, a breakdown in studies and family life, and an incapacity for intimate relations represent a dramatic development to outsiders, while the adolescent patient appears to be strangely indifferent to his plight, carefully confronting the patient with this discrepancy over a period of time usually permits differential diagnosis between a severe schizoid or schizotypal personality disorder and a simple form of schizophrenic development.

Second, in cases of paranoid psychosis, often the adolescent patient still knows well enough what the diagnostician might consider psychotic and withholds the corresponding information: The diagnosis is that of an extremely paranoid development in the diagnostic interviews, and the differential diagnosis may take much longer than in most other cases, although it may be

strengthened by independent information from projective psychological testing, observations derived from the patient's life outside the diagnostic situation, family interviews, and psychiatric social work.

The third difficult diagnostic situation is presented by patients with a severely defiant, negativistic reaction in the diagnostic interviews, so that not
even reality testing regarding this striking behavior may be successfully attempted. Here again, a careful assessment of the patient's functioning at home,
at school, and in his social environment, psychological testing, and psychiatric
social work evaluation, together with a series of diagnostic interviews, may
gradually facilitate the diagnosis. Nonpsychotic negativism usually tends to decrease over time throughout the diagnostic interviews; a truly psychotic negativism is much more resistant to the relatively brief period of diagnostic evaluation.

The final type of case in which evaluation of reality testing proves very difficult, and a relatively rare one, is that of patients who relate hallucinatory or
delusional experiences of many years' duration, predating the symptomatology
that has brought them to the attention of a psychiatrist, for example, patients
who harbor the delusion over many years, sometimes from childhood onward,
that they will die at a certain early age or who have had chronic hallucinatory
experiences over many years without other indications of emotional illness.
Once again, repeated evaluation of reality testing, projective diagnostic testing,
and an effort to evaluate reality testing in all other areas will eventually provide
an adequate diagnostic judgment. Some cases with chronic hallucinatory or
delusional symptoms, particularly if they have a depressive tone, reflect an
atypical major affective illness, and the search for other symptoms confirming
chronic depression embedded in the personality structure may facilitate establishment of this diagnosis.

THE DIAGNOSIS OF NARCISSISTIC PATHOLOGY

The more severe the narcissistic character pathology, the earlier it becomes noticeable. School-age children with narcissistic personality disorder may present
severe problems in their relationships at home and at school, a replacement of
ordinary friendships by a tendency toward exclusive relationships of dominance and submission, the enactment of grandiose fantasies, the exercise of
omnipotent control at home, and intolerance of any relationship in which they
are not dominant or the center of attention. Lack of the capacity for mutuality,
gratitude, and nonnarcissistically gratifying object investments differentiates

pathological narcissism in childhood from normal infantile narcissistic attitudes.

Cases whose pathology first appears during adolescence are less severe than those diagnosed in childhood and yet are usually more severe than those that first emerge in early adulthood; this is reflected in the incapacity to establish intimate love relations and in a breakdown in studies and work. This relation between the severity of the pathology and the age of emergence of symptoms parallels that for borderline personality organization in general, but the narcissistic personality disorder has some features that permit its differentiation within the broader range of patients with borderline personality organization. First, as noted above, in the narcissistic personality, the syndrome of identity diffusion shows an apparently good integration of the self-concept—except that it is a pathological grandiose self-concept—whereas the representations of significant others usually show severe lack of integration. Those with narcissistic personality disorders have very little capacity for empathy with others. Their relationships are dominated by conscious and unconscious envy; they evince a combination of devaluation of others, symbolic spoiling of what they receive from others, exploitativeness, greediness, a sense of entitlement, incapacity to truly depend, and an incapacity for commitment and loyalty in friendships. Regarding the pathological grandiose self, these adolescents show an exaggerated self-reference and self-centeredness, grandiose fantasies very often expressed in exhibitionistic traits, an attitude of superiority, recklessness, and a discrepancy between high ambitions and limited capacities. They are overly dependent on the admiration of others but evince little or no gratitude toward those on whom they depend. The shallowness of their emotional life and self-experience is often reflected in a sense of emptiness, boredom, and stimulus hunger.

Frequently a dominant symptom is significant failure at school. These adolescents have great difficulty in learning from others or from books, despite their fantasy that all knowledge stems from themselves or from their effortless incorporation of what they come in contact with. If the narcissistic adolescent is very bright, he may be an excellent student as long as he does not have to make any effort; and often these youngsters show excellent functioning in subjects in which they are at the top and total breakdown in subjects in which they are not at the top, in which they would have to make an effort, and in which such an effort—and the unconscious envy it stirs up—is experienced as an insult to their self-esteem. Secondary devaluation of the subjects in which they do not succeed then leads to a vicious cycle of school failure. One patient was able to swim immediately from early childhood onward and excelled in swimming, but he was never able to learn to ski: The experience of the first lesson—the comparison with his older siblings, who were much better skiers than he—interfered with his willingness to learn.

The sense of grandiosity and entitlement, inordinate envy and devaluation, and the limitations in empathy and commitment are cardinal symptoms of the narcissistic personality, easily observable in narcissistic adolescents. Their surface behavior, however, may be quite variable. In the typical case, an attitude of superiority and self-assurance and a charming, engaging, seductive friendliness may characterize the patient's early contacts, reflecting the underlying pathological grandiose self. In atypical cases, however, the surface behavior may be one of anxiety, tension, insecurity, or timidity, where fear that their superiority may not be recognized or that their narcissistic demands may not be met predominates. Bouts of insecurity, in sharp contrast to the usual sense of self-reliance and superiority, characterize most narcissistic patients, and the severity of such bouts may bring about the secondary defense of a timid surface behavior that protects them from actual disappointment of their narcissistic aspirations. Sometimes a certain conventional rigidity dominates in better-functioning patients; the normal capacity for relationships in depth with significant others is replaced by a rigid adherence to conventional clichés.

The lack of superego integration of borderline personality organization is accentuated in narcissistic pathology because of the absorption of the idealizing layer of superego precursors—that is, the ego ideal is absorbed into the pathological grandiose self. This brings about a kind of false identity integration and facilitates nonspecific manifestations of ego strength (anxiety tolerance, impulse control, some capacity for sublimatory functioning) that make these patients appear to be functioning much better than the ordinary borderline patient. This absorption of the ego ideal into the self causes not only deterioration of the world of internalized object relations and of the capacity for nonnarcissistic object investment, however, but significant weakening of the maturation of the normal superego. In relatively mild cases, this deterioration shows in the persistence of childish values such as the search for external admiration of one's physical attractiveness, clothing, possessions, or some conventionally determined personal decor, the surface manifestations of which depend on the cultural background of the narcissistic adolescent patient. The lack of superego integration is reflected in an incapacity to experience normal, mournful grief reactions and a tendency toward self-regulation by severe mood swings rather than by differentiated self-criticism—the dominance of "shame" culture over "guilt" culture.

In more severe cases, lack of superego integration is reflected directly in anti-social behavior, in tolerance of aggression that has infiltrated the pathological grandiose self and is manifest in forms of egosyntonic sadistic or self-aggressive, self-mutilating, suicidal behavior, and in strong paranoid characterological features derived from the reprojection of the earliest layer of persecutory superego precursors onto the external environment. Because of the absorption of the ego ideal into the pathological grandiose self, the persecutory superego precursors cannot easily be absorbed into an overall integrated superego and are reprojected as paranoid traits. The combination, in these severe cases, of narcissistic personality disorder, antisocial behavior, egosyntonic aggression, and a paranoid orientation constitutes, as mentioned above, the syndrome of malignant narcissism. Where superego deterioration proceeds to the extent of total deterioration or absence of superego functions, the result is the antisocial personality disorder in a strict sense (as opposed to the less precise definition offered in the DSM classification system).

THE ANTISOCIAL PERSONALITY DISORDER IN ADOLESCENCE

Although virtually all antisocial personality disorders, on careful exploration, show symptoms from early childhood, the tendency in the DSM-III and DSM-IV nomenclature is to separate "conduct disorders" in childhood from the antisocial personality disorder in adulthood, setting an artificial limit of age eighteen before the diagnosis of an antisocial personality may be established (Hare 1970; Hare and Shalling 1978; P. Kernberg 1989). This distinction seems absurd from a psychopathological and clinical viewpoint. Given the grave implications of an antisocial personality disorder at any age, it is important that the clinician examining an adolescent with significant antisocial behavior be prepared to diagnose this disorder. I explored the differential diagnosis of the antisocial personality disorder, the syndrome of malignant narcissism, and the narcissistic personality disorder in Chapter 3; here I shall briefly summarize these differences.

Keep in mind that the passive-parasitic type of antisocial personality is less likely to be noticed during early childhood, particularly if antisocial features of the patient's family and social background "submerge" the patient's antisocial behavior into culturally tolerated patterns. Thus, for example, early cheating in school, stealing, or habitual lying may appear less severe in an ambiance of social disorganization and severe family pathology than in a relatively stable and healthy social and family environment. Antisocial tendencies or severe narcissistic pathology of the parents may provide convenient cover-ups for passive-parasitic antisocial behavior in a child.

The predominantly aggressive type of antisocial personality disorder usually is much more apparent because of its impact on the immediate social environment of the child. As Paulina Kernberg (1989) has pointed out, this disorder is characterized by extreme aggression from early childhood onward, to the extent of violent and dangerous behavior toward siblings or animals and the destruction of property. These children show an "affectless" expression of aggression, chronic manipulativeness and paranoid tendencies, and a marked incapacity to keep friends. Sometimes they establish a true reign of terror at home or in their immediate social circle at school. In early adolescence, this aggression extends beyond the family circle and may include frankly criminal behavior. The parents are usually exhausted by and afraid of them but are often unable to convince mental health professionals of the gravity of the situation.

From a diagnostic viewpoint, the essential characteristics of the antisocial personality proper begin with the presence of a narcissistic personality disorder. Second, in the case of the antisocial personality of a predominantly aggressive type, the symptoms of malignant narcissism are present. In the predominantly passive-parasitic type, there is no violence, only passive-exploitative behavior such as lying, cheating, stealing, and ruthless exploitation. Third, careful evaluation of the history reveals corresponding antisocial behavior from early childhood onward. Fourth, and very fundamentally, these patients present an incapacity to feel guilt for their antisocial behavior. They may express remorse for behavior that has been discovered but not for behavior that they believe is still secret or unknown to anybody else. It is also striking that they are unable to identify with the moral dimension in the mind of the diagnostician although they may be very skilled in assessing other people's motivations and behavior; the possibility of an ethical motivation is so foreign to them that exploration of this issue—for example, in wondering how the therapist may be reacting to their antisocial behavior—often reveals their striking incapacity to imagine another's sadness, concern, and even moral shock regarding their acts of cruelty or exploitation.

Fifth, these youngsters show a total incapacity for any nonexploitative investment in others, an indifference and callousness that also extend to pets, which they may mistreat or abandon without any feelings. Sixth, they show no concern for themselves or any other person and present a lack of sense of time, of future, of planning. Often, although a concrete antisocial behavior may be carried out with a perfectly coordinated short-term plan, the long-term effects of cumulative antisocial behavior are totally ignored and emotionally insignificant to these patients: a sense of future is a superego function, in addition to an ego function, and is glaringly absent in these cases. Seventh, the lack of an affective investment in significant others is matched by a lack of normal love for the self, expressed in defiant, fearless, potentially self-destructive behavior and a proneness to impulsive acts of suicide when they experience themselves as driven into a corner. Under the impact of intense rage, they present the risk of severely aggressive and homicidal behavior toward others.

Eighth, these patients show a remarkable incapacity for depressive mourning and grief and an ability to tolerate anxiety; they immediately develop additional symptoms or antisocial behavior when they feel threatened or controlled by external structure. Ninth, these patients show a remarkable lack of learning from experience and an incapacity to absorb anything provided by the therapist; behind this symptom is a radical devaluation of all value systems, a sense that life is an ongoing struggle either among wolves or between wolves and sheep, with many wolves disguised as sheep.

Finally, these patients are incapable of falling in love, of experiencing an integration of tenderness and sexuality, and their sexual involvements have a mechanical quality that is eternally unsatisfactory to them. When antisocial personalities suffer from a sadistic perversion, they may become extremely dangerous to others. The combination of severe aggression, the absence of the capacity for compassion, and the lack of superego development is the basis for the psychopathology of mass murder as well as for murder in the context of sexual involvements.

In diagnostic interviews, the manipulativeness, pathological lying, and shifting rationalizations of these patients create what Paulina Kernberg (personal communication) has called "holographic men": These patients are able to evoke flimsy, rapidly changing, completely contradictory images of themselves, their lives, and their interactions. They impress the interviewer as profoundly inauthentic, as having a void in place of their identity (P. Kernberg et al. 2000). The diagnostic evaluation of these cases requires taking a complete history in order to compare references to their past that are communicated on different occasions, to observe their interactions with the therapist as well as with significant others, and to compare external observations and information with the patients' communications.

Exploration of these patients' lives should include tactful questions about why they did not engage in what would seem, under some specific circumstances, to be expectable antisocial behaviors; this often reveals patients' lack of the capacity to identify with ethical systems even while they are trying to portray themselves as honest and reliable. Naturally, patients who lie to the diagnostician should be confronted with that in nonpunitive ways, mainly to assess whether the capacity for guilt, remorse, or shame is still available. The narcissistic personality disorder with passive-parasitic tendencies will show the same general characteristics as the aggressive type except for direct aggressive attacks on others, on property, on animals, and on the self. Patients with the syndrome of malignant narcissism but without an antisocial personality proper will present the capacity for guilt, concern for self, some nonexploitive relations, some remnants of authentic superego functions, and some capacity for dependency; their prognosis is significantly better.

Antisocial behavior may present in patients who do not have a narcissistic personality disorder, that is, who do not belong to the continuum I have described, from the narcissistic personality disorder to the syndrome of malignant narcissism to the antisocial personality proper. Some patients with borderline personality organization and other than narcissistic types of personality disorders as well as some with neurotic personality organization and good ego identity integration may show antisocial behavior. In addition, antisocial behavior in an adolescent may, at times, reflect a neurosis with strong rebellious features and even a "normal" adaptation to a pathological social subgroup (the "dissocial" reaction). In all these cases, the antisocial behavior has a much better prognosis—in fact, an excellent prognosis—with psychotherapeutic treatment of the underlying character pathology or neurotic syndrome. Therefore, in adolescent patients with antisocial behavior, it is essential to evaluate the presence or absence of the syndrome of identity diffusion, narcissistic personality disorder, malignant narcissism, and antisocial personality disorder.

SOME GENERAL CONSIDERATIONS ABOUT THE DIAGNOSTIC EVALUATION OF CHARACTER PATHOLOGY IN ADOLESCENTS

It is very important to obtain a full picture of all the existing symptoms and their respective severities. Severe suicidal or self-mutilating tendencies, alcohol or drug abuse or dependency, severe depression, and eating disturbances may require immediate intervention; emergencies have to be taken care of first, and evaluation of the adolescent's personality structure may have to wait until he is in a stable, safe, protected environment.

In all cases, the study of personality functioning in all areas of the patient's life has precedence over taking a history; the history needs to be evaluated in light of the patient's current functioning. The information provided by the patient, his family, and other sources such as the school or psychiatric social worker also needs to be matched with a careful analysis of the interactional features of the relationship between the diagnostician and the patient. This requires honest communication from the therapist to the patient regarding the information that he is obtaining and a careful discussion of the issue of confidentiality in their interactions.

If an adolescent shows up first with his family, there may be an advantage in seeing all of them jointly before seeing the patient alone and not seeing family members first without the patient, even if they insist in doing that. Should the therapist have received information about the patient before seeing him, it is important to share this information with the patient. In families with a culture of keeping secrets from each other, an important part of the diagnostic evaluation is opening all channels of communication tactfully but decisively.

Experience in the long-term treatment of patients with severe personality disorders has taught us that there are some situations that require immediate attention: a threat to the physical survival of the patient or of others, the possibility of acute disruption of the diagnostic or therapeutic process, severe interference with these processes by the patient's or a family member's lack of honesty, and the danger of rapid breakdown of the support system that enables the diagnostic process to continue.

If severely regressive developments occur during the diagnostic process, such as a strong negative reaction to the diagnostician, it is important to abandon temporarily the pursuit of other information and focus on the adolescent's experience of the immediate situation. Here, psychoanalytic principles of evaluating the acting out of severe negative transferences come into play. The clinician may have to spend some time ventilating such negative transference developments without losing sight of the fact that he is still in the midst of a diagnostic process. It should be clearly understood that treatment will have to await the availability of complete information regarding the patient's difficulties. Primitive mechanisms of projective identification, omnipotent control, and severe denial color such early difficulties and may be used to evaluate the existence of identity diffusion, narcissistic pathology, and antisocial behavior.

If the adolescent patient refuses to come to the session, work with the family may facilitate the creation of a social structure that will bring the patient back. For example, the diagnostician may discuss with the family the measures they can take to bring the patient to consultations and help them deal with the patient under these circumstances. Should the patient come back to the diagnostic sessions, all these preliminary discussions will have to be shared with him as well. If there is acute danger to the physical survival of the patient or his family, or if a differential diagnosis with a psychotic process proves impossible to achieve in an outpatient situation, a brief period of hospitalization may be indicated in order to permit such evaluation in a controlled, supportive environment.

It is always helpful to study the family situation of adolescents being evaluated for character pathology: Pathology in the social structure of the family interacts with the patient's character pathology. Assessment of the extent to which the patient's pathology represents a relatively nonspecific reaction to severe family pathology, as opposed to the presence of severe character pathology in the patient himself, is an important aspect of this diagnostic process and will affect the choice of treatment strategies.

Careful evaluation of the adolescent patient's social life outside the family structure will provide invaluable data concerning the relation of family pathology and character pathology. For example, an adolescent who shows severe behavior disturbances at home and initially in the diagnostic interviews may be revealed to have a very active, intense, involved, in-depth life of relationships with significant friends or admired adults outside the family setting and may gradually normalize his interaction in the diagnostic setting as he begins to differentiate the diagnostician from the family authorities. The family's denial of severe character pathology in their child may be exposed by the information the adolescent patient gives about the restriction and poverty of his emotional investment in significant others and his severe conflicts and failure in school. In all cases of significant school failure, intelligence testing and, when indicated, testing for learning disabilities will further clarify the extent to which character pathology, in particular, a narcissistic personality disorder, contributes to the school failure.

Evaluation of the adolescent patient's sexual life provides very important data regarding his capacity for the development of object relations in depth, the existence of severe disturbances in sexual functions, regardless of the severity of character pathology, and the existence of potentially destructive and self-destructive behaviors that put the adolescent at immediate risk. A tendency toward sexual promiscuity in the age of AIDS may signify an urgent danger that requires prompt therapeutic intervention. At the same time, as mentioned above, the capacity for romantic idealization and falling in love and in particular the capacity to integrate sexual and tender feelings and involvement indicate significant maturation in object relations.

The adolescent's adaptation to group processes also provides important information regarding his character structure. A complete absorption in the group process—the uncritical acceptance of group mores without personal reflection and differentiation of self within the group—may protect an adolescent from behavioral manifestations of severe identity diffusion (O. Kernberg 1988). This capacity for subtle and critical evaluation of the individual members of his group will reveal identity integration or identity diffusion regardless of his surface adaptation to the group process.

An adolescent's orientation to the predominant ideology of his particular group, be it a general political ideology or an ad hoc one, will provide important information regarding his superego development: The difference between forming a primitive identification with an idealized group while splitting off severely hostile evaluations of outgroups, on one hand, and awareness that the world is not simply divided between "all good" and "all bad" people, on the other, is significant. Most political ideologies fluctuate along a spectrum from a very paranoid extreme to a trivialized and flat conventionalism at the other extreme, with a "humanistic" differentiated middle zone that respects individual differences, sexual intimacy and privacy, and the autonomy of the individual. Where the adolescent patient fits within such an ideological continuum will also reveal important information about his superego maturation.

Chapter 5 Perversion, Perversity,

and Normality: Diagnostic and

Therapeutic Considerations

THE PROBLEM OF SEXUAL
"NORMALITY"

Culturally determined value judgments and ideological cross-currents unavoidably influence our evaluation of human sexual life. When "normal" is considered to be equivalent to average or to a predominant pattern, treatment may become a matter of promoting "adjustment," and we lose the usefulness of normality as a standard of health. On the other hand, if the concept of normality refers to an ideal pattern of behavior, we run the risk of imposing ideologically motivated measures. And if, in ideologically motivated opposition to conventional notions, we proclaim the equivalent nature of any and all manifestations of human sexuality, we may miss significant, even crippling limitations of sexual enjoyment and of the integration of eroticism and emotional intimacy. An "objective, scientific" view would seem

---

This is a modified version of a paper published in *Psychoanalysis and Psychotherapy*. Madison, Conn.: International Universities Press, 1997, 14:19–40.

ideal if the human sciences were not, in their turn, contaminated by conventionality.

I believe that psychoanalysis, with all its limitations as an instrument for the evaluation of human behavior, provides the optimal combination of nonconventional exploration of the intimate life of the individual and an evaluation of how sexual patterns enrich, modify, or restrict the potential for enjoyment, autonomy, adaptation, and effectiveness. The unavoidable ideological and cultural biases embedded in psychoanalytic theory have tended to self-correct over time. It is, however, sobering to recall that only a hundred years ago psychoanalysis was at one with a scientific community that regarded masturbation as a dangerous form of pathology and that our literature lumped homosexuality and sexual perversions together without much concern for their significantly differentiating features. In fact, few if any psychoanalytic studies of the affective nature of sexual excitement have been undertaken since Freud's (1905) pathbreaking discoveries. And in contrast to Freud's revolutionary insights regarding how unconscious sexual strivings from infancy and early childhood onward influence the development and structure of intrapsychic life, recent psychoanalytic formulations have tended to underemphasize and even neglect the importance of unconscious sexuality (see Green 1997).

CLINICAL AND PSYCHOANALYTIC CRITERIA

I would propose as the most general criteria of normality the capacity to enjoy a broad range of sexual fantasy and activity and to integrate these forms of sexual involvement with a tender, loving relationship reinforced by the mutuality of sexual pleasure, of the emotional relationship, and of the idealization of that relationship (O. Kernberg 1995). By implication, these criteria imply control over the aggressive components of sexual behavior to the extent of eliminating the expression of hostile, dangerous, exploitive intentions and actions in the sexual encounter. They do not exclude autoerotic sexual activity that is neither dangerous nor actively self-destructive.

From a psychoanalytic viewpoint, normality implies the integration of early, pregenital fantasy and activity with genital fantasy and activity—the capacity to achieve sexual excitement and orgasm in intercourse and the capacity to integrate aspects of the sadistic, masochistic, voyeuristic, exhibitionistic, and fetishistic components of polymorphous perverse infantile sexuality into sexual fantasy, play, and activity. In fact, from a psychoanalytic viewpoint, the integration of polymorphous perverse infantile sexuality into a tender and loving relationship within which mutual emotional gratification and idealization rein-force and are reinforced by the sexual encounter reflects the optimum of psy-chological freedom and normality.

At a deeper level, the capacity for full sexual enjoyment implies integration of preoedipal and archaic oedipal object relations into the advanced oedipal re-lationship enacted in a sublimatory way. In every love relationship, an uncon-scious fantasy life is activated that maintains the idealization of sexual excite-ment and gratification both in polymorphous perverse infantile play and fantasy and in sexual intercourse. An aggressive element is an essential compo-nent of normal sexual excitement and, in fact, contributes crucially to the full development of eroticism (O. Kernberg 1991; Stoller 1979). Thus human sexu-ality, in conclusion, as André Green (1997) has pointed out, signals the integra-tion of the sexual drive with an object relation that incorporates the full invest-ment of the libidinal drive in that relation.

What these proposed criteria leave out are the issues of the exclusiveness, the duration of the relationship with, and the gender of the sexual object; and it is in these areas that a scientific approach is particularly vulnerable to contamina-tion by ideological and cultural bias. There are good theoretical reasons for considering a stable heterosexual relationship to be a normal outcome of the oedipal conflicts and their sublimatory resolution in adulthood. Biological de-terminants and a primary intrapsychic bisexuality, however, may powerfully in-fluence object choice and, under the influence of cultural factors, may codeter-mine different paths to object choice in both genders (O. Kernberg 1995). André Green (1997) has recently proposed a clinical clarification of male ho-mosexualities derived from psychoanalytic observations that points to the broad spectrum of psychodynamic features involved.

DEFINITION AND PSYCHODYNAMICS
OF PERVERSION

Clinically, perversions can be defined as stable, chronic, rigid restrictions of sexual behavior characterized by the expression of one of the polymorphous perverse infantile partial drives as an obligatory, indispensable precondition for the achievement of sexual excitement and orgasm (O. Kernberg 1989b, 1991; Stoller 1975). All sexual perversions combine severe inhibition of sexual free-dom and flexibility with idealization of the sexual scenario derived from the particular polymorphous perverse infantile drive that is dominant. The diag-nosis of sexual sadism, masochism, voyeurism, exhibitionism, fetishism, and transvestism is not difficult if one keeps this definition in mind. It also applies to cases of episodic perversion in which dissociative phenomena permit the expression of perversion alternating with and completely split off from conventional though somewhat impoverished sexual behavior.

From a descriptive viewpoint, perversions can be classified along a continuum of severity according to the degree to which aggression dominates the perversion and dangerous or life-threatening behavior invades the potential object relation within which the perversion becomes manifest. Such aggressive infiltration is particularly marked in the cases of pedophilia and in the rarer perversions of zoophilia, coprophilia, urophilia, and, of course, necrophilia.

From a psychodynamic viewpoint, in the psychoanalytic literature a consensus has been evolving to divide the perversions into two major groups according to the severity of the illness. The work of André Lussier (1982) on fetishism, I believe, has become a standard reference. Both levels of pathology have in common a rigid perverse pattern, the development of an idiosyncratic scenario linked to the particular perversion, and a remarkable inhibition of sexual fantasy and exploration outside this scenario. An important common feature of perverse scenarios at the less severe level is the containment of aggression and in fact the recruitment of aggression in the service of love and eroticism. This provides a sense of safety as well as an intense erotic experience within which fusion with the object in sexual excitement and orgasm is reinforced by the sadomasochistic identification of the partners as perpetrator and victim. This level of perversion is best described by the classical constellation originally conceptualized by Freud (1905, 1919, 1927, 1940). Here fixation at the level of a partial drive serves to deny castration anxiety, and enactment of a pregenital sexual scenario serves as a defense against oedipal genital conflicts. Genital sexuality is feared as a realization of oedipal wishes. There is severe castration anxiety linked to powerful aggressive components of the positive oedipal complex. All sexual interaction becomes a symbolic enactment of the primal scene, and any regression to preoedipal levels of development that has occurred has a clearly defensive nature. Preoedipal aggression is not a major component of the aggressive aspects of the oedipal conflict in these patients. Clinically, perversions at this level typically appear in the context of neurotic personality organization, that is, in patients with obsessive-compulsive, depressive-masochistic, or hysterical personality disorders (O. Kernberg 1996b).

The more severely pathological level of perversion, described by Chasseguet-Smirgel (1984) and Lussier (1982), has a typical two-layered defensive organization, with oedipal conflicts condensed with severe preoedipal conflicts whose aggressive aspects dominate the clinical picture. These perversions are typically found in patients with borderline personality organization. In fact, the characteristic psychodynamics of borderline personality organization I described on the basis of the experience of the psychotherapy research project of the Menninger Foundation (O. Kernberg 1975) turned out to overlap dramatically with the dynamics of the severe level of perversion described by Lussier in his study of fetishism.

This severe level of perversion appears in two major personality organizations: first, in the ordinary borderline personality organization, with dominant reliance on splitting mechanisms affecting ego and superego and a combination of sadistic and masochistic features in sexual behavior and in the general character structure, reflecting the abnormal "metabolism" of aggression; and second, in the narcissistic personality structure, in which the perverse scenario is infiltrated by the aggressive aspects of the condensed oedipal and preoedipal conflicts. In the case of the syndrome of malignant narcissism, the aggressive drive derivatives are integrated into the grandiose pathological self with consequent dangerous sadistic deterioration of the perversion (O. Kernberg 1989a).

In the psychoanalytic literature concerning perversion, narcissistic features have been suggested as a general characteristic. From a clinical perspective, however, it is extremely important to differentiate patients with "narcissistic conflicts" in a nonspecific sense from those whose narcissistic character structure has particular implications for prognosis and treatment. The anal and oral regression at this severe level of perversion is reflected in what Donald Meltzer (1977) has called "zonal confusion," the symbolic equivalence of all protruding or invaginated sexual areas of both genders with corresponding condensation of oral, anal, and genital strivings. Unconscious anal fantasies dominate the sexual life of these patients, with "fecalization" of genital organs and genital intercourse. Their anal-sadistic regression involves an attack on and destruction of object relations, while the oral regression is reflected in their oral-sadistic expression of envy and destructive greed.

The perversions of narcissistic personalities reveal the most dramatic combination of these dynamics: the unconscious fantasy of a fecal penis and a fecal vagina, the unconscious equalization of genders and ages, a primitive idealization of the perversion linked with the denial of castration, and the tendency to equalize all object relations and all sexual activities, which, in the process, become "spoiled," "digested," and "expelled" as feces. Here the perverse scenario may succeed in containing the aggression, but the aggressive impulses overshadow the libidinal ones, threatening to neutralize erotic excitement and to corrode or destroy the object relation. The defensive idealization of the perversion may express itself in a stress on the aesthetic qualities of both the sexual object and the sexual scenario, reflecting both the defense against and the expression of the image of fecalized sexual organs and an illusory surface adaptation in the form of "as if" relationships.

From a psychostructural viewpoint, the pathology of perversion may be classified into six major groups, which I shall briefly describe from the least to the most severe in terms of the pathology of object relations and the sexual life of these patients, as well as their prognosis for psychoanalytic treatment (O. Kernberg 1992a).

1. Perversions in the context of neurotic personality organization have excellent prognosis with psychoanalytic treatment. The presenting obligatory scenarios vary from patient to patient but are typically clearly defined. As in all perversions, they form an indispensable precondition for the gratification of the patient's sexual needs and the achievement of orgasm. Idealization of the perversion goes hand in hand with sexual inhibition in other areas. The patient's capacity for object relatedness is deep and solid, and oedipal conflicts clearly predominate in the transference.

2. In perversions at the level of borderline personality organization we typically find the condensed preoedipal-oedipal conflicts with dominance of preoedipal aggression. Specific perversions at this level are usually combined with a pathology of object relations that makes the scenario less clearly circumscribed or differentiated; it tends to blend with the general character pathology of these patients. It is important to differentiate a generalized polymorphous perverse infantile sexuality in these cases—that is, a chaotic combination of many infantile perverse trends—from the consolidation of a typical perversion. Paradoxically, the chaotic combination of polymorphous perverse impulses significantly improves the prognosis for borderline patients treated with psychoanalytic psychotherapy or psychoanalysis. By contrast, a subgroup of borderline patients with severe inhibition of all eroticism carries a poor prognosis because, as the borderline personality organization is resolved in treatment, the sexual inhibition tends to become more intense. A specific perversion in these cases is prognostically favorable, although the treatment is, of course, more complex than in the case of neurotic personality organization.

3. A perversion combined with a narcissistic personality disorder is particularly difficult to treat because the idealization of the perversion is condensed with idealization of the pathological grandiose self in a defensive structure that is often hard to dismantle. As in the borderline cases, it is important to differ-

entiate generalized polymorphous perverse infantile behavior from a specific perversion. Such polymorphous perverse behavior in narcissistic patients may reflect a replacement of object relations by the compulsive use of sexual behavior to relieve anxiety.

4. In perversion in cases of malignant narcissism, egosyntonic aggression may infiltrate the particular perversion and transform it into a sadomasochistic pattern that objectively endangers both patient and partner. In fact, it is because the syndrome of malignant narcissism is at the very limit of treatability that it deserves to be classified as a fourth group. Here we encounter the more severe and dangerous forms of sadism, masochism, pedophilia, and anally regressed perversions such as coprophilia.

5. A fifth group is constituted by the antisocial personality disorder in a strict sense as originally described by Cleckley (1941) and under study by Robert Hare (Hare et al. 1991; Hare and Hart 1995), Michael Stone (1980), and myself (O. Kernberg 1992a). These cases represent the most severe type of narcissistic character disorder, in which superego development has failed entirely. A consolidated perversion in an antisocial personality always has to be considered extremely dangerous until proved otherwise. Here we find sexual murderers and serial killers, in whom the remnants of eroticism are totally overshadowed by extreme forms of primitive aggression. The prognosis of any known treatment for the antisocial personality proper is practically zero.

6. The sixth group consists of perversions as part of psychotic personality organization, in schizophrenic illness, and in particular, pseudopsychopathic schizophrenia (O. Kernberg 1996b). A perversion in a schizophrenic illness might be psychopharmacologically controlled if the schizophrenic illness itself responds to such treatment.

PERVERSION AND PERVERSITY

The syndrome of perversity in the transference consists, in essence, in the recruitment of eroticism and love in the service of aggression. That this important and severe form of negative therapeutic reaction has been equated with perversion as a specific sexual pathology is due to a semantic confusion to which, unfortunately, psychoanalytic literature has contributed. In fact, some of the most important contributors to the study of both perversion and perversity, such as Herbert Rosenfeld (1987), Donald Meltzer (1977), and Wilfred Bion (1968, 1970), tend not to differentiate clearly between the terms *perversion* and *perversity* in the transference. In British and French psychoanalytic literature one finds the term *perverse structure,* implying a particular and unique personality organization or psychodynamic constellation characteristic of perversion. This does not do justice to the broad spectrum of personality organizations in which perversion appears.

At the same time, these authors have given us the most specific description of the syndrome of perversity in the transference. This may occur in patients who suffer from a sexual perversion, but it occurs as well in patients without such a perversion—for example, patients with narcissistic personality disorder or the syndrome of malignant narcissism.

I have pointed in earlier work (O. Kernberg 1992a) to some patients' efforts to extract goodness, concern, and love from the analyst precisely to destroy him, in an envious feast that goes beyond the need to demonstrate the analyst's incompetence and impotence and instead expresses the wish to destroy the sources of his equanimity and creativity. Because the syndrome of perversity appears with particular frequency in patients with severe narcissistic personality structure who, at the same time, may present a sexual perversion in a narrow sense, both syndromes may go together.

THE DIAGNOSTIC EVALUATION OF PATIENTS
WITH SEXUAL PERVERSIONS

In all cases, it is important first to evaluate completely the patient's sexual life, activities, fantasies, daydreams, dreams, and masturbatory fantasies, as well as the fantasies linked with actual sexual interactions. The patient's sexual preferences, their continuity or discontinuity, and the entire spectrum of his sexual responses need to be evaluated. Second, the basic aspects of core sexual identity, dominant object choice, gender role identity, and intensity of sexual desire should be evaluated, because these four features jointly define the patient's sexual identity (O. Kernberg 1995). Third, it is important to evaluate the linkage between the tender and loving capabilities of the patient and his sexual life: Does he have the capacity to fall in love? Is there a capacity to integrate love and eroticism, or are they usually or always dissociated from each other? Are sexual inhibitions present and, if so, of what type and severity? Fourth, what is the predominant personality constellation, the level of severity of personality pathology? The presence or absence of pathological narcissism and the syndrome of malignant narcissism, the quality of object relations, the presence of antisocial features, and the degree to which the expression of aggression is pathological and egosyntonic should all be assessed.

And fifth, we are interested in evaluating the couple in cases in which marital or couple conflicts are an essential aspect of the presenting symptom. Under particularly complex circumstances, a combined team of a specialist in personality disorders, a couples or family therapist, and a sex therapist may jointly formulate a diagnosis and treatment plan, a methodology that I have found very helpful in especially difficult cases.

From all these data flow the essential considerations that will determine prognosis and treatment: the level of personality organization and predominant personality disorder, the quality of object relations, the presence or absence of pathological narcissism, the severity of the disturbance of expressed aggression, the organization and level of superego functioning, the degree of sexual freedom, and the particular prognostic implications for the relationship of a couple (see Dicks 1967).

PSYCHOANALYSIS AND PSYCHOANALYTIC
PSYCHOTHERAPY FOR THE PERVERSIONS

Psychoanalysis is the treatment of choice for sexual perversions in patients with a neurotic personality organization and for patients with a narcissistic personality disorder who have sufficient capacities for anxiety tolerance, impulse control, and sublimatory functioning and who are able to maintain reasonable stability with regard to work, social adaptation, and some degree of emotional intimacy.

Psychoanalysis proper is usually contraindicated for patients with the syndrome of malignant narcissism, but there are exceptions to this rule. Patients with a combined hysterical-histrionic personality disorder may respond to psychoanalytic treatment, as do some patients with paranoid and schizoid personalities, although the large majority of patients with borderline personality organization should be treated by psychoanalytic psychotherapy rather than by standard psychoanalysis. The overall prognosis is strongly influenced by the extent to which antisocial features are present (that is, the relative integrity of the superego) as well as by the capacity for maintaining object relations in depth over a period of time, neurotic as they may be, as long as they are not purely parasitic or exploitive (O. Kernberg 1992a).

The most crucial aspect of the treatment of perversion, in my experience, is to focus on the activation or enactment of the underlying unconscious fantasies in the transference. The patient may attempt to draw the analyst into being a spectator of the patient's relationship with the external object of his perverse scenario, thus fulfilling aspects of the perverse fantasy itself as it involves the analyst. It is of course important to explore the unconscious fantasies experienced by the patient in the course of the enactment of the perverse scenario, as long as the analyst remains aware that this is only a preliminary exploration of what eventually will become a transference enactment.

For example, a patient was impotent with his wife but fully potent in sexual engagements with other women. These women had to submit to him in a masochistic scenario in which he would tie them up and have them carry out self-demeaning acts that symbolically represented their humiliation and his total control over them. In contrast, he behaved like a shy little boy with his wife. With me he displayed almost a caricature of submissiveness: He became interested in psychoanalytic ideas, sought out my published papers, and, in an overblown identification with me, used the ideas he found there to argue with his friends and colleagues about alternative psychological theories.

In the course of the treatment, as the image of a violent father who was sexually promiscuous and a tyrant at home came into focus, the patient gradually became aware of his inhibited behavior as a fear of rebelling against such a violent father and of the fantasy that the only way to rebel against him would be a violent, bloody overthrow. An underlying fantasy slowly emerged in which he would sexually submit to powerful father representatives and thus solve the conflict with the father by becoming his sexual love object.

What made the analysis of the transference particularly difficult was the surface, "as if" submission of the patient, which protected him against the underlying wish for a dependent, sexual relation with me. The analysis of that underlying wish was interfered with by the patient's "guessing" my thoughts and immediately accepting what he thought were my theories, fully endorsing them in intellectual speculations. I had serious doubts as to whether all this had any emotional meaning. After a period of time it dawned on me that I had become the bound-up victim of the patient's sadistic control in the transference; his ready acceptance of what he thought was my train of thought and his way of disorganizing my thinking had led to a temporary paralysis of all work in the sessions. The analysis of that "as if" quality in his relationship with me eventually induced in the patient a sense of confusion, intense anxiety, and the fear of me as a threatening father who wanted to keep him in the role of a little child and stood ready to castrate him if he were to penetrate his wife, who in his unconscious represented the oedipal mother.

This case illustrates the "as if" quality of perversion in the transference even under conditions of neurotic personality organization. The patient presented a typical sadistic scenario in the context of an overall psychological functioning that was remarkably normal in terms of his emotional relationship with his wife as well as his capacity for effective and mature object relations in his work and social life. He had initiated the treatment with a hidden idealization of his perversion that he only gradually dared to express in the sessions.

Another patient, in contrast, presented a sadistic perversion in the context of a borderline personality organization, a narcissistic personality structure, and polymorphous perverse infantile features strongly reflected in conscious anal sadistic fantasies and behaviors that infiltrated his entire life. He was obese as a result of overeating and abused multiple drugs; although he was very effective in his business, his chaotic style of management created continuous problems with associates and subordinates.

This patient was able to have intercourse with his wife only if he subjected her to physical abuse. Her willingness to undergo significant pain was a precondition for his achieving orgasm. What brought him to treatment was the fact that she became unwilling to continue this situation, not because of the nature of their sexual interaction per se but because of aspects of his behavior that she considered disgusting, such as not cleaning himself appropriately after defecating, to the extent that small segments of feces would be found in their bedclothes. He would almost never flush the toilet, and because he used hand towels for cleaning his genitals and anal region, his wife felt obliged to hide the towels that she used.

In the course of his treatment, the patient talked about present reality and fantasy, childhood memories, and emotional reactions to the analyst and his office in what might be described as an almost "perfect" style of free association, speculating about the deep motivations of his behavior and dramatically displaying affects that shifted from moment to moment. What was striking was his manner of throwing out ideas and feelings without assuming any responsibility for them, in what impressed me as a thoughtless spreading of chaotic material for me to pick up and make sense of. It was as if little pieces of excrement were being thrown around in a general devaluation and equalization of all thoughts, feelings, and behaviors that were the unconscious equivalent of covering the analyst and his office with excrement while the patient maintained the illusion of superiority as the producer of this digested material. Any expression of my interest in any particular material would lead to immediate ironic speculations by the patient regarding what I now had in mind and a derogatory attack on my capacity to understand him. Implicit in these enactments was the fantasy that I would make sense of the fecal chaos and in so doing bolster the patient's belief in his own superiority. These developments could eventually be understood as the symbolic equivalents of the sadistic attacks on his wife as an essential requirement for orgasmic climax.

Only the systematic interpretation and working through of this massive defense, expressed in the patient's nonverbal communications and my countertransference, led to his underlying hatred of the oedipal couple and his effort to deny the possibility of a sexual relation that could be mutually gratifying and creative. In contrast, he identified with a sadistic and mutually destructive couple, and he replicated this relationship in the transference.

In the psychoanalytic treatment of perversion, it is essential, I believe, to focus on the areas of significant inhibition in the patient's sexual life. Efforts to draw the analyst into an excited, voyeuristic countertransference engagement may permit a subtle acting out of the transference rather than leading to further understanding. The perverse scenario, with its tightly knit construction and defensive idealization, may successfully resist the analysis of the repressed, dissociated, or projected fears and fantasies against which it serves as a defense. In contrast, the areas of sexual inhibition that perverse patients strenuously attempt to avoid exploring may provide a direct link to the repressed conflicts concerning castration anxiety and preoedipal aggression that are condensed with archaic oedipal material.

For example, a patient with a masochistic perversion was able to achieve sexual excitement and orgasm only when he was controlled by two women who would force him into a subservient position while showing their excitement and desire for him when he was physically immobilized and sexually stimulated. This man experienced a total lack of sexual interest in the woman he loved and with whom he had lived without any sexual intimacy for several years.

At one point I began to focus our work on the almost bizarre split between his intense sexual life with any pair of women he could induce to participate in his particular scenario and his total lack of sexual desire for the woman who loved him and was willing to live with him in spite of his avoidance of sexual engagement with her. My efforts to explore what he felt in relation to his girlfriend, whom he described as objectively attractive and who, in the distant past, had been one of a pair of women engaged in the masochistic scenario with him, at first created intense anxiety and perplexity in the patient. Any effort to explore his thoughts or feelings when she undressed in his presence would lead him to express of boredom; he even fell asleep in the sessions when that subject was mentioned. It gradually emerged that he did not dare to depend on his girlfriend because of the unconscious conviction that all women would try to sadistically control and brainwash him if he became dependent on them; therefore, only intense sexual encounters orchestrated by him with women for whom he had no feelings permitted him any sexual gratification. Fantasies of swimming underwater and being approached by a huge fish that wanted to swallow him up and memories of humiliating experiences when his mother took him to doctors because she thought his penis was distorted toward one side alternated with the patient's attempt to talk about the relationship with his girlfriend when in fact he could only describe her behavior toward him. He was completely oblivious to any emotion he might have in relation to her or what her internal life might be: The patient described himself as feeling as if a glass wall separated him from her.

This strange combination of frightening fantasies of oral castration, interspersed with total repression of thoughts and feelings about his girlfriend and the patient's irresistible somnolence in the hours, made me aware that some parallel development was occurring in his relationship with me. His empty talk about the actual interchanges with his girlfriend produced a somnolence in me that at times made me struggle with the temptation to fall asleep. I observed that the patient's attitude on the couch was one of growing tension, and his associations became more and more strenuous efforts to carry out the task of understanding what was happening in the relationship with his girlfriend. It was as if he was in some kind of cognitive-behavioral therapy, carrying out concrete tasks of fantasy formation rather than simply letting himself depend on his relationship with me.

In short, powerful narcissistic defenses against dependency on a maternal object (because such dependency would mean a dangerous sexualization leading to castration) were gradually discovered in the transference, leading to the understanding of the idealized masochistic perversion. In that masochistic scenario, his erect penis emerged as a most desirable object in the context of humiliation and physical restraint. He allayed his deep fears of castration by arranging for the dependent position to be forced on him while eliminating any emotional involvement with his paired partners. He did not dare to depend on his girlfriend because of his oedipal prohibition, condensed with the fear of an invasive, castrating preoedipal mother, and he did not dare to depend on me, replicating the same relationship. Dependence on me would imply sexually submitting to the oedipal father and being castrated by an invasive mother at the same time.

This case, I believe, illustrates the indirect road to understanding the perversion by focusing on the patient's inhibitions as the corresponding conflicts become activated in the transference. In my somnolence, I was identifying with the patient's masochistic submission to and avoidance of a dangerous mother, while his intellectualized speculations implied his identification with an omnipotent and castrating mother.

Patients with borderline personality organization and narcissistic personality structure invariably stir up countertransference responses that are not easy to use effectively. But the analyst's skill in the therapeutic use of his countertransference disposition will be put to a serious test in the analysis of all patients with perversions, including those with neurotic personality organization, where the idealization of the perverse scenario may be particularly effective. The analyst may either be seduced by fascination with the perverse scenario or be so unable to identify with it that the patient seems strange and robotlike. Countertransference defenses against a threatened unclear identification with the couple of a perverse scenario interfere with the appropriate subtlety in empathizing with the emotional experiences of both the patient and his object.

The analyst's access to his own polymorphous perverse infantile erotic fantasies and memories is as important in these cases as is the ability in general to identify with both homosexual and heterosexual impulses of patients of both genders. Obviously, when the main purpose of the perverse scenario is to mount a destructive attack on the object, such an identification with the patient's aggressive impulses may be particularly anxiety-producing in the analyst. It is important, when the patient fantasizes or potentially enacts dangerous perverse behaviors, to apply the general principles for limit-setting that are useful in life-threatening situations of borderline patients (O. Kernberg et al. 1989). Concretely, if the patient's sexual behavior would endanger his life or his object's or would threaten severe social and legal consequences, it is necessary to make it a precondition for analysis that the patient refrain from such behavior.

For example, a female patient would walk at night into a dangerous part of town with the wish to prostitute herself as an enactment of masochistic submission to sadistic men; thus she objectively created potential dangers for herself that required limit-setting before the unconscious meanings of that behavior could be analyzed. Such limit-setting is not only perfectly compatible with analytic work but may be an essential precondition for it, if the meaning attached to it is immediately taken up in the analysis of the transference. The combination of limit-setting and an analytic approach to its implications in the sessions may provide not only the necessary space to resolve the particular symptomatology but also the freedom for the analyst to engage in an exploration of his countertransference, in which either excitement or disgust with the particular behavior of the patient may provide important cues to its meanings. For example, one adult male patient's pedophilic perversion, his sexual seduction of little girls, could be analyzed only after enactment of the perversion was prohibited. Limit-setting created a safe countertransferential space that permitted the analyst to identify with the patient's excited response to the hairless genitals of little girls, which reassured him against the frightening aspect of adult women's genitals, while their submission to him powerfully confirmed that there was no threat of castration in being faced with a split genital on the body's surface.

The issue of technical neutrality is important in the analytic treatment of patients with sexual perversion because the patient's defiant assertion of the perversion as much superior to ordinary sexual encounters may provoke the analyst into a countertransference defense of "normal" sex. The analyst's general value system regarding the protection of life, the opposition to destructiveness and self-destructiveness, and the affirmation of enjoyment and mutuality in a sexual experience might—rightly, I believe—limit his technical neutrality. In the context of such broad values, it seems important to me that the analyst honestly tolerate very different solutions to the patient's dilemma of how to deal with love and the erotic dimension of life. If a patient is happy with a perversion that provides a safe island of ecstasy within a reasonably gratifying and effective context of love and work, there is no reason for the analyst to urge him, even implicitly, to adopt a different sexual pattern. If patients seek treatment for their perversion, it is because there are aspects of the perverse solution that are unsatisfactory to them, that limit them in their erotic experience and in their love life, and that they intuitively sense as a restrictive imprisonment.

The counterpart of perversion is the deadening of the erotic, a frequent and insufficiently recognized pathology of daily life. As George Bataille (1957) has suggested, erotic ecstasy, together with the ecstasy stimulated by works of art and religious experiences, constitutes a fundamental counterbalance to ordinary life focused on work and conventional social existence: This would seem to be an important contribution of psychoanalysis that often tends to be neglected.

Although all types of ecstasy, as Freud suggested, derive from erotic sources, the psychoanalyst's personal experience confirming the erotic dimension of life would seem an important precondition for treating all sexual inhibitions, including the perversions. I would not have found it necessary to say this had clinical experience not shown how often the anti-erotic aspects of conventional culture influence psychoanalytic perspectives. The capacity for an object relation in depth is a fundamental precondition for a full erotic capability. This is a contribution from psychoanalysis that, although originally presented in a theoretical frame by Freud, has found important confirmation in our knowledge regarding the deterioration of the erotic capability under conditions of severe destruction of internalized object relations in severe narcissistic personality structures. The recovery of both normal object relations and the capacity for a synthesis of love and the erotic is a crucial treatment goal with borderline patients. It is also a realistic goal in the treatment of the perversions.

Part Two **Psychoanalytic Psychotherapy**

Chapter 6 Psychoanalysis, Psychoanalytic Psychotherapy, and Supportive Psychotherapy: Contemporary Controversies

The relation between psychoanalysis and psychoanalytic psychotherapy is becoming a major concern of the psychoanalytic community for several reasons: (1) A broad spectrum of psychoanalytic psychotherapies has been derived from psychoanalysis as a basic underlying theory and a method of treatment, and the usefulness of these widely recognized methods for many patients too ill to participate in a standard psychoanalysis has been widely recognized; thus they create the possibility of reaching a large number of patients by methods carried out in less frequent sessions and at less financial cost than standard psychoanalysis. (2) The conceptual challenges presented by developments in psychoanalytic theory and practice have broadened or changed psychoanalytic technique within some schools, implicitly blurring the differentiation between psychoanalysis and psychoanalytic psychotherapies. (3) Independent schools of psychoanalytic psychotherapies are training practitioners in theories and techniques that

A previous version of this chapter was published in the *International Journal of Psychoanalysis* 80 (1999):1075–1091.

appear to be in competition with those taught in psychoanalytic institutes. (4) The question has been raised as to whether psychoanalytic psychotherapies should be taught as part of the training of psychoanalytic candidates or left to institutions other than psychoanalytic institutes or to postgraduate programs to be developed by psychoanalytic societies. (5) There is growing controversy within psychoanalytic circles regarding whether psychoanalytic institutes should train psychoanalytic psychotherapists who do not receive full training as psychoanalysts and the related question of what requirements for personal analysis, supervision, and seminar experiences would be adequate to this task. (6) There is the challenging question of what attitude psychoanalytic institutes and societies should take toward the certification of, national or federal recognition of, and third-party reimbursement for psychoanalysis and how they should define the boundaries with nonpsychoanalytic practices and organizations. The relation of psychoanalysis to psychoanalytic psychotherapy has therefore raised conceptual, clinical, educational, and political issues.

Exploring the *conceptual* question would seem to require a clear definition of the psychoanalytic method of treatment (or "psychoanalytic technique"), of the boundary between psychoanalysis and psychoanalytic psychotherapy and between these modalities, and of the supportive psychotherapies derived from psychoanalysis. Given the development of alternative psychoanalytic theories and technical approaches, however, are such definitions possible at this time?

The *clinical* issues involve the indications and contraindications for psychoanalysis and its derived methods of treatment and the prognostic and technical implications of these different treatment modalities.

From an *educational* perspective, the role of psychoanalytic institutes and societies in providing training in psychoanalytic psychotherapies raises questions of educational methodology, the possibility of several tracks of training, the advantages and disadvantages of providing training in psychoanalytic psychotherapy outside psychoanalytic institutes proper (for example, in psychiatric residency training programs and in other public or private institutions), and, finally, the relation of psychoanalytic institutions to other institutions that train practitioners in psychoanalytic psychotherapy.

Regarding the *political* issues, the alliance or competition with other psychotherapy institutions and their approaches to national health-delivery and third-party payer systems—in short, the professionalization and legalization of psychoanalytic and psychotherapeutic practice (how to protect the public from "wild therapies")—all have important political implications. The political strategies and tactics followed by psychoanalytic institutions appear to be so dependent on local situations that vary from country to country that any generalization at this point would seem premature. In this chapter, therefore, I shall limit myself to conceptual, clinical, and educational issues.

In a previous publication (O. Kernberg 1993b), I examined the developing convergences and divergences in contemporary psychoanalytic technique, concluding that extensive mutual rapprochement among the ego-psychological, Kleinian, British Independent, and French mainstream psychoanalytic approaches now permits the definition of a common basic technique. This technique includes maintaining a central focus on transference analysis, remaining alert to character analysis ("pathological organizations" [J. Steiner 1987, 1990] in Kleinian terminology), and focusing sharply on unconscious meanings in the "here and now." There is an increasing trend toward translating unconscious conflicts into object relations terminology and an increasing emphasis on countertransference analysis and on the importance of patients' affective experience as an entrance point into the exploration of unconscious meanings. Additional areas of convergence of the different psychoanalytic approaches include increasing concern about the "indoctrination" of patients (Kernberg 1996a), the consideration of a multiplicity of "royal roads" to the unconscious (Blum 1985), and a questioning of linear models of development.

Meanwhile, a new psychoanalytic current is gradually diverging from the mainstream just summarized (O. Kernberg 1997b). In the United States in particular, this new current involves the development of intersubjective and interpersonal psychoanalytic approaches including self-psychology, on one hand, and the cultural psychoanalytic tradition expressed in contemporary relational or interpersonal psychoanalysis, on the other. Insofar as self-psychology focuses on self self-object transferences as the major matrix of psychoanalytic treatment, it implies a movement away from technical neutrality and an emphasis on emotional attunement and the analyst's subjective immersion in the patient's subjective experience. This approach also accentuates an anti-authoritarian attitude on the part of the analyst, questioning the privileged nature of his subjectivity. Present-day intersubjective and interpersonal approaches similarly focus on the "real" aspects of the transference-countertransference bind and on the analyst's role in compensating for past over- or understimulation of the patient's archaic self; they consider that the personality develops continuously within a relationship matrix (rather than in the context of expressing conflicts between drives and defenses against them). This concept requires a consistent focus on the intersubjective field in the relation between patient and analyst and assumes that the patient's emotional growth depends on the integration of new affective interpersonal experiences. A major consequence of this overall shift in psychoanalytic perspectives is the questioning of the traditional, positivist view of the analyst's objectivity in interpreting the patient's transference distortions and their origins. The intersubjective and interpersonal approach favors a constructivist model, in which exploration of new affective relations in the psychoanalytic encounter is the basic source of interpretation and the patient's incorporation of this affective experience is considered a major therapeutic factor.

Most North American analysts apparently still operate within an ego-psychology approach, increasingly enriched by object relations theory. This version of psychoanalysis can be clearly differentiated from psychoanalytic psychotherapies. It is more difficult to establish conceptual boundaries between psychoanalytic psychotherapy and the British Independent, French mainstream, and American constructivist approaches, a reflection of their greater flexibility and expansion of technique and, at the same time, a threatening challenge to the identity of their practitioners. In this regard, the widespread practice of psychoanalytic psychotherapy by analysts in the United States has made this less of a problem for American psychoanalysts than it has become for the mainstream in France, where a broader range of psychoanalytic methods and a reluctance to accept the constraints of a specific "analytic technique" accentuate the problem (Cahn 1996; Gibeault 1998; Israel 1998; Widlöcher and Braconnier 1996; Widlöcher and Prot 1996).

Considering these complications, I propose that a basic common boundary between psychoanalytic method and that of psychoanalytic psychotherapy can be established. This conceptual boundary may apply to all the psychoanalytic schools to which I refer. A further issue needs to be spelled out first, however. In the traditional American approach to psychoanalytic psychotherapies, strictly psychoanalytic techniques have tended to be combined with supportive interventions, and in practice the inclusion of supportive elements is singled out as that which differentiates psychoanalytic psychotherapy from psychoanalysis. This issue has been explored in great detail by Wallerstein (1995) and by Rockland (1989), the former in presenting the arguments for a continuum of psychoanalytic techniques from a psychoanalytic-expressive polarity to a suggestive-supportive polarity, the latter in differentiating distinctively supportive from expressive or exploratory psychotherapy. In what follows I propose a rather strict differentiation of standard psychoanalysis, psychoanalytic psychotherapy, and psychoanalytically based supportive psychotherapy. To clarify a minor semantic issue: Psychoanalytic psychotherapy has also been referred to as exploratory or expressive psychotherapy. The terms *psychoanalytic psychotherapy* and *supportive therapy* imply that both modalities of treatment are based on psychoanalytic theory (O. Kernberg 1984). There are, of course, nonpsychoanalytic supportive psychotherapies that are effective and validated by research, but I shall not deal with them here.

MODALITIES OF PSYCHOANALYTICALLY BASED TREATMENTS

In order to differentiate psychoanalysis, psychoanalytic psychotherapy, and supportive psychotherapy from each other, it is important, first of all, to distinguish the overall theory of the treatment from its objectives and to separate the techniques employed from the resulting process.

The underlying theory of unconscious motivation (unconscious conflicts between aggression and libido, on one hand, and the defenses against them, on the other, including the structural implications of impulse-defense configurations and the internalized object relations within which such unconscious conflicts are embedded) is common to all three modalities of treatment, although the emphasis on and relations between drive theory, object relations theory, and structural organization vary.

These treatment modalities also vary in their objectives. The objective of psychoanalysis is fundamental structural change—the integration of repressed or dissociated unconscious conflict into the conscious ego. In expressive or psychoanalytic psychotherapy, the objective is a partial reorganization of psychic structure in the context of significant symptomatic change. The objective of supportive psychotherapy is symptomatic improvement by means of a better adaptive equilibrium of impulse-defense configurations, with a reinforcement of adaptive defenses as well as adaptive impulse derivatives. In my view, however, the objectives of treatment do not sufficiently differentiate these modalities. It is the translation of these objectives into a technical approach that characterizes each treatment. Also, we still have serious methodological difficulties in assessing structural change. Surprisingly fundamental structural changes have been observed in patients treated with psychoanalytic psychotherapy, including patients with severe personality disorders (O. Kernberg 1984, 1992b).

It might be argued that it is not technique per se that differentiates these treatment modalities but the interaction between technique and the patient's response, or between the therapist's personality and technique, on one hand, and the patient's personality and interaction with the therapist, on the other.

But this broad approach would confuse, for example, a psychoanalytic stale-mate in which the patient is unable to proceed any further in a psychoanalytic modality of treatment with a therapeutic stalemate in a psychoanalytic psy-chotherapy. It is true that the patient's ability or inability to participate in a given modality may induce the therapist to shift his technique; a clear defini-tion of techniques may permit diagnosis of such a shift. From a conceptual viewpoint, I believe that a differential definition of the three modalities exclu-sively in terms of the technique employed, apart from the therapeutic interac-tion and its effectiveness in the individual case, permits the clearest and most clinically meaningful differentiations. Obviously, in clinical practice, the atti-tude and personality of the therapist will color the application of any technical approach, and the patient's reaction, in turn, will affect it. Clinical and research experience, however, convincingly indicate the possibility of defining a consis-tent, basic technique applied in each case in the light of the following guide-lines.

Starting from Gill's (1954) definition of psychoanalysis—namely, the facili-tation of the development of a regressive transference neurosis and its resolu-tion by interpretation alone, carried out by a psychoanalyst from a position of technical neutrality—I would define *interpretation, transference analysis,* and *technical neutrality* as three essential features of the psychoanalytic method (O. Kernberg 1984; O. Kernberg et al. 1989). Although Gill himself questioned that definition in later years, I strongly believe that this is the simplest and the most clinically and theoretically useful definition of the psychoanalytic method. With the underlying assumption that a regressive transference neurosis reproduces, in the psychoanalytic situation, the pathogenic unconscious impulse-defense configurations dominant in a patient's psychopathology, most English-language psychoanalysts will probably still feel comfortable with such a definition. If, at the same time, it is specified that impulse-defense configurations are embedded in partial and total internalized object relations, so that both the impulsive and the defensive sides of pathogenic unconscious conflicts are represented by in-ternalized object relations, a broad spectrum of object relations theoreticians in all three regions of the psychoanalytic community should feel comfortable. If, finally, it is spelled out that the content of these unconscious conflicts involves aggressive and libidinal impulses centering on infantile sexuality, the archaic and advanced oedipal constellation, primary seduction, castration anxiety, and the primal scene, French psychoanalytic authors also should feel reassured, leaving open the extent to which archaic oedipal issues and preoedipal conflicts are intimately linked.

This definition of psychoanalysis in terms of its technique should satisfy the conceptual requirements of the psychoanalytic "mainstream." It may not satisfy those of the American intersubjectivist, interpersonal, and self-psychology approaches, but it may help clarify the extent to which these approaches incorporate psychotherapeutic (in contrast to strictly psychoanalytic) techniques and where they would draw the boundaries of the three modalities of treatment. Thus, for example, these schools' emphasis on countertransference analysis and on the intricate nature of transference-countertransference binds may be compatible with the proposed definition of psychoanalysis except when countertransference communication or enactment decreases or eliminates technical neutrality. If not interpretively reduced, this would shift the treatment modality into psychoanalytic psychotherapy—or to a supportive modality.

The technique of *interpretation* includes clarification of the patient's conscious and preconscious experience, confrontation, or the tactful focus on verbal and nonverbal behavior that complements the patient's communication of his subjective experience by free association, and interpretation per se of the unconscious meaning of what has been clarified and confronted. Unconscious meaning in the "here and now" is usually an important bridge to the interpretation of the unconscious meaning in the "there and then" (Sandler and Sandler 1987).

Transference analysis is the main interpretive focus in standard psychoanalysis, carried out systematically in the sense that an actually emerging sequence of transference developments is systematically explored without a biased presumption of the genetic order of these transference dispositions. The consideration of synchronic and diachronic expressions of the transference—that is, condensations of conflicts from different stages of development, contrasting with a sequential narrative of a particular period of development—has conceptually replaced older models of linear development (O. Kernberg 1993b). Although transference analysis, particularly from the Kleinian perspective of analysis of the "total transference situation" (Joseph 1989), always incorporates developments outside the sessions, it essentially focuses on unconscious developments in the patient-analyst relationship, with countertransference analysis an essential component of the analysis of the therapeutic relationship. Granting significant differences regarding the approach to the transference—for example, the sharp focus on linguistic communication and structure in French analysis, the focus on the activation of primitive object relations in Kleinian and British Independent approaches, and the focus on character defenses in ego psychology—the dominance of systematic transference analysis may be considered an essential characteristic of the psychoanalytic method.

Technical neutrality refers to the analyst's interpretive equidistance from the patient's superego, id, acting ego, and external reality—that is, his approach to the material from the position of the observing segment of the patient's ego (O. Kernberg 1997a). Technical neutrality implies a concerned objectivity that permits the highlighting of the transference and its analysis as an implicit distortion of the "normal" therapeutic relationship established at the outset by setting up the frame and defining the tasks of both participants (free association for the patient, interpretation for the analyst).

Free association is a method common to psychoanalysis and psychoanalytic psychotherapy. The former differs from the latter only in the greater frequency of sessions and the use of the couch. Most psychoanalysts would agree that three or four sessions constitute the minimum for psychoanalytic work to be effective. But in my view neither frequency of sessions nor the use of the couch is a conceptually significant defining feature of psychoanalysis.

Psychoanalytic psychotherapy uses the same basic techniques as psychoanalysis but with quantitative modifications that, in combination, result in a qualitatively different treatment. Any given session of the former may be indistinguishable from a psychoanalytic session, but over time the differences emerge quite clearly. Psychoanalytic psychotherapy utilizes interpretation, but with patients with severe psychopathology, for many of whom this is the treatment of choice, clarification and confrontation occupy a significantly larger space than interpretation per se, and interpretation of unconscious meanings in the here and now, a larger space than interpretation of those in the there and then. For practical purposes, clarification, confrontation, and interpretation in the here and now are the major aspects of interpretive techniques utilized in psychoanalytic psychotherapy, with a clear predominance of clarifications and confrontations (O. Kernberg 1984; O. Kernberg et al. 1989).

In the treatment of patients with severe character pathology, transference analysis is the essential focus of psychoanalytic psychotherapy from the very beginning, but it is modified by an active interpretive exploration in depth of the patient's daily life, an approach made necessary by the predominance of primitive defense operations in these patients. Splitting operations in particular tend to dissociate the therapeutic situation from the patient's external life and may lead to severe, dissociated acting out either in or outside the sessions. Therefore, interpretive linkage of the patient's external reality and transference developments in the hours becomes central.

In psychoanalysis, technical neutrality ideally is maintained throughout the treatment. In the psychotherapeutic treatment of patients with severe character pathology, by contrast, the need to set limits necessitates abandoning neutrality again and again, in order to control life-threatening or treatment-threatening acting out. The self-perpetuating nature of acting out may prove impossible to resolve interpretively without structuring or setting limits. In practice, this means that, for example, characterologically determined suicidal behavior (as contrasted to suicide in the context of severe depression) requires limit-setting. An initial therapeutic contract, in which the patient commits himself to either becoming hospitalized or controlling his suicidal behavior rather than acting on it, may become a precondition for treatment. Any such abandonment of technical neutrality should be explored immediately after its establishment in terms of the transference implications of the therapist's structuring behavior, followed by the analysis of the transference implications of that very behavior, followed in turn by the gradual resolution of the structure or limit-setting by interpretive means, thus restoring technical neutrality. In short, technical neutrality in psychoanalytic psychotherapy is an ideal working state, again and again preventively abandoned and interpretively reinstated (O. Kernberg 1984, 1992a; O. Kernberg et al. 1989).

Psychoanalytic psychotherapy usually requires two to four sessions per week, but no fewer than two, in order to explore transference developments and to follow the changing reality of the patient's daily life. It is not possible to carry out these tasks with patients with severe psychopathology on a once-weekly schedule; either the time would be utilized completely by updating developments in the patient's life, thus precluding transference analysis, or systematic transference analysis under these circumstances may foster the splitting-off of important developments (and acting out) in the patient's external life. Psychoanalytic psychotherapy should be carried out in face-to-face sessions, in order to permit highlighting the patient's nonverbal behavior—a predominant mode of communication in severe personality disorders—and to facilitate the therapist's simultaneous attention to the patient's communication of subjective experience by means of free association, to nonverbal behavior, and to the therapist's countertransference analysis. As in psychoanalysis, analysis of the information coming from these three sources permits the establishment of a "selected fact" (Bion 1968, 1970), signaling the main thrust of interpretation.

Psychoanalytic psychotherapy thus does not dilute the "gold" of psychoanalysis with the "copper" of support but maintains an essentially psychoanalytic technique geared to analyze unconscious conflicts activated in the transference within a modified frame, spelled out by the analyst and explicitly agreed to by the patient in advance. The attention to developments in the patient's external life represents a shift in focus from the standard psychoanalytic approach; it contrasts with the "goallessness" of each psychoanalytic hour within an ego-psychological frame or the "absence of memory and desire" (Bion 1967) within a Kleinian frame. Concern about the patient's external life in psychoanalytic psychotherapy also extends to the analyst's alertness to the relation between transference developments and the long-range treatment goals, that is, the extent to which the treatment itself, as a sheltered haven, may acquire secondary gain functions as a protection against external reality in the case of patients with severe psychopathology (O. Kernberg et al. 1989).

Supportive psychotherapy, which is based on psychoanalytic theory, utilizes the preliminary steps of interpretive technique—clarification and confrontation—but does not use interpretation per se. Rather, it utilizes cognitive and emotional support—statements by the therapist that tend to reinforce adaptive compromises between impulse and defense by providing cognitive information (such as persuasion and advice) and emotional support (including suggestion, reassurance, encouragement, and praise). In addition, supportive psychotherapy utilizes direct environmental intervention by the therapist, the patient's relatives, or mental health personnel engaged in auxiliary therapeutic functions (Rockland 1989).

The transference, therefore, is not interpreted in supportive psychotherapy, but it is not ignored, either. Careful attention to transference developments helps the therapist analyze, in a tactful way, the "inappropriate" nature of transference developments and the reproduction in the hours of the pathological interactions the patient generally engages in with significant others. He encourages the patient to reduce such pathological behavior in the hour, pointing out the distorted, unproductive, destructive, or confusing nature of the behavior, clarifying the conscious reasons for it, and confronting its inappropriate nature, followed by the transfer or "export" of the knowledge thus achieved to the patient's relationships outside the treatment. In short, supportive psychotherapy includes the clarification, reduction, and export of transference, together with the direct cognitive and affective support of adaptive combinations of impulse and defense and direct supportive environmental interventions.

Technical neutrality is systematically abandoned in supportive psychotherapy; the therapist takes a stance alternately on the side of the ego, the superego, the id, or external reality, according to which agency represents the most adaptive potential for the patient at a given point. The major dangers in supportive psychotherapy, of course, are, on one hand, infantilizing the patient by means of an excessively supportive stance and, on the other, countertransference acting out as a consequence of abandoning of the position of technical neutrality. The therapist carrying out supportive psychotherapy, therefore, needs a heightened awareness of these risks. Like psychoanalytic psychotherapy, supportive psychotherapy is carried out in face-to-face sessions and has the advantage of considerable flexibility regarding frequency, from several sessions per week to weekly sessions to one or two sessions per month, according to the urgency of the patient's present difficulties and the long-range objectives of the treatment.

The proposed differentiation of psychoanalytic psychotherapy from supportive psychotherapy may be criticized from the viewpoint of actual practice, in which supportive and interpretive techniques are often combined in treatments ranging from eclectic to "wild" psychotherapy. From a theoretical viewpoint, all treatments based on psychoanalytic theory are supposed to contain supportive elements. I believe, however, that the supportive effects of any intervention must be differentiated from supportive techniques proper, and that the combination of interpretive and supportive techniques in clinical practice interferes with the possibility of transference analysis in depth, because of the abandoning of technical neutrality, and also with the full deployment of supportive techniques in order to reduce the deviation from technical neutrality and protect some possibility for transference analysis. In this regard, I believe that a thorough psychoanalytic training facilitates both the learning of a strictly psychoanalytic psychotherapy and its differentiation from supportive psychotherapy. In addition, such training can facilitate learning in-depth the methodology of supportive psychotherapy based on psychoanalytic theory.

INDICATIONS AND CONTRAINDICATIONS

Summarizing the characteristics of the three treatments described, we may say that the techniques of psychoanalysis and psychoanalytic psychotherapy are essentially identical, with quantitative modifications that create a different ambiance in the latter over time. Insofar as the proportion of clarification and confrontation to interpretation may shift in the course of any psychoanalytic treatment, the differentiation of psychoanalysis from psychoanalytic psychotherapy cannot be ascertained in any particular session but can be established only by evaluation of the treatment over time. The clearly different prevalence of interpretation per se, of unwavering adherence to technical neutrality, and of systematic transference interpretation makes the differential diagnosis of these methods easy in most cases. Primitive defensive operations are systematically interpreted in both modalities as they enter the transference, in the context of the analysis of the activation of primitive object relations that represent the unconscious intrapsychic conflicts between drives and defenses against them. In addition, because of the systematic elaboration of the transference neurosis— that is, the naturally evolving sequence of transference paradigms—during psychoanalytic treatment, the atmosphere of the analytic situation gradually shifts from predominance of the analysis of the intersubjective nature of transference-countertransference formations to the gradual predominance of the exploration of the deeper levels of the patient's intrapsychic experience (André Green, personal communication). In contrast, the consistent dominance of the exploration of the intersubjective developments in psychoanalytic psychotherapy without that gradual shift signals the relatively limited nature of the transference analysis in these cases. By the same token, the techniques of supportive psychotherapy—the absence of interpretation of unconscious conflicts (particularly of the transference), the utilization of cognitive and affective supportive techniques and direct environmental intervention, the utilization of the transference for reeducative purposes, and the consistent abandonment of technical neutrality in the service of fostering adaptive impulse-defense configurations—clearly signal the definite difference of this approach from psychoanalysis and psychoanalytic psychotherapy.

How does psychoanalytic theory influence supportive psychotherapy? It does so, first, by the use of techniques derived from psychoanalysis (clarification and confrontation). It renders the therapist alert to transference developments, and it facilitates the diagnosis of primitive defensive operations in the therapeutic interactions, enabling the therapist to clarify their present function of protecting the patient's security and self-esteem without pointing to their unconscious roots. Alertness to the countertransference also helps sharpen the therapist's approach in supportive psychotherapy.

The strategy of psychoanalysis is the resolution of the transference neurosis; the strategy of psychoanalytic psychotherapy, with patients with severe personality disorders or borderline personality organization, involves resolving the syndrome of identity diffusion and permitting the integration of normal ego identity. Pathological character constellations operating within a normal identity structure may not be elaborated sufficiently in the treatment of these patients in spite of radical personality changes and resolution of their neurotic symptoms (O. Kernberg 1984, 1992a; O. Kernberg et al. 1989). The strategy in supportive psychotherapy is the careful, gradual mapping out of the patient's dominant interpersonal difficulties and neurotic symptoms, which are reflections of unconscious conflicts, and their psychotherapeutic modification in the direction of reinforcing adaptive solutions, principally by means of the clarification, confrontation, reduction, and export of transference reduction as a major treatment technique. In supportive psychotherapy, the strategy involves fostering a better adaptation to intrapsychic and external needs rather than structural intrapsychic change.

Regarding the tactics of these treatments—that is, the approach to the patient's material in each session in both psychoanalysis and psychoanalytic psychotherapy—the therapist attempts to diagnose the predominant transference issue on the basis of the simultaneous exploration of the patient's verbal communication, his nonverbal communication, and the countertransference, in order to establish a "selected fact," and then works interpretively with the affectively dominant unconscious conflict that this selected fact represents. The analyst's free-floating attention permits him to capture that material. In supportive psychotherapy, the patient's dominant symptomatology and behavioral disturbances dictate the point of entry of the therapist's interventions. The therapist focuses on the transference (as previously described) only when transference complications interfere with the effort to change impulse-defense configurations by means of supportive interventions. Thus, strategy, tactics, and techniques jointly clarify the differences among these three modalities of treatment based on psychoanalytic theory.

COMPARISONS

The indications for these three modalities are still subject to debate, and the clinical experience we currently have needs to be strengthened (or confronted) with empirical data. *Psychoanalytic psychotherapy* has proved to be highly effective for many but by no means all patients with severe, chronic, life-threatening self-destructive behavior such as chronic suicidal behavior, severe eating disorders, drug dependence and alcoholism, and severely antisocial behavior. The differential diagnosis of cases of severe self-destructive and antisocial behavior that are amenable to treatment with psychoanalytic psychotherapy has been one of the important by-products of the psychoanalytic exploration of these cases (O. Kernberg 1992a). The indications of this modality for patients with neurotic personality organization, for whom psychoanalysis per se would be the treatment of choice, is still controversial. It may be indicated as an alternative treatment when individualized contraindications play a significant role. It often is chosen instead of psychoanalysis for financial reasons or because of geographic or time considerations: This is precisely the controversial area. I believe it is fair to say that, given the present cultural and financial climate and the very recent nature of empirical research regarding the effectiveness of these treatments, at this time, financial and cultural pressures often tend to override the clinical evidence for psychoanalysis as the treatment of choice.

Supportive psychotherapy, originally conceived as the treatment of choice for patients with severe personality disorders, may now be considered the alternative treatment for patients with severe personality disorders who are unable to participate in psychoanalytic psychotherapy. The Menninger Foundation Psychotherapy Research Project showed that patients with the least severe psychoneurotic disturbances tend to respond very positively to all three modalities, although they respond best to standard psychoanalysis (O. Kernberg et al. 1972).

Standard psychoanalysis is the treatment of choice for patients with neurotic personality organization. Psychoanalysis has also expanded its scope to include some of the severe personality disorders, in particular, a large spectrum of patients with narcissistic personality disorders, patients with mixed hysterical-histrionic features, and some patients with severe paranoid, schizoid, and sadomasochistic features.

Although we still lack systematic studies of the relation between particular types of psychopathology and outcomes with psychotherapeutic treatments derived from psychoanalytic theory, it may be stated that, as a tentative generalization for the least severe cases, brief psychoanalytic psychotherapy, supportive psychotherapy, or psychoanalysis is the treatment of choice, psychoanalysis representing the opportunity for the greatest improvement if the severity of the case warrants such treatment. For cases that are of moderate severity but still within neurotic personality organization, psychoanalysis is the treatment of choice, and definitely less can be expected from psychoanalytic psychotherapy. As mentioned above, because of financial restrictions, in many countries, and perhaps the United States in particular, psychoanalytic psychotherapy has become a prevalent treatment for cases in which optimal improvement might be expected with psychoanalysis per se. For the most severe cases, psychoanalysis is the treatment of choice only for selected individuals, psychoanalytic psychotherapy for the large majority, with supportive psychotherapy a second choice if contraindications for psychoanalytic psychotherapy dominate.

In all cases, individualized *contraindications* for the respective treatments are important. With regard to psychoanalysis, individual contraindications depend on the ego strength, motivation, introspection or insight, secondary gain, intelligence, and age of the patient. In the case of psychoanalytic psychotherapy, secondary gain, the impossibility of controlling life- or treatment-threatening acting out, limited intelligence, significant antisocial features, and a desperate life situation may constitute individual contraindications, especially when they occur in combination. As mentioned above, when psychoanalytic psychotherapy is contraindicated for individual reasons, supportive psychotherapy becomes the treatment of choice. In that case, finally, a sufficient capacity for commitment to an ongoing treatment arrangement and absence of severe antisocial features are minimal individual requirements. This is not meant to be a complete list but an illustration of the criteria that become dominant in individual decisions regarding the selection of the treatment and its contraindications.

I must point out that the definitions of technique, the differentiation of these three modalities of treatment, and the criteria for indications and contraindications that I outlined are quite controversial at this time. What folllows are major critiques of my approach that have been expressed within the psychoanalytic community.

1. To utilize highly specialized psychiatric diagnostic criteria to decide indications for treatment does injustice to the psychoanalytic concept of the universality of unconscious intrapsychic conflicts and to the determination of psychic equilibrium by the nature of these conflicts rather than by means of psychiatric diagnoses. Psychiatric diagnostic considerations may restrict and bias the mind of the psychoanalyst and preclude his open engagement in exploring the unconscious.

2. The prognosis for treatment depends on highly individualized features of the analyst-patient couple. In its prognostic implications, the nature of the particular relation established by the therapeutic couple overrides all aspects of psychiatric diagnosis or psychotherapeutic modality.

3. The transformation of psychoanalytic methodology into a circumscribed theory of technique does injustice to the complexity of the analyst's intuitive understanding, his psychoanalytic instrument, his creativity, and the many ways in which unconscious communications from both participants stimulate the activation of understanding in self and other. All "techniques" restrict the richness of intuitive grasping and communication of the manifestation of the unconscious.

4. The need that arises from the proposed model of indications for treatment—to examine patients initially in great detail and depth in order to establish not only a descriptive but a structural diagnosis and so to clarify their predomi-

nant personality organization—runs counter to the principles of open exploration of unconscious meanings in the patient's presentation and threatens to distort the transference by the active and intrusive intervention of the
psychoanalyst. The spontaneous development of transference-countertransference binds will give more information to the psychoanalyst than a diagnostic psychiatric evaluation.

5. The differences do not take into consideration the range of or variations
among psychoanalytic approaches. Given the proposed definitions of interpretation, transference analysis, and technical neutrality, for example, insofar
as self-psychology recommends an interpretive approach from the psychoanalyst's position as a self-object of the patient, it runs counter to the concept of
technical neutrality as an essential characteristic of psychoanalytic technique; or insofar as intersubjective psychoanalytic approaches tolerate partial
expression ("enactment"? acting out?) of the countertransference as a stimulus to transference activation and interpretation, again, transference analysis
as proposed is too restrictive in ruling out the introduction of supportive
techniques into the psychoanalytic setting. Interpretive interventions within
the French psychoanalytic model may attempt to contact the patient's unconscious directly by focusing on the linguistic aspects of a segment of the
patient's communication, on metaphor or metonymy in the patient's free associations. Addressing that segment with an interpretive comment that has
an elusive quality so as to avoid a premature saturation of meaning, preserving an "enigmatic" aspect of the interpretation in order to stimulate the unexpected in the patient's unconscious, may not be consonant with the restrictive definition of clarification, confrontation, and interpretation in the
here and now and the there and then.

In response to these critiques, I propose that a sophisticated initial psychiatric diagnosis can only help by providing the analyst with a richer and more in-
depth picture of the patient, facilitating the exploration of potential limitations
or risks to the treatment approach. Such a diagnostic evaluation also may provide a frame that becomes helpful at later stages in analysis by relating the unconscious present to the unconscious past. This is not a matter of requiring the
analyst to keep the historical data in mind throughout the sessions, thus re-
stricting his freedom to react to the patient's material, but rather of letting diagnostic and historical knowledge emerge spontaneously when, in the analyst's
mind, it contacts the currently selected fact.

Evaluation of the patient's psychopathology needs to be carried out from a position of technical neutrality, and, should it affect transference developments, these should be readily detected and analyzed once the treatment starts. In more general terms, clarity of thinking and the precision of categories in the analyst's mind should not interfere with his free-floating attention once he is engaged with the patient. Clinical experience, even when a manual of psychoanalytic psychotherapy for borderline patients is used (O. Kernberg et al. 1989), has demonstrated that a well-defined technical approach leaves ample room for variations in individual approaches to patients and for very different styles within the same general intervention. Clarity of conceptualization and planned mode of intervention, in short, do not need to conflict with intuitive openness and creative formulations.

Perhaps the most important critique of the proposed model is that, given developments within the self-psychology, intersubjectivity, and interpersonal schools, with the shifts in transference analysis, countertransference utilization, and flexibility with regard to technical neutrality advocated by these approaches, the differences between psychoanalysis and psychoanalytic psychotherapy and their common differences from supportive psychotherapy become so blurred that the model no longer applies. In this regard, indeed, the proposed model better fits the psychoanalytic mainstream (ego psychology, Kleinian analysis, French psychoanalysis, British Independents). But the differences between psychoanalysis and psychoanalytic psychotherapy, on one hand, and supportive psychotherapy, on the other, are definite and clear enough to override all existing differences within psychoanalytic approaches proper.

If my theoretical and technical assumptions are valid, then psychoanalytic psychotherapy and supportive psychotherapy are important derivatives of psychoanalytic treatment that can be differentiated from it, that vastly expand the realm of psychoanalytically based interventions, and that may be helpful to a large segment of the population who cannot or should not be treated by psychoanalysis proper.

I have not examined the psychoanalytic psychotherapy of couples (Dicks 1967), psychoanalytic group psychotherapy (Bion 1961; Ezriel 1950; Foulkes and Anthony 1957; Scheidlinger 1980), or psychoanalytic psychodrama (Gibeault 1998; Jeammet 1996), all of which are also derivatives of psychoanalytic theory. The exploration of individual psychoanalytic modalities of treatment in this chapter should facilitate the definition and description of related modalities of psychoanalytic psychotherapy and supportive psychotherapies.

TRAINING IN PSYCHOANALYTIC
PSYCHOTHERAPY

To What Extent Should Psychoanalytic Education Teach Such Modalities of Treatment?

I referred to the fact that, in some circles, because of the difficulty in clearly differentiating psychoanalytic psychotherapy from psychoanalysis proper and the tendency to view psychotherapy as a mixture of psychoanalytic and supportive techniques, concern has been expressed that exposure to training in psychoanalytic psychotherapy might threaten the psychoanalytic identity of candidates in training. I believe that a solid grounding in the theory of psychoanalytic technique and its precise delimitation should help the advanced candidate in psychoanalytic training learn to work with patients for whom psychoanalysis proper is contraindicated or not feasible.

The systematic teaching of psychoanalytic psychotherapy in psychoanalytic institutes should provide candidates with a greater flexibility of technique, prevent "wild psychotherapy," and put an end to the problematic contradiction, in many places, between teaching and learning the techniques of standard psychoanalysis and of psychoanalytic psychotherapy. In the long run, it should contribute significantly to the clinical expertise and sophistication of our graduates while providing a degree of quality control to the practice of psychotherapy by candidates, many of whom have had little or no systematic training in psychotherapeutic modalities before entering a psychoanalytic institute.

One highly controversial issue is whether psychoanalytic institutes should also offer training in psychoanalytic psychotherapy to nonanalysts such as psychoanalytically oriented psychiatrists and psychologists. Can and should nonanalytically trained psychotherapists carry out psychoanalytic psychotherapy as defined in this chapter? What would the requirements for such training be? And how would such a training program affect the psychoanalytic institute?

I believe that we cannot avoid this question. The widely divergent responses to it within the psychoanalytic community illustrate its importance. At the same time, it is unquestionably the most politically influenced issue regarding psychoanalytic psychotherapy. In the United States, several psychoanalytic institutes offer training programs in psychoanalytic psychotherapy for psychiatrists and psychologists and experience these programs as positive outreach activities, given the generally indifferent or hostile ambiance in departments of clinical psychology and psychiatry in universities and medical schools. They also see such programs as potential sources of recruitment for future psychoanalytic candidates. In some European institutes, by contrast—for example, those in France and Italy—such programs would be strongly opposed and rejected because of deep-seated concern for the identity of psychoanalytic education in a social environment filled with psychoanalytic psychotherapy programs of varying degrees of professional quality offered by questionable training institutions. In these countries the major concern is to protect psychoanalytic training from contamination by diluted and "wild" forms of psychotherapy.

A more pressing question is the recruitment of experienced faculty. Many experienced psychoanalysts who also systematically practice psychoanalytic psychotherapy carry out research and teaching on this subject in university settings rather than in psychoanalytic institutes, thus depriving the institutes of their educational contributions. I propose that psychoanalytic institutes make active efforts to engage these experts in teaching psychoanalytic psychotherapy within the institute. The tendency to shift the responsibility for this endeavor to the psychoanalytic society in the form of postgraduate courses tends to deny the essential nature of this educational experience by placing it outside the institute. This fits with the traditional approach to psychoanalytic psychotherapy in psychoanalytic institutions, which have tended to regard it as a second-rate treatment, a degraded or diluted form of psychoanalysis. As I see it, it is a highly sophisticated, specialized technique with indications and contraindications that expands the realm of the therapeutic effects of psychoanalysis rather than competing with it. From a theoretical and clinical viewpoint, as well as from that of the social responsibilities of the psychoanalytic profession, the teaching of the psychoanalytic psychotherapies deserves to be in the hands of the highest levels of teachers, practitioners, and researchers.

Last but not least, the technique's built-in flexibility, derived from the combination of limit-setting, the interpretive resolution of movements away from technical neutrality, the concern with protecting the patient's and the treatment's survival by means of specialized types of contract-setting, and, above all, experience with the most severe types of transference regressions (severely psychopathic, paranoid, and depressive transferences [O. Kernberg 1992a]) has facilitated the development of new technical approaches that may be transferred to psychoanalysis proper. Thus, psychoanalytic psychotherapy may be considered an experimental setting in which new psychoanalytic techniques for the standard treatment situation may be explored—in parallel, of course, to the application of technical approaches derived from standard psychoanalysis. I have in mind techniques described by the research group studying psychoanalytic psychotherapy with borderline patients at the Westchester Division of the New York Hospital (Clarkin et al. 1998), including technical approaches to patients with chronic dishonesty in the transference, patients who develop micropsychotic episodes and paranoid transference psychosis, severe types of acting out within the treatment sessions, perversity in the transference, chronic sadomasochistic transference stalemates, and defensive social parasitism. For all these conditions, new technical approaches derived from psychoanalytic psychotherapy may broaden the range of action and protect the frame of standard psychoanalysis as well. In conclusion, the teaching and learning of psychoanalytic psychotherapy in the context of psychoanalytic training may significantly enrich the educational experience and the clinical expertise of the analyst in training, and strengthen our research efforts and our therapeutic contributions to a changing social, cultural, and economic environment.

RESPONSE TO AN EMAIL DISCUSSION
OF THIS PAPER

I am very appreciative of the thoughtful and intense discussion stimulated by the original publication of this material in the *International Journal of Psychoanalysis*. I cannot do justice to all the original, challenging, and controversial issues raised and shall limit myself to what I consider to be some essential points of controversy.

I believe that it is clear that there is no direct relation between psychoanalytic theory and psychoanalytic technique or method: The same theory has led to alternative techniques. Therefore, to call "psychoanalysis" everything that is done on the basis of a common theory must be to confuse all issues regarding the differentiation of derivative treatment modalities. For the same reason, I believe that we should reject the proposal that "everything done by a psychoanalyst is psychoanalysis." We cannot escape the need to define specific theories of technique and their translation into practical interventions, even if we find that there are alternative theories of technique and clinical interventions.

I also believe that it is problematic to question the importance of the definition of the interventions by the analyst on the ground that patients may interpret or experience any of these interventions in highly diverse ways, so that only the specific dyadic interaction between analyst and patient can be evaluated and not a general body of technique. If we cannot define what we are doing because it may be experienced in different ways by the patient, we are implicitly renouncing a scientific approach to the study of our clinical practice. Also, from a psychoanalytic viewpoint, the patient's experience of our interventions needs to be subjected to psychoanalytic exploration, so that significant distortions may be analyzed in terms of their transference implications (and possible countertransferential acting out).

I conclude, therefore, that we cannot avoid founding our exploration of alternative psychoanalytic modalities of treatment or derived psychotherapeutic modalities only on a theory of technique. We need a definition of our essential interventions that is based on our theory of technique; we must define the psychoanalytic method or technique per se, then trace the boundaries of this technical approach and be able to define derivative psychotherapies as well.

This brings me to a major critique of my proposed classification of modalities of psychoanalytic therapies. Paolo Migone suggests that we adopt Merton Gill's 1954 definition of psychoanalytic technique as referring to all treatments centered on the analysis of transference as Gill defined it. I think that Migone clearly understands the relevance of a definition of the theory of technique for differentiating the psychoanalytic method from other methods, and that he is correct in stating that one implication of Gill's proposal is the inclusion of what I call psychoanalytic psychotherapy as part of psychoanalysis proper. In simple terms, Migone and Gill believe that whether the patient is seen once per week or five times per week, on the couch or in face-to-face interviews, it is still psychoanalysis, as long as the analyst focuses on transference interpretation; therefore, my differentiation between psychoanalysis and psychoanalytic psychotherapy would be irrelevant. Migone, in referring to the "transference-focused psychotherapy" that I have developed for the treatment of borderline patients, proposes to consider that psychotherapy to be psychoanalysis proper.

I disagree, first, because I believe that, although the frequency of sessions and the use of the couch are not essential paradigms of psychoanalytic techniques per se, these aspects of the setting are sufficiently important to affect the psychoanalytic process in fundamental ways. In low-frequency, face-to-face sessions, psychoanalysis becomes "anemic," as Ernst Ticho put it. Second, I believe that Gill's definition of transference broadens this concept excessively. Gill includes the analyst's actual behavior as an aspect of the transference rather than as reality that needs to be differentiated from reality distortions that reflect the patient's transference dispositions. He changes the analytic process into an almost exclusive exploration of intersubjective developments in the here and now, that may gradually may lose the connection with deeper levels of the patient's unconscious reality. Gill's statement that "it also implies a shift from the view of the reality of the analytic situation as objectively definable by the analyst to a view of the reality of the analytic situation as defined by the progressive elucidation of the manner in which that situation is experienced by the patient" tends to privilege the patient's subjective experience and to eliminate the analyst's function as a "third excluded other." In other words, Gill neglects the analyst's responsibility to explore honestly his actual contributions to the patient's experience—his countertransference—as well as the patient's transference and to facilitate, by means of interpretation, the patient's gradual development of awareness of his unconscious past beyond the interactions in the present dyadic situation.

My long experience in carrying out the psychoanalytic psychotherapy with borderline patients to which Migone refers approvingly has convinced me that this treatment approach generates an atmosphere different from that of psychoanalysis.

It is true, however, that individual psychotherapy sessions may not be differentiated from psychoanalytic sessions proper and that the differences between them that I have described are only quantitative, although they do lead to qualitative change over time. In this connection, I agree with Maria Ponsi's critique in the sense that I believe that structural change can be obtained with both modalities and that there is an overlap of the interpretive interventions, although in psychotherapy the preliminary aspects of interpretation dominate.

In contrast, I also believe that Gill's 1954 definition of psychoanalysis and psychoanalytic technique is still valid and is very compatible with recent developments in what I have described as the psychoanalytic mainstream, constituted by the convergent aspects of the contemporary ego-psychology, contemporary Kleinian, British Independent, and French approaches (referring to non-Lacanian approaches). I think that the intersubjective, relational, interpersonal, and self-psychology approaches lend themselves less clearly to the differentiation between psychoanalysis and psychoanalytic psychotherapy that I proposed. I believe, however, that even within those psychoanalytic approaches, most clinicians would still differentiate between psychoanalysis proper and psychoanalytic psychotherapy; it would be an interesting task to relate such differentiations with those proposed in my paper.

Alain Gibeault, in a comprehensive discussion, presents an elegant and cogent model of the relation between certain key elements of psychoanalytic theory, on one hand, and a derived, coherent theory of psychoanalytic method or technique, on the other, and differentiates psychoanalysis proper from psychoanalytic psychotherapy.

Gibeault and I agree that there are patients who have such severe psychopathology that the standard psychoanalytic method is contraindicated or cannot be tolerated and that an alternative treatment based on the same psychoanalytic theory is indicated, with the objective of bringing about structural intrapsychic change. I fully agree with his observation that these patients are not able to contain their unconscious conflicts in the sense of having a capacity for representation, fantasy formation, and dreaming that would reflect an ability to elaborate intrapsychically unconscious conflicts, in contrast to their intolerance of primitive anxiety, or their expression of unconscious conflicts in violent action, discharge, and somatization, with a serious deficit in their capacity for symbolization. We also agree that the objective of psychoanalytic psychotherapy in these cases is to help them develop the ability to contain the unconscious conflicts, to transform violent acting out and somatization into intrapsychic experience, representational development and fantasy, and into tolerance of affective experience instead of discharge and elimination in action.

A major difference in our assessment of such patients stems from our diagnostic instruments. Gibeault utilizes a metapsychological approach, evaluating patients' capacity for topographical regression—that is, for preconscious functioning and formal regression—and their tolerance of primary process discourse that permits the analysis of condensation and displacement. A capacity for topographic regression to preconscious functioning and for formal regression to primary process functioning is the precondition for temporal regression as well and for differentiation of the present from the unconscious past. In contrast, the incapacity for such topographic and formal regression would contraindicate psychoanalytic technique proper and indicate such psychotherapeutic techniques as the French model of psychodrama, which permits imaging and visualization by means of the enactment of scenarios of unconscious conflicts that cannot be symbolized, with a secondary integration of such enacted scenarios into a tolerable representational narrative.

My diagnostic approach, in contrast, utilizing structural psychoanalytic criteria, differentiates borderline from neurotic personality organization on the basis of the evaluation of normal identity formation as opposed to identity diffusion, the predominance of advanced as opposed to primitive defensive operations, and the maintenance of reality testing in contrast to structurally psychotic personality organization. This assessment is achieved in a series of diagnostic interviews that lead to a differential treatment indication, an approach that differs from Gibeault's proposal. At this point, I may clarify a misunderstanding of various contributors to our discussion who assume that I am using descriptive psychiatric criteria for indications of alternative treatment modalities based on psychoanalytic theory. I certainly do believe that there are psychiatric descriptions of personality disorders that are diagnostically relevant and that can and should be used as part of a psychoanalyst's assessment of his patients, but I also believe that the diagnosis should be not a descriptive one but a structural one in that it assesses the dominant organization of the patient's personality. This psychoanalytic evaluation transcends the ordinary psychiatric one and, I believe, is actually an important contribution that psychoanalysis has to offer to psychiatry.

It is interesting that Gibeault compares the "tactical" Kleinian method of transference interpretation—that is, the systematic exploration of the total transference as a major focus of the psychoanalyst—to the "strategic" interpretation of the French approach, which is discontinuous and "punctuates" the patient's exploration of his unconscious as part of the therapeutic regression. The latter approach to transference interpretation, different from mine, is relevant to the required frequency of sessions. My approach is closer to that of the Kleinian school. I believe that various discussants are correct in interpreting my "metaphorical" approach to the diagnosis of primitive transferences in the psychoanalytic psychotherapy of borderline patients as an interpretive method geared to facilitate the patient's capacity to resume representational processes and symbolization.

Although Gibeault and several others, such as Gertrude Blanck and Maria Ponsi, agree with my differentiation between psychoanalysis and psychoanalytic psychotherapy, most of the discussants do not. The disagreement stems in part from their agreement with Merton Gill's perspective, a "relational-intersubjective" viewpoint that would incorporate what I designate as psychoanalytic psychotherapy into psychoanalysis proper. Others disagree because they feel that, in clinical practice, the psychoanalyst's interventions are a complex mixture of interpretive and noninterpretive actions and that, when a patient in analysis requires support, it would be appropriate for the analyst to provide it. This line of reasoning also includes Winnicott's concept of "holding" as a basis for the stress on noninterpretive interventions with some patients or at certain times during an ordinary psychoanalytic process.

Once again, I believe that one has to differentiate the supportive effects of the psychoanalyst's interventions from supportive techniques proper. I also believe that there are semantic problems in using the expression "holding" to rationalize very different attitudes of the psychoanalyst. In my view, "holding" is the analyst's emotional tolerance of the onslaught of intense transference regression, his maintaining a concerned objectivity in the face of violent attacks or efforts at erotic seduction. It is related to Bion's "containing," a concept that stresses the cognitive aspects of this analytic attitude, whereas Winnicott stresses its emotional ones. In my proposed classification, "holding" is not a supportive technique, nor are clarification and confrontation, which discussants have misinterpreted as educational measures.

It is true, of course, that in clinical practice psychoanalysts do not carry out "pure" technical approaches and that any theoretical map is only a frame or guideline that permits an overall approach to classifying the nature of the treatment. The messiness of day-to-day work should not, however, preclude clarity in our conceptual frame, including the specific modality of treatment we are attempting to employ, its indications and contraindications, and the kinds of change we expect as a result of our interventions. Ponsi rightly points to the many noninterpretive interventions that are yet to be spelled out and classified. I would argue only that I have attempted to focus on the essential interventions that characterize supportive psychotherapy, namely, cognitive and affective support measures, direct environmental intervention, a reeducative reduction of transference regression, and its export to patient behavior outside the treatment situation. Supportive psychotherapy thus defined implies the abandonment of technical neutrality limited by an effort not to infantilize the patient or to facilitate countertransferential acting out.

Most discussants have agreed with me in distinguishing supportive psychotherapy from the other psychoanalytic modalities. The only question is whether such a technical approach can justifiably be said to be derived from psychoanalytic theory. I believe that, as long as the psychoanalytic theory of unconscious conflicts and defense, transference and countertransference, determines the analyst's understanding of the patient's psychopathology and the impact of the supportive interventions on the patient's impulse-defense configurations, it is warranted to state that this is supportive psychotherapy based on psychoanalytic principles.

In conclusion, I am very grateful for this opportunity for interchange with colleagues and, beyond my personal views, for the opportunity to highlight an issue of great importance and concern for the psychoanalytic community. Our discussion of psychoanalysis and psychotherapy evolves in a sociocultural climate of competing procedures that challenge psychoanalytic theory and technique, the unfortunate misuse of the term *psychoanalysis* for problematic and at times highly questionable treatments, and the political challenges that our component societies are experiencing with regard to accreditation, reimbursement, and, at the bottom, respect for psychoanalytic treatment.

Chapter 7 Psychodynamic Psychotherapy for Patients with Borderline Personality Organization: An Overview

THERAPEUTIC STRATEGY

From a therapeutic perspective, psychodynamic psychotherapy as described in this chapter is a psychoanalytic psychotherapy that explores the syndrome of identity diffusion, its expression in primitive tranferences as they reflect early internalized object relations of an idealized and persecutory kind. The goal of the treatment is to identify these paradigms and then to facilitate their gradual integration, so that splitting and other primitive defensive operations are replaced by more mature defensive operations and identity diffusion is eventually resolved (O. Kernberg 1984).

The strategy involves three consecutive steps: (1) The dominant primitive object relation is identified in the transference and is described in an appropriate metaphorical statement that includes a hypothesized relation between two people linked by a dominant peak affective state. (2) Within this dominant relation, the patient's repre-

Published in *Highlights of Modern Psychiatry,* edited by K. Achté and T. Tamminen. Klaukkala, Finland: Recallmed, 2000, 246–261.

sentation of self relating to the representation of a significant other ("object representation") is described, and the patient is shown how that self-representation, linked to its corresponding object representation by a specific affect, is activated within the transference in frequent role reversals in which the patient alternately enacts his representation of self and of the corresponding object, while projecting the other member of the internalized object relation onto the therapist. In this phase the patient learns not only to understand how the same transference disposition may manifest itself in completely contradictory behaviors but to tolerate his identification with both self-representations and object representations in this interaction. (3) The idealized internalized object relations are interpretively integrated with their opposite, split-off persecutory ones, so that the patient, who already has learned to accept his identification with contradictory internalized representations of self and object at different points in his treatment experience, now learns to integrate them and to accept that he harbors both loving and hateful feelings toward the same object, that his self-concept is both "good" and "bad," and that his objects are neither exclusively good nor exclusively bad, as he originally perceived them to be.

This gradual integration of the internal world of object relations leads to a tolerance for ambivalence, a toning down and maturing of all affective experiences and emotional relations with significant others, a decrease in impulsive behaviors, and a growing capacity for self-reflection and empathy with significant others.

In practice, then, the resolution of identity diffusion and of primitive defensive mechanisms appears in several successive steps: In successfully treated cases, one may first observe a significant decrease in impulsive behavior; later, a toning down of the patient's contradictory and explosive affects; and, eventually, the integration of normal ego identity.

THERAPEUTIC TECHNIQUES

Psychodynamic psychotherapy for borderline personality organization derives from psychoanalytic concepts and techniques, modified in specific ways that make this treatment clearly different from psychoanalysis proper. In fact, this treatment was developed, in part, because of the failure of standard psychoanalysis to help many patients with severe personality disorders, an experience captured in the psychotherapy research project of the Menninger Foundation, in particular (O. Kernberg et al. 1972). The psychoanalytic techniques that, appropriately modified, characterize the technique of this psychodynamic psychotherapy are interpretation, transference analysis, and technical neutrality.

The technique of *interpretation* includes clarification of the patient's subjective experience, the tactful confrontation of aspects of his nonverbal behavior that are dissociated or split off from his subjective experience, the interpretation in the here and now of the hypothesized unconscious meanings of the patient's total behavior and their implicit conflictual nature, and the interpretation of a hypothesized origin in the patient's past of that unconscious meaning in the here and now.

Clarification, confrontation, and interpretation of unconscious meanings in the here and now predominate in the early stages of the treatment; the linkage to the patient's unconscious past is emphasized only in advanced stages. The initial avoidance of genetic interpretations protects the patient from confusion between present and past and from defensive intellectualization.

Transference analysis refers to the clarification, confrontation, and interpretation of unconscious pathogenic internalized object relations from the past, which are typically activated very early in the relationship with the therapist. In simplest terms, the transference reflects the distortion of the initial therapist-patient relationship by the emergence of an unconscious, fantasized relationship from the patient's past that he unwittingly or unwillingly enacts in the current treatment situation. In psychoanalysis, a systematic analysis of transference developments is an essential technical tool; in psychodynamic psychotherapy, transference analysis is modified by an ongoing linking of such transference activations in the therapy hours with the pathological enactments the patient experiences outside the treatment situation. Such pathological interactions are also immediately explored in terms of their corresponding transference implications. This modification of the technique of transference analysis protects the treatment from splitting treatment hours from the patient's external life.

Technical neutrality refers to the therapist's avoidance of taking sides regarding the patient's unconscious conflicts and thus helping the patient understand these conflicts. The therapist, in his total emotional reaction to the patient—that is, his countertransference reaction—may experience powerful feelings and the temptation to react in specific ways in response to the patient's transference challenges. Utilizing his countertransference response to better understand the transference without reacting to it, the therapist interprets the meanings of the transference from a position of concerned objectivity, which is the most important application of the therapist's position of technical neutrality.

In borderline patients, tendencies toward expression in action rather than in verbal communication—"acting out"—may threaten the patient's life, other people's lives, the continuity of the treatment, or the frame of the psychotherapeutic sessions. The therapist may have to establish limits to the patient's behavior both within and outside the sessions; this implies a movement away from technical neutrality. That is, the therapist takes the side of preserving life and safety when the patient's behavior places these in jeopardy. Interpretation of the transference conflict that has motivated such abandonment of technical neutrality, interpretation of the patient's interpretation of the therapist's intervention, and the gradual reinstatement of technical neutrality as a consequence of such interpretations form an essential sequence that is often performed repeatedly in psychodynamic psychotherapy, differentiating it from psychoanalysis, in which technical neutrality can be maintained in a much more stable and consistent way.

The establishment of a realistic therapeutic relationship between patient and therapist—which permits the diagnosis of its distortion by means of transference activation—is reflected by the treatment setting and the therapeutic frame. *Treatment setting* refers to the time, space, and regularity of therapeutic sessions. *Therapeutic frame* refers to specific tasks assigned to patient and therapist, namely, the patient's free and full communication of his subjective experiences ("free association") and the therapist's consistently attentive, respectful, concerned, and objective exploration of the patient's communications and the total treatment situation. These arrangements differ from those of standard psychoanalysis in the frequency of sessions (a minimum of two or three per week in psychotherapy, in contrast to three to five in standard psychoanalysis) and in the physical positioning (face-to-face interviews in psychodynamic psychotherapy, in contrast to the use of the couch in standard psychoanalysis). The minimal (and, in most cases, sufficient) frequency of two sessions per week permits the simultaneous analysis of what is going on in the patient's external life and in the transference: A lower frequency tends to weaken the possibility of the patient's fully grasping either external reality or the transference.

The more severe the personality disorder, the more the patient's pathological behavior patterns and transference enactments are reflected in his nonverbal behavior; the face-to-face position permits a full observation of this behavior. In fact, the database for the therapist's interventions originates from three sources: the patient's verbal communication of his subjective experience; his nonverbal behavior, including his communicative style; and the countertransference. Whereas in standard psychoanalytic treatment most information derives from the first of these sources (although the others are important as well), in psychodynamic psychotherapy more information stems from the patient's nonverbal behavior and the therapist's emotional responses to it, which at times reflect empathy with the patient's central subjective experience (concordant identification in the countertransference) and at other times reflect identification with what the patient cannot tolerate in himself and is projecting onto the therapist (complementary identification in the countertransference). Both reactions, when the therapist is able to identify and observe them, are valuable sources of information.

Countertransference analysis is in fact an essential aspect of this psychotherapy. The countertransference, defined as the total emotional reaction of the therapist to the patient at any particular point in time, needs to be explored fully by the therapist's self-reflective function, controlled by staying firmly in role, and utilized as material to be integrated into the therapist's interpretive interventions. Thus, the therapist's use of the countertransference as part of the total material of each hour, rather than its communication to the patient, characterizes this psychotherapeutic approach. In Chapter 10 I explore the utilization of countertransference reactions in more detail, together with clinical illustrations.

The treatment contract includes not only the treatment setting and frame but also specific, highly individualized conditions that derive from the life-threatening and treatment-threatening aspects of the patient's psychopathology, particularly the establishment of realistic controls and limits that protect the patient from suicidal and other destructive behaviors. The initial contract setting is a major aspect of the psychodynamic psychotherapy of borderline patients and can constitute a formidable preventative against the tendency to drop out of treatment prematurely, a tendency typical of patients with borderline personality organization.

TACTICAL APPROACHES IN EACH HOUR

Within each session, the strategic and general technical approach to transference analysis is facilitated by tactical aspects that include, first of all, the effort to establish a joint view of reality with the patient, thus reinforcing his reality testing before interpreting unconscious meanings in his present behavior. The patient's interpretation of the therapist's interpretations needs to be clarified, as well as the extent to which his actual experiences reflect fantasies or have delusional characteristics. In each session, positive and negative transference dispositions are analyzed; primitive defensive mechanisms activated as part of transference enactments are interpreted; acting out is controlled; and the patient's capacity for self-observation and reflection is tested as part of each interpretive effort.

In general, the interpretive focus in each session is determined by what is affectively dominant at any point. Affect dominance takes precedence over transference dominance in the sense that transference analysis is not the unique, exclusive focus.

Because of the severity of the symptoms these patients frequently present, in particular their destructive and self-destructive behaviors, suicidal and parasuicidal tendencies, eating disturbances, abuse of drugs or alcohol, and antisocial behavior, a set of priorities for intervention has been established as another essential aspect of the psychodynamic psychotherapy of borderline patients (O. Kernberg 1992a; O. Kernberg et al. 1989). These priorities protect the patient and the treatment from the effects of such complications while highlighting the need for their interpretive resolution as part of transference analysis. In practice, the following priorities should override other affectively present material as the first focus of the therapist's attention.

Whenever a sense of danger to the patient's life, other people's lives, or the patient's physical integrity emerges in the session, that particular subject matter represents the highest priority for immediate therapeutic intervention. Threatened interruptions of the treatment constitute the second highest priority, and severe distortions in verbal communication, particularly chronic deceptiveness (which is typical in patients with both antisocial behavior and severe paranoid tendencies), constitute the third priority. Severe acting out, both in and outside the sessions, is fourth, followed by the development of severe narcissistic resistances. The analysis of narcissistic resistances follows the general principles of psychoanalytically derived techniques of dealing with such material in the transference. In essence, narcissistic defenses become specific transference resistances against authentic dependency on the therapist, which would threaten the narcissistic patient's pathological grandiose self and expose him to the activation of underlying conflicts with unconscious aggression, and in particular, severe conflicts concerning envy.

The treatment also includes particular techniques to deal with severe paranoid regressions and the development of delusional and hallucinatory manifestations in the sessions. The analysis of "incompatible realities" (O. Kernberg 1992a) as part of the exploration of transference psychosis usually makes it possible to resolve severe paranoid regressions in the transference and the shift into depressive transference developments (see Chapter 8).

Transferences can generally be classified as predominantly psychopathic, paranoid, and depressive, signaling three degrees of severity. Psychopathic transferences are particularly likely to emerge in patients with significant antisocial behavior and corresponding superego pathology. Systematic interpretation tends to transform them into paranoid transferences, which, when successfully interpreted, give way to depressive transferences, the more normal level of development, in which the patient is able to experience ambivalence, guilt, and concern, to acknowledge her own aggressive tendencies toward self and others, to mourn lost opportunities, and to express wishes for reparation and sublimatory trends in general. At this stage, the patient is on her way to improvement. Excessively severe depressive transferences, however, clearly indicate pathological submission to unconscious guilt, and this may constitute a problem in advanced stages of the treatment. The general principle applies that psychopathic transferences need to be resolved before paranoid ones and paranoid ones before depressive ones. This principle reflects another aspect of the general strategy of transference interpretation (see Chapter 8).

It should be clear from what has been said so far that transference analysis is a major aspect of psychodynamic psychotherapy for borderline conditions. This implies transformation of the patient's pathological expression of intolerable unconscious conflict between love and hatred, derived from pathogenic experiences in the past, into conscious elaboration of these conflicts. The gradual transformation of pathological character patterns into an emotional experience and self-reflection in the transference implies the therapist's active effort throughout the treatment to retranslate repetitive pathological behaviors and acting out, on one hand, and defensive somatizations, hypochondriacal reactions, and attacks on the patient's own body, on the other, into emotional developments in the transference.

In this process, very primitive traumatic experiences from the past are reactivated as traumatic transference episodes, and the patient may unconsciously attempt to repeat past traumas in order to overcome them. Primitive fears and fantasies regarding murderous and sexual attacks, primitive hatred, and efforts to deny all psychological reality in order to escape from psychic pain are the order of the day in the psychodynamic psychotherapy of these patients. Severely traumatized patients, whose experience of physical or sexual abuse or witnessing such abuse has had significant etiological influence on their present psychopathology—in particular, a severe personality disorder with borderline, narcissistic, or antisocial features—typically evince the unconscious dominance of a hateful, paralyzed, panic-ridden victim self-representation relating to a hateful, overpowering, sadistic object representation, a perpetrator-persecutor object representation linked to the self-representation by hatred and its objective of inducing pain, sadistic control, humiliation, and destruction.

This internalized object relation, which has transformed the primitive affect of rage into a characterologically anchored, chronic disposition of hatred, is activated in the transference with alternating role distribution. The patient's identification, for periods of time, with his victim self while projecting the sadistic persecutor onto the therapist will be followed rapidly, in equally extended periods of time, by the projection of his victimized self onto the therapist while the patient identifies himself unconsciously with the sadistic perpetrator. In my experience, only a systematic interpretation of the patient's unconscious identification with both victim and perpetrator can resolve this pathological constellation and lead to a gradual integration of the dissociated or split-off self-representation into the patient's normal self. The effects of the traumatic past reside in the patient's internalized object relations; the key to therapeutic resolution is to come to terms with this double identification.

In order to explore and resolve such conflicts, the therapist has to maintain a stable and steady treatment frame. In case of the development of intense and chronic countertransference reactions he may require ongoing supervision or consultation. The very sheltered nature of the therapeutic situation fosters the patient's expression of his unconscious conflictual needs and conflicts in this relationship. When everything goes well, severe regression in the psychotherapeutic sessions goes hand in hand with dramatic improvement in the patient's life, often observable from very early in the treatment. If no such intense enactments occur in the hours, or intense transference regression coincides with unremitting manifestations of these behavior patterns outside the hours as well, these are indications that the treatment is not going well, and provide signals to explore and correct the therapeutic approach. Ongoing supervision and consultation usually resolve therapeutic stalemates.

Frequently the question arises as to what it takes to become expert in this treatment. In my experience, psychiatric residents who have had a good background and general training in psychodynamic techniques are able in advanced stages of their training to carry out such treatments under supervision, as are postdoctoral fellows in clinical psychology who also have a good background and training in psychodynamic psychotherapy and appropriate supervision. Parallel psychoanalytic training greatly helps the talented psychotherapist improve his technical approach. This treatment modality follows very naturally the lines of general psychoanalytic psychotherapy and thus is more easily taught than its complexity would seem to indicate.

Insofar as the treatment requires at least two sessions per week over the course of many months, it would appear to be an expensive form of long-term psychotherapy. The fact is, however, that these patients typically require repeated hospitalizations, present chronic failure at work, and need medical attention for specific symptomatic complications. The expensive long-term social support they require may lead to secondary gain and social parasitism. Psychotherapy geared to resolving severe personality disorders rather than simply providing an ongoing social support system may be less expensive than it would seem on the surface. Also, because this treatment aims at fundamental changes in the patient's personality as well as in his dominant symptoms, it has therapeutic aims unmatched by other treatments geared to the specific symptoms of severe personality disorders. Research regarding the effectiveness, the process, and the outcome of this treatment is under way, and the manual currently being expanded should help researchers and clinicians in the field deal with one of our most challenging pathologies in clinical practice.

A recent study (Clarkin et al. 2001) examines the efficacy of transference-focused psychotherapy (TFP), an approach to the psychotherapeutic treatment of severely ill patients that has been developed at the Personality Disorders Institute of the New York Hospital, Westchester Division. Twenty-three female patients diagnosed with DSM-IV borderline personality disorder began twice-weekly TFP. The patients were assessed using measures of suicidality, self-injurious behavior, symptomatology, social functioning, interpersonal relations, and medical and psychiatric service utilization. They were reevaluated four, eight, and twelve months after entering the study. Compared to the year prior to treatment, the number of patients who made suicide attempts and the medical risk and seriousness of their medical condition following these attempts declined significantly. Study patients had significantly fewer emergency room visits, psychiatric hospitalizations, and days of inpatient hospitalization during the treatment year, and in this time severity ratings of bipolar criteria and symptoms significantly decreased and reasons for living significantly increased. The dropout rate was 19.1 percent. This uncontrolled study strongly suggests that extended outpatient TFP may result in considerable improvement in functioning in a broad range of areas.

We have also examined treatment process in terms of factors related to early dropout (Yeomans et al. 1994) and symptom response (Hull, Clarkin, and Kakuma 1993). Preliminary treatment data indicate that the different subgroups of Cluster B patients have a different response to treatment, suggesting that these subgroups would have different trajectories across longer periods of time. The treatment course was found to be significantly associated with the level of antisocial behavior reported at Time 1; the more antisocial patients had a worse trajectory of symptom change.

Chapter 8 The Psychodynamics and Psychotherapeutic Management of Psychopathic, Narcissistic, and Paranoid Transferences

DIAGNOSTIC AND PROGNOSTIC IMPLICATIONS OF THE SPECTRUM OF NARCISSISTIC DISORDERS

It is essential to the treatment of any case in which antisocial features are at issue to evaluate (1) the presence or absence of pathological narcissism; (2) the extent to which superego pathology dominates—that is, where the patient falls in the continuum from the narcissistic to the antisocial personality disorders; (3) the intensity of egosyntonic aggression and whether it is directed against the self in the form of suicidal, parasuicidal, or self-mutilating and self-destructive behavior or against others in the form of physical violence, homicidal tendencies, or a life-endangering sadistic perversion; (4) the severity of the paranoid tendency; and (5) the stability of the individual's reality testing (O. Kernberg et al. 1989). Such an evaluation makes it possible to as-

Published in *Psychopathy: Antisocial, Criminal, and Violent Behavior*, edited by T. Millon, E. Simonsen, M. Birket-Smith, and R. D. Davis. London: Guilford Press, 1998, 372–392.

sess the extent to which the therapist can rely on the patient's honest communication, his dangerousness to himself and others, and the overall likelihood that he can sustain a psychotherapeutic relationship rather than dropping out of treatment prematurely. The most general rule—that the degree of antisocial tendencies and the quality of object relations determine the prognosis for any psychotherapeutic treatment—thus becomes much more specific and immediately useful in planning the treatment of such patients (O. Kernberg 1984).

As we saw in Chapter 3, the spectrum of narcissistic pathology with antisocial behavior ranges, in order of ascending severity, from the narcissistic personality to the syndrome of malignant narcissism to the antisocial personality disorder proper.

THE ANTISOCIAL PERSONALITY DISORDER
PROPER (APD)

The essential structural characteristic of the antisocial personality disorder proper as here defined, that constitutes the most severe form of pathological narcissism is the marked distortion, deterioration, or absence of the superego system. In these patients, the earliest layer of superego precursors—namely, primitive, persecutory, aversive representations of significant others (onto whom primitive aggressive impulses have been projected)—has not been neutralized by the internalization of idealized, all-good, demanding yet gratifying representations of significant others that normally constitute the second layer of superego precursors, or the early ego ideal. As a consequence, the demands and prohibitions of the third level (corresponding to the advanced oedipal stage) cannot be assessed realistically and internalized and are hence experienced in a highly distorted way under the impact of projected aggression. Thus, the third layer of superego precursors—the internalization of realistic demands and prohibitions from the oedipal phase—cannot develop.

The absence of a normally integrated superego makes the individual totally dependent on immediate external cues for the regulation of interpersonal behavior; for example, he needs immediate admiration from others or indications of triumph and dominance over the external world in order to have a sense of security and self-esteem. There is no capacity for ethical self-regulation or for empathy with the moral and ethical dimensions of others as a significant motivational system in interpersonal relations. By means of projective mechanisms, the selfish, suspicious, combative attitude of a self that is deprived of superego regulation is attributed to all others, precluding the capacity for trust, intimacy, dependency, and gratification by the experience of love from others. Thus the overall structural characteristics of the individual include the absence of a functioning, integrated superego and the hypertrophy of a threatened, endangered, violent self geared to face an essentially dangerous, violent world. This pathological, grandiose, aggressively infiltrated self is the most primitive type of "identification with the aggressor."

To translate this pathological structural system into the language of unconscious fantasies: The world of the APD reflects the pathology of internalized object relations and thus is characterized by a basic experience of savage aggression from the parental objects, a world of violence experienced as a constant background for all interpersonal interactions. The lack of any good, reliable object relation results in the sense that the good are weak and unreliable; a reaction of rage and hatred to the inevitable disappointments by potentially gratifying objects; and unconscious envy of others who act as if they are not dominated by a violent inner world. The painful state of envy and resentment fosters the devaluation and contempt that characterize the pathological grandiose self of such individuals. Only the powerful matter in the external world, but they must be controlled, submitted to, manipulated, and, above all, feared, because the powerful are also sadistic and unpredictable.

The transformation of pain into rage and of chronic rage into hatred is a central affective development of these patients. The structural characteristics of hatred imply a relation between an endangered self and a hateful and hated object that must be controlled, made to suffer in revenge, and ultimately destroyed. The projection of hatred brings about a basic paranoid orientation toward a world perceived as hateful and against which one must defend oneself by means of dishonesty, treachery, and aggression. Given crude self-interest as the only standard of behavior, and given the basic assumptions that impulsive rage and hatred determine the unpredictability of the dangerous behavior of powerful others, the assessment and internalization of a value system are irrelevant: Survival depends on cautious submission and evasion, a consistent manipulation of assumed aggressors.

Thus the basic paranoid orientation of the antisocial individual and his psychopathic defenses against it (O. Kernberg 1993d) interfere with any possible internalization of value systems, even those of potential aggressors. In this regard, the antisocial personality proper differs from the syndrome of malignant narcissism, in which there is at least some idealization of the value systems of the powerful, an idealization of the pathological grandiose self in terms of self-righteous aggression, and some capacity for identification with other powerful, idealized figures as part of a cohesive "gang" (Meltzer 1977) that permits the internalization of at least some loyalty and good object relations. For the psychopath, in contrast, only power itself is reliable, and the pleasure of sadistic control is the major motivational system in a world clearly divided between the all-powerful and the despicable weak.

Henderson's (Henderson 1939; Henderson and Gillespie 1969) clinical differentiation of passive and aggressive psychopaths seems to me to be of significant clinical value. The passive type is much less dangerous and therefore provides some potential "space" for a psychotherapeutic intervention, questionable as its effectiveness may be. The eminent dangerousness of the violent psychopath, in contrast, calls for protection of the family, of society—and of the therapist—as the highest priority. The passive psychopath has learned to deal with the powerful by pseudosubmission and by outsmarting them, a passive-parasitic exploitiveness that, at least, implies the capacity to control immediate anger and rage and to transform it into the slow-motion aggression of a "wolf in sheep's clothing." These patients can deny their own aggression, and the division of the world into wolves and sheep is complemented by the adaptive function of the wolf disguised among the sheep.

Whether the psychopath is predominantly aggressive or passive, the gratification he seeks is exclusively linked to bodily functions, to eating, drinking, drugs and alcohol, and a sexuality divested of its object relations implications and thus devoid of love and tenderness. In the most severe cases of aggressive psychopathy, sexual sadism may become an invitation to murder, making these individuals extremely dangerous. Or early aggression may dominate their emotional life to the extent that even the sensuality of bodily contact and skin eroticism are eliminated; all capacity for sexual gratification is extinguished, to be replaced by senseless physical destructiveness, self-mutilation, and murder.

MALIGNANT NARCISSISM

The syndrome of malignant narcissism is a somewhat less severe form of pathological narcissism, with significant antisocial features, paranoid traits, and ego-syntonic aggression directed against self or others, but without total destruction of superego functions (Kernberg 1989a). In this syndrome, the process by which the earliest aggressive superego precursors are either projected or internalized in the form of a violent, grandiose, pathological self is modified by the capacity to internalize at least some idealized superego precursors as well. These patients admire powerful people and can depend on sadistic and powerful but reliable parental images. The pathological grandiose self of the syndrome of malignant narcissism internalizes both aggressive and idealized superego precursors, leading to idealization of the aggressive, sadistic features of the pathological grandiose self; "justified indignation" becomes justified violence against the self or others. Idealization of the powerful self goes hand in hand with the capacity for some loyalty and a certain tolerance of realistic superego demands and prohibitions.

THE NARCISSISTIC PERSONALITY

In the narcissistic personality proper, the least severe form of pathological narcissism, a certain degree of superego development with internalization of the third level of more realistic demands and prohibitions has evolved, while the pathological grandiose self constitutes, by its idealized nature, a massive defense against awareness of unconscious aggression, particularly in its form of primitive, dominant envy. In fact, the defenses against unconscious envy, in particular, devaluation and contempt, predominate in a majority of cases, and their elaboration in the transference may become the major focus of the treatment for extended periods of time. By the same token, the defenses against envy signal these patients' capacity to recognize good aspects of others that are envied and that they would want to incorporate. The antisocial behavior of these individuals reflects the egosyntonic, rationalized entitlement and greed of a pathological grandiose self; potential conflicts between areas of superego deterioration and remnants of internalized value systems may evolve in the course of successful treatment.

PROGNOSTIC CONSIDERATIONS

Once a malignant intrapsychic structure has evolved—that is, once a pathological grandiose self infiltrated by aggression dominates psychic functioning in the absence of the moderating and maturing reliance on an integrated superego—can later psychosocial influences and, in particular, psychotherapeutic treatment help? We were made dramatically aware of the susceptibility of ordinary people to social influences that may promote antisocial behavior by the experiments of Stanley Milgram (1963) in the United States and by Zinoviev's (1984) analysis of socialized dishonesty as a major cultural characteristic of the totalitarian system of the former Soviet Union. Edith Jacobson (1971b) has pointed to the "paranoid urge to betray" that is a part of paranoid structures in general, and I have applied this analysis to the psychopathic regression of individuals in leadership positions in highly paranoiagenic organizations (Kernberg 1992b).

Are there healing influences that, either in early childhood or perhaps in later years, may alter the psychopathic structure? We have good clinical evidence that the narcissistic personality with antisocial features may be effectively treated and that even the syndrome of malignant narcissism is treatable. So far, to my knowledge, this has not yet been demonstrated for the antisocial personality proper. What complicates the question is that many studies do not differentiate sharply in the selection of subjects between individuals with APD proper and those with the less severe syndromes in which antisocial behavior dominates. I believe that it is crucial to reintroduce sharp diagnostic differentiations in this field as a precondition for evaluating the effectiveness of various treatment modalities.

PREPARATION FOR TREATMENT OF
ANTISOCIAL BEHAVIOR

The most urgent question in any case presenting with severe aggressive or self-aggressive behavior is whether there is a risk to the life of the patient or others, including the therapist. If the diagnosis is that of an antisocial personality disorder, aggressive type, it is crucial to involve the patient's family, social services, and the law in protective measures.

The prognosis for psychotherapeutic treatment of the APD proper is practically zero. The main therapeutic task is to protect the patient himself and the family, the therapist, and society from the destructiveness of such a patient. If the patient is in possession of a dangerous weapon, immediate protective separation from the weapon is obviously required. For example, one patient who consulted because of severe hypochondriacal symptoms turned out to be involved in the homosexual seduction of men whom he would lure to a hotel and then rob at gunpoint. The therapist demanded that the patient deliver his weapon before any further psychotherapeutic contacts could take place and consulted a lawyer as to his legal responsibilities in the case.

If the patient meets the criteria for an APD proper but does not present aggressive or exploitive behaviors that are of immediate threat, the diagnostician's most urgent task is to ascertain the reason for the consultation: Is the family searching for help, is the consultation exclusively geared to give the patient protection from impending legal action, is the legal system seeking help in assessing the patient's criminal responsibility, has the family or social agency pressed for this consultation as part of an effort to deal with the threats the patient represents for his environment, or is the patient being seen during a period of genuine psychotic regression? There is a small group of patients who present what traditional German psychiatry called "pseudo-psychopathic schizophrenia" (Guttmacher 1961), that is, patients who alternate between periods of psychotic illness that conforms to the criteria for chronic schizophrenia and periods of recovery of reality testing, at which time they fulfill all the criteria for an APD. Prognostically speaking, these patients are the most ominous group within the category of APDs; usually they can be managed only under conditions of practically permanent reclusion in specialized psychiatric hospitals or psychiatric prisons.

Patients with the passive or aggressive type of APD who do not pose a serious immediate threat present the clinician with the task of protecting the family and the social environment from long-term dangers derived from the patient's behavior. These patients may chronically steal from or exploit their families, may be chronically violent without actual threat to life, or may engage in behavior that threatens to bring out their involvement with the law. Protective intervention may involve the clinician in serving as consultant to the family, social agencies, and the law. It is, of course, essential not to allow the patient to exploit psychotherapeutic contacts as a means of protection against legal procedures. And the psychotherapist must take all measures to assure his own safety, including obtaining legal advice about his responsibilities, as a precondition for any interventions with the family.

A psychotherapist who decides to attempt to work with a patient presenting this diagnosis must, as the minimal precondition for treatment, secure the patient's agreement to discontinue any antisocial activity that is potentially threatening to himself or others. For example, a patient with a pedophilic perversion and who is HIV-positive would have to commit to absolute abstention from any pedophilic activity. Of course, it would be absurd to propose such a condition in the case of a patient who had not proved honest in his communication about his behavior.

One patient with antisocial and self-mutilating behavior and chronic suicidal tendencies threatened, during an early diagnostic session, to act on the impulse to cut herself with the razor blades she carried in her purse and to cut the therapist if he attempted to interfere. The therapist took immediate action to assure his own safety, summoning a colleague to join him until arrangements could be made for the patient's immediate hospitalization. A therapist should not attempt to carry out a diagnostic assessment alone in a closed room with a dangerous patient.

Another patient, with the diagnosis of a passive type of APD, had diverted the money allocated for taxes on his wife's business for several years. When this was discovered by the Internal Revenue Service, repayment bankrupted the business. The patient wanted to enter psychotherapeutic treatment in order to demonstrate to his wife his commitment to changing his behavior, in the hope of avoiding divorce. In the course of an evaluation that included the entire family, it emerged that his wife would be willing to give him another chance only if their financial activities were totally separated. This would preclude his continued economic dependency on her and force him to engage in productive work commensurate with his professional background. Psychotherapy was offered to him on the condition that he be responsible for paying for his treatment with his own earnings and with the understanding that the therapist's ongoing communication with the patient's wife and other family members would be an essential aspect of a long-term arrangement. Once it became clear to the patient that psychotherapy would not further his efforts to remain financially dependent on his wife and her family, he rejected the offer of treatment.

Psychotherapeutic treatment with APDs who are not dangerous requires open communication with the patient and the family regarding the severity of the condition, the poor prognosis, and the need to maintain open communication with the entire family system in order to monitor the patient's compliance with the requirement that all antisocial behavior be suspended. Such arrangements increase the likelihood of success in controlling potential aggression toward self and others and eliminating the secondary gains of entering psychotherapeutic treatment. They also increase the chance that the patient will reject psychotherapy, thus sparing the therapist and the family the exhaustion of their resources in pursuit of an unattainable goal.

Chronic lying as a major presenting symptom in a patient with APD does not necessarily preclude achievement of the preconditions for treatment. For example, in the case of an adolescent living with and potentially under the control of the parents, the treatment arrangements should include educational contacts with the family, since the only reliable source of information about the patient is his behavior. It should be made clear to the patient that his behavior, and not any of his statements, will determine how the family will interact with him and what rights and privileges he will be granted in the home. If the youngster's behavior threatens the well-being of the family (if, for example, he continues to steal from his parents to buy drugs), institutional or foster care placement may be the only alternative.

If the only antisocial behavior is lying, parental control may be much easier. The patient's chronic lying may then be taken up in psychotherapy as the dominant or unique transferential issue until it is either resolved or demonstrated to be impossible to resolve.

THE TREATMENT OF MALIGNANT NARCISSISM

When the diagnosis is malignant narcissism, the prognosis is somewhat better. Again, a precondition for the treatment is strict control of the antisocial behavior, open communication with family and the social system, elimination of all secondary gains from treatment, and the physical, social, and legal protection of the therapist. In my experience, most of these patients require an initial period of hospital treatment to set up the necessary treatment arrangements. Psychodynamic psychotherapy may begin in the hospital and may be continued on an outpatient basis once the patient is ready to take on responsibility for fulfilling the preconditions. There are, however, cases in which outpatient treatment may be attempted from the beginning. For example, one adolescent patient presented severe behavior problems at school, with cheating, drug dealing, and inordinate physical violence against other students and teachers; meanwhile, he lied to family members, abused alcohol and drugs, engaged in promiscuous sexual behavior, and held a leading position in a street gang. He was found to have a typical narcissistic personality structure along with egosyntonic aggression, severe paranoid traits, and antisocial behavior. But he was able to maintain loyalty to his gang and to individual members and also evinced a capacity for nonexploitative dependency on some family members. Further, he showed the capacity for authentic guilt feelings when one of his violent outbursts significantly injured another boy. I therefore agreed to attempt outpatient psychotherapy, although I made it clear to the youngster and his parents that I did not have high expectations. A tight social control system was set up involving a psychiatric social worker who maintained ongoing contact with the family and school, strict control regarding his finances and whereabouts, and ongoing contact with the local police regarding his gang-related activities. This, along with the patient's agreement to attempt to live within these restrictions, provided an adequate structure to attempt an outpatient psychotherapeutic relationship.

This patient began coming to psychotherapy sessions only under the family's threats to cut off all financial support unless he attended regularly. In the sessions, he alternated between berating me for being the agent of his parents and filling the hours with trivialities, while I systematically focused on his deceptiveness in his relationship with me and the functions of this deceptiveness in our interaction. The analysis of his perception of me as a corrupt agent of his parents, a foolish dispenser of quackery, and a dangerous enemy who was attempting to control his life while pretending to be on his side gradually helped clarify the projection of his own pathological, grandiose self onto me; his profound conviction that in a world of enemies only the powerful and the "wolves disguised as sheep" could triumph over the "suckers" shifted the transference from a typically psychopathic into a paranoid one.

GENERAL PSYCHOTHERAPEUTIC STRATEGIES

In general, if and when one can establish a solid and unbreakable treatment frame for the analysis of the antisocial psychopathology, systematic interpretation of the psychopathic transference may gradually transform it into a predominantly paranoid transference. This may now be explored in the same way in which one analyzes severe paranoid regressions in nonantisocial narcissistic personalities and in patients with borderline personality organization in general (O. Kernberg 1992a).

Patients who are able to communicate honestly can provide information about their behavioral problems outside the sessions, and this, combined with the development of severely regressive behaviors in the sessions, gradually makes it possible to transform their pathological behaviors interpretively into cognitive and affective experiences in the transference. For patients whose chronic deceptiveness makes accurate assessment of their pathological behaviors outside the sessions impossible, the therapist requires a reliable network of informants. All patients with severe acting-out tendencies require the interpretive transformation of their automatic, repetitive behavior patterns into affectively invested fantasies in the transference. The exploration and working through of these fantasies are major tasks of the treatment.

Some general psychotherapeutic principles apply to determining the issues on which to focus in the treatment hours. First, as mentioned above, the therapist should always consider the following priorities of urgency of intervention (O. Kernberg et al. 1989): (1) danger to self or others, (2) threats of treatment disruption, (3) dishonesty in communication, (4) acting out outside and inside the sessions, and (5) trivialization of the communication. Second, it is essential to look for the affectively dominant aspect of the total material—including the patient's verbal communication, nonverbal behavior, and the countertransference. The patient's verbal descriptions of his subjective experience are a relatively weak source of cues to what is affectively dominant and in need of exploration; these cues are to be found by means of careful evaluation of the patient's behavior and the therapist's countertransference.

COUNTERTRANSFERENCE ISSUES

In the treatment of patients with severely antisocial behavior, it is important that the therapist find some potentially likable, authentic human aspect of the patient, a possible area of ego growth that will constitute the basis for genuine communication. The therapist's position of technical neutrality implies a commitment to what he expects or hopes is a still-available core of ordinary humanity in the patient, a core of object-relation investment that assures a capacity for dependency and the establishment of a therapeutic relationship.

From the vantage point of an implicit alliance between the therapist in his specific role and whatever normal aspect of the patient's personality has been preserved, the therapist consistently confronts the patient's identification with primitive sadistic, corrupt, antisocial, death-desiring parts of his inner life. The internal world of object relations of these patients is populated by primitive sadistic representations of self and others and their interactions with masochistic, devalued, threatening, or corrupt enemies. At the beginning, the therapist may have to assume the existence of a somewhat normal self-representation in the midst of this nightmarish world; this assumption permits him to confront the patient's imprisonment in a destructive world systematically without causing the patient to experience these interpretations as an attack. This means that, in spite of the patient's projection of his primitive superego precursors onto the therapist and his consequent perception of any critical comment from the therapist as a savage attack to be fended off, the therapist must remain in a moral stance without becoming moralistic; he must remain in a critical attitude without letting himself be seduced into identification with projected sadistic images, nor tempted into a defensively seductive, mutually manipulative style of communication that reinforces the patient's denial of the severe aggression rooted in his internal world.

The patient, by means of his provocative behavior, will attempt to move the therapist out of that position of technical neutrality and authentic human concern into the role of a sadistic persecutor, a masochistic victim, or a manipulative, essentially indifferent authority or into a total emotional withdrawal from the patient. Paradoxically, a therapist's pseudoinvestment, a friendly surface that denies the aggression in the countertransference or reflects a basic indifference toward the patient, may bring about an apparent "warming up" of the therapeutic relationship without a resolution of the underlying dishonesty in the patient's communication or, more fundamentally, the possibility of resolving the severe denial and splitting processes that defend against the aggressive implication of the patient's antisocial behavior.

The therapist can maintain an honest investment in the relationship only as long as his objective safety is protected. Assurance of his physical, emotional, social, and legal safety must take precedence over any other consideration. An authentic investment in the psychotherapeutic endeavor precludes the therapist from "going out of his way" to try to help an impossible patient and demands the maintenance at all times of realistic boundaries for his involvement. Going overboard to provide impossible cases with a "corrective emotional experience" in the face of their provocative behavior may create the risk of the therapist's denial of the negative aspects of the countertransference, which may precipitate the end of the treatment.

THE PARANOID TRANSFERENCE

In clinical practice, the spectrum of narcissistic personality disorders, ranging from the narcissistic personality with antisocial features to malignant narcissism to the antisocial personality proper, always includes significant paranoid features. Insofar as the combination of antisocial behavior and primitive defensive mechanisms implies a projection of these antisocial tendencies onto others, fears of being found out, mistreated, manipulated, or exploited are a frequent correlate of antisocial behavior.

Once the psychopathic transference has shifted into a predominantly paranoid one—that is, once the patient's dishonest and pseudofriendly behavior has shifted into honest suspicions and distrust of the therapist—the patient may appear to be much more hostile and belligerent in the sessions but, by the same token, more honestly engaged in the psychotherapeutic relationship. Now the main question is whether the structure of the treatment adequately protects the patient, the therapist, and the treatment setting from the patient's acting out of severe aggression. The answer depends on whether the patient's superego is sufficiently intact and noncorrupted to enable him to experience some minimum of guilt and concern for the therapist and the therapeutic relationship that will prevent him from threatening the therapist or the treatment with destruction.

The task now is to examine in great detail the nature of the patient's projections, the image of the therapist as a sadistic persecutor that emerges from them, and, eventually, the projective processes by which the patient is attributing to the therapist that which he cannot tolerate in himself.

One patient had violent temper tantrums in connection with her suspicion that the therapist had been talking about her to third parties; she assumed that the therapist was attempting to obtain confidential information from her in order to use it against her later. The patient gradually became aware that she repeated the suspicious and enraged behavior of her mother, who would attempt to control the patient's communications with people outside the family and her private life in general. Eventually, the patient became aware that she had been attributing to the therapist her own proclivity for surreptitiously spying on others in order to achieve control over them, manipulating others in order to obtain information about their social life, eavesdropping on their conversations, and participating in meetings under false pretenses in order to obtain privileged information.

Sometimes a patient's paranoid regression takes on frankly psychotic features, with the development of delusions in the transference. At such points, it is important to maintain strict boundaries in the therapeutic situation, clearly stressing the kind of behavior that cannot and will not be tolerated within and outside the sessions; the therapist must then ascertain whether such delusion formation occurs only in the therapy hours or also in the patient's external life. If paranoid delusion develops outside the hours in a patient diagnosed as a borderline personality organization (that is, a nonpsychotic disorder), it is important to provide clear structure for the patient outside the hours in order to avoid dangerous aggressive and self-destructive behavior before the nature of this behavior can be understood in the transference.

Once it is established that the patient's convictions are clearly delusional, the technique of "incompatible realities" may be utilized to resolve the psychotic regression. It consists in letting the patient know that the therapist understands that the patient's conviction is unshakable and that the therapist respects that conviction. At the same time, the therapist should explain that his own conviction is quite different, so that the patient is faced with the fact that he and the therapist are living in different realities. It is important that the therapist present his conviction without attempting to convince the patient, while making it very clear that he will not be convinced by the patient's view, either. The therapist should demonstrate by his behavior that he is interested in the implications of their differences.

Patients who still have a severe unresolved psychopathic transference may see the therapist's statement about incompatible realities as evidence that he is lying. At that point a good deal of time may have to be devoted to exploring the transference implications of a "dishonest" therapist treating the patient before tracing them back to projective processes in the patient. That is, this development reflects a regression from the paranoid to the earlier stage of predominantly psychopathic transference. If, on the other hand, the patient believes that the therapist is sincere but totally misguided in his view of reality, the situation of mutually incompatible realities can be analyzed. In this way a psychotic nucleus in the transference may be circumscribed and then examined as a particular transferential problem. This approach is very effective in reducing paranoid transference regression in essentially nonpsychotic patients but is contraindicated for patients with a psychosis with paranoid features.

One patient became convinced that the therapist was presenting his comments in a sarcastic or otherwise provocative way in order to get her angry enough to lose control and thus justify treating her as if she were psychotic. She, in turn, was enraged by what she perceived as the therapist's sadistic, cynical, insensitive, and provocative behavior. Her vehement protest was condensed with ironic mimicry of the therapist's linguistic style and accent. Her indignation escalated to the point that she was considering making formal complaints to the therapist's superiors. The therapist said that he believed she was convinced that he was treating her in such sadistic and provocative ways, but in his view, nothing in his behavior objectively warranted such an accusation. He added that his conviction that her accusations were totally unfounded required an examination of the honesty of his statement. If the patient thought he was honest, how could he be so blind to the nature of his own behavior as to make statements that were in total disagreement with her experience of the situation? The patient in this case did not believe that the therapist was lying, but she could not accept that he would be unaware of something so obvious as what she was describing. This led to acute confusion on the patient's part and finally to her self-accusation that she was mistreating a good therapist. And this in turn enabled the therapist to point to her fear of asserting a view of him that, though perhaps not corresponding to reality, might nevertheless have an important function for her. Eventually, the patient was able to recognize in her view of the therapist the frightening experience of her "crazy" parents, who savagely fought with each other under the influence of severe drug intoxication. The therapist represented a psychotic parental couple destroying their relationship while oblivious to their child (the patient), an innocent victim of this savagery.

The working through of paranoid transference eventually leads to the patient's capacity to acknowledge the projection of his own aggressive needs and wishes and to integrate awareness of this "persecutory" segment of his experience with the split-off "idealized" segment. This bridging of opposite self- and object representation units initiates the development of "depressive" transference, the advanced stage of the treatment of patients with borderline personality organization.

NARCISSISTIC TRANSFERENCE

Narcissistic personalities usually show less severe antisocial behavior, so that setting up the structure for the limitation of destructive acts is much less problematic. The patient's ability to establish a therapeutic contract is not compromised by severe superego distortion, deceptiveness, or an incapacity to accept responsibility for himself, and thus the treatment can be largely devoted to the analysis of narcissistic transference.

The basic problem in the treatment of patients with predominantly narcissistic transference is their inability to acknowledge the importance of the therapist and thus to depend on him. Their objective need of help from the therapist generates intense conscious and unconscious envy and defenses against envy. Also, by projection, they may develop fears of envious attacks by the therapist, who therefore acquires dangerous features in the patients' minds. Massive devaluation of the importance of the therapist and the therapeutic relationship is an essential defense against dreaded dependency and the related unconscious envy. In severe cases, this may present as the creation of an unrealistic therapeutic atmosphere within which the therapist feels (consciously and sometimes unconsciously) excluded. As the patient's "self-analysis" goes on, the therapist, treated as a bystander, often becomes bored, restless, or sleepy during the sessions.

At other times, a primitive, frail, and unstable idealization evolves in which the patient appears to accept the therapist's interpretations but, in the long run, devalues them or "extracts" them as magical comments to be appropriated by the patient and used for his own purposes. These patients try to outguess the therapist in order to protect themselves against attack by him, unconscious envy, and essentially, dependency on the therapist.

Manifestations of omnipotent control in these cases include efforts to manipulate the therapist to respond in ways the patient expects. Should the therapist react differently and thus demonstrate his possession of knowledge that the patient did not already have, the patient would feel put down, humiliated, or attacked. By means of radical devaluation of unexpected interpretations or statements, the patient neutralizes the therapist, who has to be as good as the patient but neither better nor worse, and correspond rigidly to the patient's expectations.

In patients with significant superego pathology, even in the absence of antisocial behavior, there is a profound distrust in the therapist's genuine interest, a suspicion that he is only interested in exploiting the patient and has no authentic knowledge to contribute but only magic or quackery, "gimmicks" that the patient may appropriate in order to enhance his own manipulative skills. In the process the patient tends to deny the therapist's distinct reality as a different human being with his own internal life. In particular, it is the therapist's creativity in the therapeutic process that these patients profoundly envy and unconsciously seek to destroy.

The effect of all these mechanisms may be a severe "emptying out" of the therapeutic situation, the therapist's sense that nothing is really going on and that there is a lack of development in the transference. To the contrary, the patient's pathological grandiose self is being intensely activated in the transference relationship. In fact, the transitory idealizations of the therapist reflect the temporary projection of the patient's grandiose self-image. The patient's activation of grandiosity, omnipotent control, devaluation, and denial of dependency reflects the object relation derived from the pathological grandiose self.

When the pathological grandiose self is infiltrated by egosyntonic aggression, the manifestations of omnipotent control, devaluation, and projective identification of undesirable aspects of the self onto the therapist become much more evident. The patient may express inordinate demands, arrogant, openly controlling behavior, and the syndrome that Bion (1958, 1968) described as a combination of arrogance, curiosity about the therapist's mind and life, and pseudostupidity (the apparent incapacity to listen to ordinary logic and reasoning that do not correspond to the patient's preset ideas). Severe narcissistic devaluation may bring about premature disruption of the treatment, particularly with patients with significant antisocial features and severe superego pathology, in whom the capacity for engaging in authentic relationships is seriously compromised. Premature termination because of narcissistic devaluation of the therapist differs from the often-surprising late dropouts that occur at precisely the point when the patient has experienced the therapist as providing him with authentic help. These are negative therapeutic reactions that stem from unconscious envy. The therapist's awareness of the potential for such reactions may permit preventive interpretation when the patient seems able to acknowledge the therapist's help, perhaps for the first time.

Careful analysis of particular aspects of the patient's grandiosity, arrogance, demandingness, and devaluation may gradually reveal the components of the pathological grandiose self—that is, condensed identification with idealized self- and object representations that represent a selective takeover of the aspects of significant others that, in the patient's past, signified the possession of strength, wisdom, power, and superiority.

The more severe the superego pathology, of course, the more such powerful images, particularly parental images, include sadistic and corrupt features. Often patients with severe narcissistic personality disorders who have been victims of physical or sexual abuse or exploitation harbor a deep conscious resentment against the perpetrators while unconsciously identifying with the double role of victim and abuser. In the transference, the activation of both victim and perpetrator status must be explored together with the patient's unconscious activation of idealized aspects of past representations of self and other. Careful analysis of all these component identifications in the transference permits the gradual resolution of the pathological grandiose self and of its protective function against more primitive aggression. The emergence of conflicts involving hatred and envy tends to push narcissistic transference toward paranoid transference. Although on the surface the paranoid transference seems much more negative than the narcissistic one, at bottom it reflects the development of a more intense and dependent object relation that lends itself to gradual working through along the lines of the elaboration of paranoid transference described above.

One patient tended to dismiss as meaningless or stupid any comments of the therapist that did not fit with her preset views. At the same time, she was extremely curious about what the therapist might be thinking. Meanwhile she avoided talking openly about her own thoughts, fearing that honest communication would expose her to exploitation and mistreatment. She was immensely curious about the therapist's relationship with his family and went to considerable trouble to find out as much about them as she could. Her reaction to this information oscillated between radical devaluation of them and resentful envy.

Another patient, fearful that the therapist would try to cheat him of his allotted time, carefully checked every minute of the sessions while using every pretext to prolong them. He had a remarkable tendency to waste time in the hours, endlessly repeating the same questions and enraged demands for answers. He used the "stolen" moments after the end of the sessions to impart the apparently important information he had withheld during the regular session. It turned out that what the therapist would give "freely" of his time and interest was worthless; only what the patient could appropriate by force would gratify his sense of envious resentment.

A particularly malignant expression of narcissistic resistances may be the patient's destroying his own life in a gradual, undramatic, and yet highly effective way in fulfillment of unconscious wishes to defeat the treatment. Thus, for example, one patient neglected her academic responsibilities, repeatedly placing herself at serious risk of being expelled from her postgraduate program. She systematically withheld from her therapist the trouble she was getting into until a major crisis had reached the point at which it would be almost impossible to correct the situation. Again and again the therapist felt called upon to carry out last-minute rescue efforts that would typically fail. It was some time before he realized how the patient was successfully preventing him from becoming aware of her self-destructive behavior in time to intervene successfully.

The foregoing illustration relates to a more general dangerous development, namely, "perversity" in the transference, or the recruitment of love in the service of aggression. The patient consciously and unconsciously evokes the therapist's dedication and commitment, then sees to it that his attempts to help either fail or make matters worse. One patient, for example, implored her therapist to explain her problematic relationships with men. She listened and seemed to be thoughtfully applying the therapist's interpretations to an understanding of her difficulties. Several weeks' worth of work on this problem eventuated in the patient's making use of all she had learned from the therapist in a devastating attack on her boyfriend, using distortions of the therapist's statements to reinforce her sadistic attack. She placed a massive misuse of what she had received from the therapist at the service of destroying the relationship with her boyfriend. A dramatic type of perversity in the transference is an apparent demand for love that is eroticized and becomes an aggressive effort to seduce the therapist sexually, with the ultimate purpose of destroying the treatment and the therapist's professional life.

A particular complication with patients whose syndrome of malignant narcissism has evolved during psychotherapy into a severely regressive paranoid transference is the patient's acting out of primitive sadistic object relations by dragging the therapist into legal threats and involvements. At times this development takes the form of unremitting and even violent provocations of the therapist that eventually give rise to sadistic countertransference reactions. If the therapist enacts these responses, in no matter how attenuated a form, the patient triumphantly uses these enactments as the basis for initiating legal action against the therapist or enters a new psychotherapeutic relationship with a therapist who may be drawn into condoning or encouraging the pursuit of legal action against the previous therapist. Sooner or later, the new therapist is also transformed into a persecutor; the patient may now initiate legal action against him and look for a third therapist as part of this chronic pattern. The primitive, violent, sadistic internalized object relations of such a patient require the therapist's ongoing concern not only for his own survival but also for his efforts to liberate the patient from destructive internal tormentors.

The psychodynamic psychotherapy of narcissistic transference may be frustrating to the therapist because of the enormous amount of time required to transform the pathological grandiose self into its component transference dispositions—the primitive object relations involved—and their gradual working through. The advanced stage of treatment comes to resemble those of other patients with borderline personality organization, and the therapist may not be aware, at that point, that a major breakthrough has been achieved. Furthermore, as successful work goes on in the therapy, the patient may develop an active life of engagement outside the treatment situation while the transference appears to be monotonously narcissistic. This combination of the patient's apparent behavioral improvement and the therapist's ongoing frustration in the sessions may prompt the therapist to bring the treatment to an end prematurely rather than patiently working through the narcissistic resistances; such work, however, is an essential precondition for consolidating whatever gains the patient may have made in the extratransferential field.

THE COGNITIVE STYLE OF ANTISOCIAL DISORDERS

In his pathbreaking research, David Liberman (1983) has described six styles of verbal communication characteristic of patients with various types of character pathology. The "narrative style" is characteristic of patients with obsessive-compulsive illness; the "dramatic style" is typical of hysterical patients; the "epic style" is typical of patients with antisocial pathology; the "lyrical style" is found among depressive-masochistic patients; the "dramatic style that creates suspense" is found in phobic patients; and the "inquisitive style that does not create suspense" is typical of patients who project their own paranoid curiosity onto the analyst. Ann Applebaum (personal communication) has suggested a seventh style, the "manic" style, which is very effective in inducing the therapist to adopt a jocular, satirical, or hilarious mode of interaction.

Liberman highlighted the defensive nature of these cognitive styles and their enormous influence on the transference situation and on the analyst's capacity for thinking and interpretation. He stressed the importance of the analyst's avoiding cooptation into responding in the same defensive style as the patient's and the need for him to adopt a flexible and differentiated communicative style of his own to counteract the patient's approach. For example, the therapist's use of a modified narrative style may counteract the epic style of communication by patients with psychopathic transference.

Liberman describes the egosyntonicity of psychopathic patients' impulsive behavior, rationalized by their ad hoc "ethical" system. In these patients' episodic, egosyntonic acting out, third parties are severely damaged precisely when some collaborative interaction with them might take place. A radical devaluation of these attacked and damaged third persons protects the patients from reflecting on their own behavior. Their subtle distortions of the truth hide their tendency to impulsive action and seduce the analyst into behaviors the patients then interpret as meaning that the analyst is colluding with them in their own destructive actions.

A psychopathic patient's verbal communications may seem to be informative but, by subtly manipulating the facts, limit the knowledge that the therapist may acquire and prevent him from realizing that the patient may use his reaction to this information to support the patient's impulsive destructiveness. Such patients assume that in order to survive, one must withhold and lie. They find nothing unusual in this idea—indeed, they assume that the rest of the world operates according to a similar assumption. In order to avoid being manipulated by the therapist, they build up a dossier on him so as to be able later to prove that they are correct in thinking him dishonest and manipulative. On the surface, these patients may imitate the narrative style that characterizes obsessive patients, but their narratives change from session to session or even from moment to moment, bringing about a sense of confusion in the therapist, who may not be able to tell which participant in the therapy is responsible for it.

The antisocial patients' projection of their own dishonesty onto the therapist perpetuates their conviction that the unconscious engagement of the therapist in collusion with them is the only alternative to being victimized by him. These patients may induce the therapist to respond with certain comments that they carefully gather over a period of time, eventually to prove to the therapist and perhaps the world at large how contradictory, manipulative, and dishonest his behavior is.

The essential characteristics of this "epic" communicative style are the patients' unconscious need to induce in the therapist a potential for action and their inability to conceive of the therapist as reflecting on their behavior in order to help them reflect on it themselves. If such a patient imagines the therapist as thinking about him, he assumes that this is only in order to plan ways to manipulate the patient into action.

In Liberman's view, the major danger of the epic style of patients with antisocial behavior is that the analyst may gradually become impotent to contain the information communicated to him in ways that induce action rather than understanding. He may become fascinated with the process and, as a consequence of his growing preoccupation with the patient outside the treatment situation, he may be seduced into unconscious collusion with the patient that may end with the analyst himself as the injured third party to the patient's egosyntonic aggression. My experience has provided me with ample clinical confirmation of Liberman's descriptions.

Liberman's recommendations for dealing with these dramatic, potentially dangerous transference developments focus on the importance of guarding oneself against any tendency to be naive. The therapist must be alert to the possibility of being seduced by the patient—especially by one he find himself preoccupied with beyond the treatment sessions. Liberman also advocates limit-setting to protect the analytic frame.

He also stresses the importance of the analyst's consistently communicating with antisocial patients in a "narrative style" aimed at transforming the patients' implicit manipulation of the analyst in order to induce him to take action into a coherent cognitive statement that retranslates the intended action into its motivating unconscious fantasy. The therapist demonstrates by his interpretive behavior that he is relying on reflection rather than action in his interaction with the patient.

In this instance, Liberman's general proposal that the analyst needs to counteract the patient's defensive cognitive style by adopting a different interpretive cognitive style is expressed explicitly in the analyst's narrative response to the patient's epic presentation. The analyst, however, must preserve his capacity to respond flexibly, rapidly shifting his communicative style if shifts in the transference situation warrant it. The therapist's neutralization of a particular epic style in a patient with psychopathic transference may help resolve severe psychopathic and paranoid regressions in the transference. The narrative interpretive style may provide an important therapeutic experience for a patient who previously had consistently defended himself against reflective narratives by the induction of action in others and by his own egosyntonic, destructive actions.

THE EFFECTS OF TREATMENT

I believe that the prognosis in work with patients presenting severe antisocial behavior—who are usually not considered suitable for psychoanalytic treatment or even for psychoanalytic psychotherapy—depends in part on the structural characteristics of their illness and in part on developments that can be assessed only during the treatment (O. Kernberg 1992a). If the treatment starts out with conspicuous psychopathic transferences and the therapist is able to diagnose them in terms of chronic mendacity and an epic style of communication, the question is whether analysis of these developments will transform a psychopathic transference into an openly paranoid one. In some cases, chronic dishonesty cannot be resolved by analytic means, and the patient may abandon the treatment at a point when failure of the psychopathic defense in the transference threatens the ascendance of severe paranoid developments. By contrast, the therapist's unconscious collusion with the patient's psychopathic transference may perpetuate the treatment for many months or years, with a total absence of change in the patient's behavior outside the hours. Under these circumstances, severe antisocial behavior completely dissociated from the treatment situation may evolve over time, the treatment ending only after consequences of such external behaviors threaten its continuity.

If the therapist is successful in transforming the dominant transference from a psychopathic into a paranoid one, analytic work with incompatible realities in the transference may result in the gradual resolution of a psychotic nucleus. The perpetuation of a psychotic nucleus may itself bring about complications that threaten the treatment, however. At that point, a primitive, sadistic object relation between a fantasied, overpowering, cruel, sadistic, and dishonest object and a powerless, paralyzed, humiliated, and tortured self may crystallize in the transference, with rapid role reversals but without the possibility of being challenged by the remaining healthy, dependent part of the patient's self. This is particularly true with patients who have experienced great trauma in the first few years of life. Typically, their physical or mental suffering has been consciously and unconsciously attributed to a sadistic and overwhelming maternal figure or a combined mother-father figure with no compensating parental figure the idealization of whom would counter a conception of a universe constituted only by the powerfully cruel and their victims.

Severe pain in early life is transformed into primitive aggression, which is dispersed in action or defended against via massive denial and projective identification. These defenses against the transformation of aggression into symbolic thinking are all dramatically reenacted in the transference. The treatment situation becomes a power struggle in which the patient actively devalues and destroys everything that comes from the therapist and experiences the therapist's effort to interpret this situation as an attack on the patient's autonomy. By means of projective identification, a treatment situation may be perpetuated in which the therapist is forced, mainly by means of powerful countertransference developments, to submit helplessly to victimization in an unconscious identification with the patient as a victim, or is propelled into an identification with the aggressor in a violent reversal of the patient's desperate efforts at omnipotent control.

I have found several approaches effective in achieving significant change and resolution of the paranoid transference regression, depending on the circumstances. It is important to be alert to the potential for paranoid regression when psychopathic transference is present, and to pay attention to the chronic countertransference reactions that develop under conditions of primitive defensive operations in the transference that are derived from the patient's inability to reflect and his tendency to evacuate intolerable conflicts massively by projective identification. Ongoing countertransference analysis outside the treatment sessions often permits a clear formulation of the nature of the primitive object relation activated in the transference and makes it possible to interpret this relation.

The therapist's ability to recognize a patient-induced impulse to action as material to be interpreted and contained rather than acted on permits him to refrain from action. The transformation of an action potential into the narrative mode may become an important aspect of the therapist's interpretive style, limited only by such structure-setting as seems indispensable. In this regard, I have made it a basic rule not to make decisions about changes in my relationship to a patient or in our treatment arrangements during a session in which the impulse for change came to my mind, thus protecting the patient and myself as much as possible from countertransferential acting out. Some of it, however, is almost unavoidable in terms of shifts in the style of the therapist's communication and may have to be reflectively acknowledged at a later stage of the treatment.

When acting out is acute, I believe it is helpful to interpret the total transference situation in as much depth as possible while remaining willing to return to the surface of the immediate interaction between patient and therapist. This may mean returning, if necessary, to the initial contract of the treatment, that is, reminding the patient of what he came to treatment for, the nature of the task for therapist and patient, and what each has committed himself to doing. This can be a way of reinstating a rational frame (the "normal relationship," in contrast to the transference relation) before again examining the transference in depth. Such a restatement and consolidation of the treatment frame is sometimes indispensable if any analysis of the transference is to occur.

Finally, keep in mind that some patients cannot be helped, at least in the concrete situation of any particular psychotherapist engagement. In the end, it cannot be only the therapist who wishes to help a patient whose major gratification in life is the destruction of those who are attempting to help him.

Chapter 9 A Severe Sexual Inhibition in a Patient with Narcissistic Personality Disorder

Whereas oedipal conflicts may emerge at any phase of the psychoanalytic treatment of narcissistic personalities, it is particularly in the advanced stages of resolution of narcissistic transferences that the intimate connection between oedipal and preoedipal conflicts, with the growing dominance of oedipal conflicts, tends to become remarkable in the sessions (Grunberger 1989; O. Kernberg 1984; Rosenfeld 1987). The following case highlights how the analysis of oedipal conflicts gradually resolved a severe and extended inhibition of sexual desire that developed in the course of analytic treatment. The enactment in the countertransference of castration anxiety against which the patient was successfully defending himself by projective identification produced an extended stalemate, which was resolved once the countertransference was transformed into transference interpretations.

The patient, Mr. F, was a forty-five-year-old international lawyer, a European financial expert whose knowledge and experience in investment banking had proved to be so valuable to several corporations

---

Published in the *International Journal of Psychoanalysis* 80 (1999): 899–908.

that his financial success would have permitted him to retire comfortably. His aggressive, ironic, sharp, and intense style of management was both feared and appreciated by his colleagues. He entered psychoanalytic treatment after the failures of two marriages, in which his complete emotional indifference to the women he had married and his lack of any sexual interest in them finally drove them to such despair that they demanded and obtained a divorce.

His relatively brief periods of marriage were interspersed with a long-standing pattern of sexual promiscuity. He would become infatuated with a woman for a period of days to weeks, establish a sexual relationship that would last at most several months, and then drop her. He had felt proud of his sexual exploits until his second divorce, when he began to recognize his inability to maintain any relationship as a serious failing. He presented a rather typical pathology of narcissistic love relations (O. Kernberg 1995).

His social relations were characterized by superficial friendships with other men, business tycoons who shared his interest in travel and action sports and in arrangements for get-togethers in which relationships with women could be established and exploited. He was proud to consider himself one of the leaders of this group of "golden playboys." What was striking was his inability to provide any differentiated descriptions of his male friends or of the many women with whom he had established relationships. At a deeper level, it turned out that he was very suspicious of women's interest in his wealth; he tended to present himself in such casual and unassuming ways that he sometimes gave the impression of being an aging hippie rather than a successful businessman. He would carefully hide his financial prominence from the women he was involved with and enjoyed their surprise when he appeared in the presence of apparently powerful businessmen. He presented an engaging, superficially friendly and humorous façade; only when frustrated in his demands for total dedication to him would he show abrupt, derogatory, and occasionally arrogant behavior.

He was the youngest of three brothers; the others were, respectively, five and eight years older than he. He obviously enjoyed describing them as relatively unsuccessful businessmen with whom he maintained very distant relations and toward whom he still harbored deep resentments because of what he had experienced as their hostile and dismissive behavior toward him during their childhood in a lower-middle-class household in a northern European city. His memories of childhood included his resentment of the privileged position of his older brothers when it came to space and privacy in the home, freedom to do as they wanted, and their early rebellion against what all three experienced as the chronically irritated, scolding and nagging, suspicious and controlling attitude of both parents.

The patient's parents came from traditional, upper-middle-class European families. His mother had been by far the dominant person in his childhood. What he described as her overpowering, suspicious, manipulative, and hypochondriacal attitude, her unrealistic and constant concerns regarding real and imaginary illnesses in herself and the rest of the family, conveyed an almost psychotic picture. He described his father as chronically dissatisfied, in an ongoing struggle with his wife, resisting her efforts to control the family at every step, taking refuge in his rather esoteric business, and apparently having a very distant relationship with his children. The patient said he had never experienced any moment when his parents appeared to be in harmony with each other. Over the years he had come to depreciate his father's ineffectual attempts to stand up to the powerful mother.

What was most remarkable in Mr. F's references to his childhood were extended memory gaps, so that my early knowledge of his childhood experiences did not extend much beyond the summary provided here. He remembered that his sexual development was relatively late, that he started masturbating in his adolescence only after learning that all his schoolmates had been doing so for years, and that his relatively small stature and frail aspect made him feel less masculine than his friends, a feeling that disappeared only after his early relationships with women had turned into the promiscuous pattern I have outlined.

The first five years of the analysis were characterized by a slow but successful working through of the severely narcissistic character structure. At the beginning of the treatment, he was quite ambivalent about whether he needed psychoanalysis. He oscillated between concerns about his difficulty in maintaining a relationship with a woman for more than a few weeks and his failure to maintain any emotional or sexual relationship with the two women whom he had married after a few weeks of infatuated involvements. A strikingly contradictory emotional reaction emerged in his early relationship with me. In this opposite state of mind, he considered his behavior with women to be perfectly normal and regarded men who maintained long-term relationships with women as "squares, bourgeois types"; he felt himself to be in danger of being brainwashed by the questionable wisdom of a conventional psychoanalyst presumably identified with such values.

He was so impatient with the slow course of psychoanalytic treatment that he offered to pay for his entire treatment at its initiation if I committed myself to reducing it by at least one-third of its usual time; in other words, he wanted to tempt me, quite seriously, with an incentive to do my work faster; he proudly told me how paying such awards had enabled him to triumph over business competitors.

His initial surface friendliness toward me rapidly turned into an ironic expression of superiority as he found himself uncovering various ridiculous peculiarities in my behavior. He had noticed, for instance, a "panic button" in my office (corresponding to a general physical arrangement of the hospital setting within which my private office functions take place) and speculated on the absurd location of that panic button in terms of the location of the couch and my chair. He also thought that, because he could occasionally hear the voice of my secretary in spite of the double doors separating our rooms, she must be hearing his voice, and therefore, privacy was not assured. Because I did not take any actions to correct what he considered obvious shortcomings in my physical arrangements, he oscillated between considering me either stupid for not realizing that these were absurd conditions or extremely stubborn because, although I silently recognized that he was right, I persisted in my behavior rather than give in to him.

These initially trivial "foibles" of mine gradually turned into frightening experiences for him as he realized that he was attributing to me the bizarre, rigid, and controlling behaviors that he associated with his mother. The gradual shift from a view of me as a weak, somewhat pathetic, and rigid person who reminded him of his father to a view of me as a dangerously manipulative and almost "crazy" replica of his mother signaled a transformation of his narcissistic superiority into paranoid fearfulness as a dominant transference development.

At the same time, he became increasingly aware of his intense envy of me. He started to consider the possibility that I might not be imprisoned as he was by the incapacity for a relationship in depth with a woman. His initial devaluation of my wife, whom he had seen accidentally in a few casual encounters at cultural events and whom he compared triumphantly with the beautiful young women he considered his "specialty," gradually turned into painful feelings of envy and resentment of what he thought my possible enjoyment of my wife and of our life might be. When we carefully explored the chaotic relationships with women that characterized Mr. F's daily life, it also became evident that he was studiously staying away from women whom he might have appreciated and admired for their intelligence, integrity, sensitivity, interest, and achievements. He was selecting women who, despite their physical attractiveness, he could depreciate for their inferiority, as he saw it, in comparison with him. Unconscious envy of women, in short, became a major issue to be explored in the transference and in his acting-out behavior.

This state of affairs shifted rather abruptly when, after several years of treatment, he established a lengthy relationship with a woman who seemed to be a severe and chronic liar. The information he had about her indicated a pattern of exploitiveness and irresponsibility that raised serious questions in my mind. It turned out that, while Mr. F was superficially denying his awareness of these issues, projecting his fear and concerns onto me, at a deeper level he was fascinated by this sexual involvement with a woman who seemed to resemble his mother closely.

Over several months he developed a sadomasochistic relationship with her, in the context of which he asserted his triumph in being able to achieve a long-standing, highly gratifying sexual relationship that included the enactment of sadomasochistic scenarios, all the while proclaiming his total emotional indifference toward the woman. This period coincided with a remarkable distancing in the transference that was eventually revealed as a complex combination of strong homosexual impulses toward me as a concerned, warm, caring father and fear of the development of a negative oedipal transference, while he revengefully tried to destroy the sadistically perceived preoedipal-oedipal mother. At one point, fantasies of a "menage à trois" involving him, myself, and a woman whom I would "generously" cede to him reflected a condensation of his wish for a sexual submission to me as the price for access to women and his reliance on my sexual strength in order to be able to subjugate and sexually attack a feared and hated woman.

The sexual relationship ended when the woman's behavior finally convinced him that she was indeed out to exploit him financially and when her dishonesty and deviousness became well known and documented in their social circle. At the same time, he began to recognize one of his "temporary" girlfriends as a gifted professional as well as a very attractive and loving companion who had maintained her interest in him in spite of his erratic behavior toward her. For the first time in his life, Mr. F fell in love and was able to have a tender and sexual relationship with a young woman that evolved into the decision to marry her.

This third marriage turned out to be very satisfactory in an emotional and sexual sense. They decided to have children (a decision that Mr. F had strenuously resisted in his earlier marriages) and in fact had three children during the next three years. It was at a point when we were beginning to consider the possibility of ending his psychoanalysis that he developed an extreme sexual inhibition, to the extent that he lost all desire for sexual intercourse; in fact he could not be excited by any sexual stimuli. For a period of almost six months he had no masturbatory or other sexual activity. It is on this episode of his psychoanalysis that I wish to focus now.

When we were beginning to discuss the potential date for the end of his analysis, Mr. F started to report a loss of interest in having sex with his wife while what he described as a warm, committed relationship with her continued. In the past, he had been erotically stimulated by a multitude of erotic material as well as in his social interactions with women, but now a total lack of interest in and capacity for sexual arousal set in. He sounded genuinely concerned about this latest development and attempted to overcome it by creating "artificial" romantic scenarios that included his wife and involved smoking marijuana—which in the past had intensified his sexual desire. At first, I thought that anxiety about his capacity to achieve an erection with his wife might reflect the upsurge of deeper levels of oedipal anxieties and guilt about the successful establishment of his marriage and his fatherhood, and there was some material indicating his fear of losing the protection of a benign and powerful father image in connection with the planned termination of his treatment. I also explored with him the possibility that, rather than tolerating a full-fledged mourning reaction in connection with the termination, he might be regressing to a display of symptoms as an unconscious plea for me not to abandon him. These developments in the transference, however, remained feeble, and there was a lack of development of new elements in the sessions that I found disconcerting.

As the patient's anxiety about this unprecedented loss of his sexual interest increased, he started reading the literature about impotence and wondering whether there might be organic factors determining this development. His capacity to absorb specialized medical literature about this problem was impressive. I asked about the extent to which he might be competing with me regarding the understanding of the origin and meanings of his difficulty and the extent to which his sexual inhibition might be expressing a split-off fear of competing with me.

This did not lead anywhere, and in the course of several months he reported the disappearance not only of all sexual fantasy and arousal but of all morning erections, as well as a disquieting inability to masturbate in his effort to generate sexual arousal. He considered the advisability of seeking a medical consultation, and during several weeks' discussion I made it clear that he was, of course, free to pursue such a course while he expressed his reluctance to do so without my explicit "authorization." I eventually expressed my agreement: he had gradually managed to convince me that some organic condition might be determining his impotence and that medical exploration was indicated. Beyond this "rational" conviction, however, I developed an uneasy sense of hopelessness about his impotence that was vaguely related to an image in my mind of his wife as totally unattractive and a feeling of impotence on my part—as if no further psychoanalytic exploration of this symptom was feasible. At times, I found myself imagining my own erotic responses to hypothetical situations similar to those reported by my patient in relating to his wife, as if to reassure myself against the "hopelessness" of the patient's condition.

Let me clarify that, on general principles, I would refer a patient to a urologist or a medical specialist for symptoms that seem indicative of an organically caused impotence or when there are concurrent medical treatments with known sexual side effects. I also should mention that I saw this patient before the availability of Viagra and the related culture of self-medication by men with feelings of insecurity about their sexual functioning.

I referred Mr. F to a urologist with expertise in the diagnosis and treatment of impotence. The patient underwent a complete medical and neurological checkup, with an exhaustive endocrinological study as well as an examination in the sleep laboratory; he was found to be functioning perfectly normally from a medical viewpoint. The urologist recommended that he continue his psychoanalytic treatment!

When Mr. F informed me of these developments, what struck me as particularly significant was his sense of satisfaction and relaxation. Indicating that his impotence and lack of sexual desire had now become my problem, not his, he wondered whether I would be able to live up to this challenge or whether he would have to accept that he might have resolved his difficulties with women, but at the cost of giving up his sexual life.

It was at that point that I realized—with a shock—that I had been imprisoned for the previous six months in a chronic countertransference fixation, in the sense of defending myself against a profound feeling of insecurity and impotence with regard to Mr. F's analysis. I could now see how I had been utilizing my increasing concern about the possibility that a medical illness might be underlying his sexual inhibition as a defense against my identification with the patient's sense of impotence and castration anxiety. Freed internally to resume thinking analytically, I found it easier to realize that the patient was split between a rational and urgent wish to resolve his loss of sexual desire and indifference to this problem: He had projected his insecurity and anxiety onto me. I also realized, again with a shock, that the patient had successfully communicated to me an image of his wife as having become utterly uninteresting from a sexual viewpoint, a warm, nice, but unfeminine and sexually boring companion, in marked contrast to the previous image of her as an exciting, highly sexual, responsive partner with whom Mr. F had had a highly gratifying sexual relationship. In fact, he had communicated to me over an extended period of time how his future wife was "coming on like a sex bomb," triumphantly implying that his sexual experiences surely exceeded mine.

I now interpreted his indifference toward resolving the sexual inhibition with his wife except by magical, "as if" means that would bypass his emotional relationship with her. I suggested that he was attempting to protect himself against a deep-seated insecurity about his sexual power, a fear of failure and impotence, by attempting to make these my problems and perceiving himself in the position of an interested bystander, observing my efforts and wondering whether I would be successful or fail in my task to restore his sexual power. In short, a reactivation of his narcissistic defenses had occurred, in the context of projecting his sexual inhibition and anxiety onto me.

In response to this approach, Mr. F's relaxation shifted into a growing sense of anxiety along with a reactivation in the transference of an ambivalently admiring and yet helplessly doubtful relation to a warm but weak father image. Memories of his childhood emerged in which he had been "dragged" to doctors because of his mother's hypochondriacal preoccupation with the underdevelopment of his genitals. There were painful recollections of being shamefully exhibited before doctors who repeatedly reassured his mother that his penis was not deformed or twisted toward one side, that his testicles were of normal size, and that they were definitely descended. He remembered now that he was smaller than most of his classmates, that he had experienced relatively late development of pubic hair and other secondary sexual characteristics, and, he reported with great shame and resentment, that his mother used to call him a "shrimp." He gradually became aware of the frightening fantasy that it was inconceivable that he, a little "shrimp" boy with a "shrimp" penis, would be able to penetrate his wife, an attractive, adult woman and the mother of his children.

At the same time, behind the helpful and idealized but also competitively devalued image of me as warm and friendly yet impotent in solving his sexual difficulty, an image of me as dangerous and threatening emerged in a series of dreams. In that image, my face changed to a mysterious figure with a mustache that he could trace back to nightmares from his childhood and that he associated with the murderous enemies of "007," with whom he identified in fantasy.

The patient now became aware of once again being aroused by his wife, but at such moments he developed intense anxiety, fearful that he would be unable to achieve or maintain an erection and that she would make fun of him or depreciate him. These developments occurred against the background of significant victories over business competitors and renewed efforts to deny the importance of his sexual difficulties by focusing on his professional and social triumphs. His behavior toward his wife became quite domineering and controlling, and, for the first time, conflicts developed because she resented his authoritarian attitude and confronted him with his aggressive demands. This increased Mr. F's anxiety, and he found himself relating to his wife in the resentful and grudging manner that had typified his father's behavior toward his mother. He also experienced me, once again, as irrationally controlling him and as disturbing his well-being by confronting him with his sexual difficulties. It is in this context that the following session took place, illustrating, I believe, the intense oedipal rivalry and castration anxiety underlying his lack of sexual desire and illuminating the transference-countertransference enactment related to the urological consultation.

As Mr. F came into my office, he looked at a wire connected to a television set in a corner of the room. He was accustomed to seeing this equipment (utilized for research purposes) from time to time and knew it was turned off. He now commented that this wire was dangerous because people could trip on it and that I should dispose it differently—for example, along the wall or under the carpet. He became quite angry, remarking that he knew from experience that it was useless to give me good advice. I would stubbornly do what I wanted, even if it was obvious that this wire could really be dangerous for patients. While telling himself that it was ridiculous to become upset about this, he was getting increasingly angry with me. I pointed out that he was afraid of the intensity of his anger at what he perceived as my arbitrary, stubbornly provocative attitude toward him.

After a few minutes of silence, he said, "I now have the image of your balls, just your balls, no penis there. Not even a small one." He added, "Not even a shriveled one." I said that, in this image, I shifted from being dangerous and provocative to being a sexless shrimp, and the patient said, "I knew you were going to say that." He added that, while he was silent, he had also had the fantasy that I might have laid down that wire specifically to make him trip, and he had imagined an electrical discharge taking place if that happened.

He then went on to describe a successful meeting in which his side had effectively dismantled the efforts of the lawyers for the other side to change the terms of a highly lucrative contract that he had engineered. He mentioned proudly that he had outsmarted those lawyers in their own area of competence. This had given him a sense of well-being and power. He commented derisively on the uncertainty of the business partners on the other side. Earlier he had referred to them with a sense of resentment and envy because they had freely made sexual jokes during an informal party, thus indicating their sexual security, while he had to struggle with all these problems in his life.

He then returned to the wire running across my room and said that there was no reason to get irritated, it probably only indicated my bungling way of arranging things in my office. He added some comments regarding the disorderly state in which my books had been stacked in the bookshelves. I said that the triumph over his adversaries and the thought that my wire-laying reflected a bungling attitude on my part reassured him against a sense that he could not compete sexually with them or with me. His fantasy of my not having a penis, my being castrated, was part of this effort to reassure himself against the fantasy that he himself possessed a small, deficient penis.

The patient then said that he felt very tired all of a sudden, and in fact, while taking up once more the successful business deal he had recently completed, he sounded more and more monotonous and sleepy. I should mention that, in recent weeks, as we were exploring his intense fears about sexual engagements with his wife, on several occasions he had fallen asleep immediately following moments at which intense anxiety had been stirred up in him; in fact, once when I simply drew his attention to the anxiety in his relationship with his wife, Mr. F actually fell asleep for a few moments in the session.

I said that he seemed to me to be falling asleep, and that if that were so, I would think that thoughts about the relationship with his wife had come into his mind together with an effort to avoid exploring this issue in the session. He said that he had just remembered looking at his wife that morning, from the back, and finding her very attractive, and that was painful. He said he didn't know why it was painful, but she looked very beautiful and he had tried to dismiss this image from his mind.

I wondered whether it was painful to tell me that his wife was attractive to him because this would mean that he would want to have sex with her and feared that he would not be able to function sexually with her, and that he would experience it as humiliating to share that fear with me. I added that perhaps his protest about the wire in my office and my incompetence, and his excited triumph over his rivals, were efforts to avoid a very shameful and humiliating sense of fear of not being able to function sexually because this confirmed in his mind his being a "shrimp" and my thinking that he was a shrimp. The patient remained silent for a while, and I had a sense that there was a shift in his attitude, so that I no longer experienced him as being in the competitive or fearful relation with me that had seemed dominant earlier in the session.

He then said, "It is true that I have to struggle with this image of myself. But then you confirmed it because, after all, you sent me to the doctor, the same as my mother." I was impressed by what seemed to me Mr. F's genuine reflection about that difficult period in our work, and, after a silent moment, I said I understood that he had felt that I had been contaminated by his uncertainty about his sexual functioning and that I had reacted with the same behavior as his mother, thus reconfirming his view that I saw him as sexually inferior. Then Mr. F mentioned that he had had sex with his wife the night before the session. At first, he wanted to have sex but didn't have an erection, and then she caressed him and they were talking, and she smiled at him in a loving way, and he realized that she loved him and that he did not have to present himself as a big businessman to be accepted by her, and all of a sudden he was able to respond and to have sex with her. He added that he didn't fear the intensity of her movements and reaction before she reached orgasm, whereas previously at such moments he had doubted he was enough of a man to respond to such an adult woman's behavior.

Now I had a brief experience of confusion; a significant shift in the transference seemed to occur. The patient conveyed the impression of having been able both to tolerate his insecurity in relating to his wife and to accept her love without being overwhelmed by his fantasies that she must be depreciating him or that he was not an adult man but only a small child in relating to her. I would have expected him to be very pleased to tell me about this, but instead his derogatory comments and ironic teasing earlier in the session had seemed to reflect a defensive competitiveness with me. I wondered whether he might have told me this experience expecting me to feel relieved, thus reconfirming my anxiety about his sexual performance. I also wondered whether, at a still deeper level, castration fears, in which I would be a dangerous father image, might have something to do with his underplaying his satisfaction with a good sexual relation with his wife. I said nothing at this point.

For some time Mr. F remained silent, and then he said that he was thinking of his wife. He liked her body after she had recovered her shape following the birth of their third child but found it difficult to talk about that for some reason. She also had fuller breasts now, and that was very attractive, and then he went back to the feeling of pain he had when she had seemed so extremely desirable that morning. He looked increasingly uneasy as he was talking about his wife's attractiveness, and I pointed this out to him. He said he didn't know what this was about, and I suggested that, for some reason, talking about his sexual excitement as well as his sexual interactions with his wife was difficult for him, perhaps because of fears about how I would react. In fact, I had experienced a sense of satisfaction with the good sexual experience my patient had communicated to me, in a transient and mild but definite identification with his erotic interest in his wife.

He said that there was no reason for him to feel uncomfortable, because he had talked to me about his sexual feelings and experiences many times before, so this was strange. And then, with a laugh: "You wouldn't get sexually excited with what I am telling you here, would you?" I said it sounded as if he was trying to protect himself against fears that I might get sexually excited and against fantasies about what that would mean. He said that the thought had never occurred to him before, and in fact, he considered me an analyst with so much experience that I wouldn't react to patients' telling me about their sexual life.

I reminded Mr. F that, early in his treatment, he had experienced himself as an expert on women while I appeared to him as a "square," a conventional bourgeois. Later on—in fact, very recently—he had experienced me as a very secure and effective man with women who would depreciate him because of his insecurity with his wife. Then Mr. F said, "Well, perhaps you might become envious of me if things go well with my wife; after all, you know that I am much more successful than you when it comes to business and earning money, and that I probably earn more in a month than you earn in a year." He remained silent again and then thought of his father, his father's failing health, and the fact that he was unreasoningly dependent on the care of the patient's mother; Mr. F thought this was pathetic given the constant fights in which his parents engaged. And he became very angry with the doctors who were treating his father and were not being as effective as they should be in the management of his medical problems.

I thought that this reflected his feelings of guilt about triumphing over me as father image, displaced onto his father, but it was toward the end of the session, and I decided not to say anything at that point. The patient then went on to talk about how difficult it was to find good doctors, making fun of a local medical doctor who was giving his father contradictory information. I wondered whether again that was a displacement of a reaction toward me.

I selected this session as a rather typical one during this stage of my patient's treatment, a fundamental phase that evolved into a gradual resolution of Mr. F's inhibition of sexual desire and impotence as his castration anxiety, his profound guilt about competing successfully with his father, and his feelings of inferiority toward the oedipal mother emerged in the context of a defensive reactivation of past narcissistic resistances. In the weeks following this session, Mr. F remembered childhood fantasies about the inordinate size of his mother's hairy genitals, in the context of both excitement about and fear of his wife's genitals. Dreams in which he was attacked by underwater predators signaled the intensity of his fear of potential damage during sexual intercourse.

In conclusion, what I have been highlighting is an extended stalemate in the treatment over several months as a consequence of a countertransference enactment derived from my defensive rejection of the patient's projective identification of his sexual fears onto me (O. Kernberg 1993a). This development led to the symbolic repetition of a childhood experience, the patient's mother taking him to a doctor because of an assumed sexual inferiority. It illustrates Joseph Sandler's concept of the role-responsiveness of the analyst, particularly his enactment of this responsiveness in actual behavior rather than his utilizing internal reaction as a countertransferential source for the integration of projective identification on the patient's part (Sandler and Sandler 1998b). This treatment also illustrates the intimate connection between preoedipal and oedipal conflicts in the advanced stages of the treatment of a narcissistic personality and the need to assess the patient's sexual functioning very carefully before deciding on terminating his psychoanalysis. As André Green (1997) has stressed, the recent focus on preoedipal pathology has often coincided with a neglect of the fundamental conflicts concerning sexuality that mark human development in normality and pathology from the beginning of life. I think the threat of separation from the analyst reactivated the threat of becoming the "third excluded other" linked to the separation from the early (symbiotic?) mother. This expression of the early or archaic oedipal situation had remained latent under the dominance of Mr. F's severe, pathological narcissistic conflicts, only to be triggered by the conflict concerning termination.

Finally, this case also illustrates how a symptom emerging in the advanced or final stage of an analysis may recapitulate an earlier symptom not fully explored previously in all its unconscious determinants. At the same time, this symptom may enter naturally in the transference; its systematic analysis may facilitate the completion of earlier analytic work related to this symptom as well as the exploration of new transference developments connected with termination.

Chapter 10 Acute and Chronic

Countertransference Reactions

The early concept of countertransference defined it as the analyst's unconscious reaction to the patient or to the transference derived from the analyst's own transference potential, to be overcome by the analyst's self-analysis in order to return to a position of technical neutrality (Little 1951; Reich 1951). This concept and our view of the importance of countertransference in the psychoanalytic situation have since undergone significant changes. Under the influence of psychoanalytic contributions made in the 1950s, particularly those of Paula Heimann (1950) and Heinrich Racker (1957), a global or totalistic view of countertransference, now defined as the analyst's total emotional reaction to the patient, emerged and gradually prevailed. Now the task became the analysis of the various components of the analyst's global countertransference, including (1) his unresolved or reactivated unconscious conflicts, (2) his external reality and reactions toward

---

Published in *Psychoanalysis on the Move: The Work of Joseph Sandler,* edited by Peter Fonagy, Arnold M. Cooper, and Robert S. Wallerstein. London: New Library of Psychoanalysis, 1999, 35:171–86.

third parties, (3) the contributions of the patient's transference, and (4) the reality of the patient's life (O. Kernberg 1965). With Racker's concepts of concordant and complementary identification in the countertransference (emphasizing the contribution of the transference), the analyst's exploration of his countertransference now permitted a sharper diagnosis of the patient's activated internalized object relations; countertransference analysis became an important tool in the analysis of the transference.

More recently, in technical contributions of the 1980s and early 1990s (Alexandris and Vaslamatzis 1993; Carpy 1989; Grinberg 1993; Hamilton 1990; O. Kernberg et al. 1989; Loewald 1986; McDougall 1993; Ogden 1993; Pick 1985; Segal 1981; Spillius 1988; Volkan 1993), countertransference analysis is emerging as a crucial aspect of psychoanalytic technique, providing fundamental information about the nature of the dominant transference at any particular time. Insofar as some (for example, Mitchell 1988) view transference developments as influenced in important ways by the analyst's unconscious contributions to the patient-analyst interaction, the pendulum may have swung in the opposite direction from what in retrospect appears to be an early phobic attitude toward countertransference.

As I have said, I believe that countertransference is one of three significant sources of information about the analytic situation, in addition to the patient's subjective experience, communicated by means of free association, and the nonverbal behavior he manifests during the hour. These sources of information are unavoidably influenced, at any particular moment, by the extent to which the analyst preserves the internal freedom to explore his own reaction to the patient and by his theoretical organizing frame and clinical experience.

The importance of countertransference as a source of information varies with the severity of the patient's illness. The more severe the patient's character pathology, and the more intense, regressive, and primitive the transference, the more countertransference reactions will come into the foreground. Particularly with severe character pathology, powerful negative countertransference reactions may dominate the analyst's observational field, at least temporarily. The most important primitive defensive operation and means of communication of the transference under such conditions—projective identification—explains the activation of such intense countertransferences. Generally speaking, one might say that the less the patient is able to contain a primitive experience in his subjective awareness, the more this experience is expressed in his behavior and in the analyst's countertransference.

Thus, by means of projective identification, the patient's threatening and intolerable self-representations or object representations, charged with primitive aggressive affect, are projected onto the therapist while the patient unconsciously attempts to induce a corresponding role response in the analyst (Sandler 1976). At the same time, he attempts to control the analyst under the impact of this projected self- or object representation and its threatening affect. Typically, it is a complementary identification in the countertransference that creates the risk of flooding the analyst's psychic experience at such moments.

In addition, the persistence of the patient's unconscious effort to repeatedly maintain or reproduce the same primitive transference reaction in severe psychopathology (as well as with some better-functioning narcissistic patients with enormous resistance against establishing a dependent relationship in the transference) may reinforce the countertransference, activating chronic countertransference reactions—in other words, chronic distortions or stagnation in the analyst's emotional disposition toward or capacity to work with the patient, rather than sudden and transitory countertransference developments (such as forgetting an appointment, a momentary irritation with the patient, or *lapsus linguae* in an interpretive comment).

Because of my experience in treating patients with severe character pathology with psychoanalysis as well as with psychoanalytic psychotherapy, my attention has been drawn to the technical implications of the activation of intense countertransference reactions in the therapist when faced with severe regression in the transference, and to the particular distortions and technical difficulties derived from chronic countertransference reactions.

ACUTE COUNTERTRANSFERENCE REACTION

A patient, Mr. A, suffered from an obsessive-compulsive personality disorder. His obsessive doubts intruded into the successful business he headed and were paralyzing his ability to make decisions. In addition, he was aware of a growing irritability with the younger men in his firm, protégés he had himself brought into the business. Arguments with them as well as his obsessive doubts resulted in significant secondary anxiety and depression and motivated him to enter psychoanalysis.

In the course of three years' worth of analysis, it had become clear that his obsessive doubts reflected an internalized submission to and rebellion against a powerful father. The father had been very successful in the same field as the patient. The patient's unconscious guilt about successfully competing with his father and his obsessive doubts were activated in the transference. Periods when he desperately tried to guess what I might counsel him to do, trying to make decisions on the basis of what he thought I would point him to, alternated with periods when he resented what he experienced as my efforts to control him and subject him to my strict rules of behavior.

When he was a child, Mr. A's mother had treated him as her preferred son, only to "betray" him to the father by passively acquiescing in the father's authoritarian behavior toward him. As a result, the patient's wishes to depend on a good mother were displaced from her to the father, and repressed homosexual impulses toward the father were split off from a romantic attachment to women who represented aspects of the mother. The patient was married, and his fear of approaching his wife sexually reflected his unconscious oedipal guilt, his deep-seated suspicion and resentment of women, and his difficulty in expressing his dependency needs vis-à-vis women.

The following situation illustrates a typical acute countertransference reaction and its management. The last session before a week-long separation during which the patient had an out-of-town commitment that coincided with my own absence started with Mr. A's obsessively discussing whether he should give in to the financial demands of an advertising agency whose services he wanted to acquire or stand firm on his counterproposal. Gradually, his anger at the director of that agency became stronger. He complained bitterly about the lack of gratitude of this young man, whom the patient had helped in the past, and expressed indignation at the defiant and inconsiderate ways in which the man was treating him. I raised the question whether, in the middle of this disappointment, there might also be disappointment with me for not helping him to make a decision. He responded with irritation that I was wrong; he wasn't expecting anything from me, and this analysis was proving to be completely useless.

I wondered aloud whether his disappointment with me might have something to do with the forthcoming week-long separation. I reminded him that I had wondered whether he had set up a business trip at the time of my absence in order to avoid a feeling of being left behind and left alone. He responded that, to the contrary, he would have to cancel an additional hour at the time of his return because of flight scheduling problems.

At that moment, I remembered that I had a similar flight problem and told the patient that I had planned to suggest a session at a later time on the day of our first appointment.

He then really became enraged at me. Why was I bringing up a change in his schedule in the middle of a session, when my usual practice was to convey new information of any kind only at the beginning of a session? I was disrupting his flow of free association, Mr. A went on, showing how distracted I was by raising issues that concerned only me and were totally neglectful of his needs. This was the last thing he would have expected at the final session before the one-week separation.

The patient's anger increased. In the next few minutes I experienced a rapidly changing set of feelings. First I felt guilty for not having remembered to make my suggestion at the beginning of the session, feeling that I had indeed been neglectful, and I wondered what might have influenced me in this regard. I remembered that I had had a fleeting sense of guilt before the session for having to make a last-minute change in Mr. A's schedule and wondered to myself whether I was acting like his mother (that is, pretending to be interested and concerned for him). Then, as his attacks on me intensified, I became irritated, feeling that he was making a mountain out of a relatively minor molehill. I thought that I had fairly acknowledged my mistake. Finally, while he continued to express his rage concerning my unreliability, I thought that I was now in a relation to him similar to the one he had experienced when confronted with his father's dissatisfaction with his performance. The patient was now enacting the role of his father and projecting his "unreliable self" onto me, replicating, at the same time, his problem in relation to the young advertising agency director.

I commented on his disappointment and its transformation into rage at me, his sense that I was unreliable because I was not helping him with his problem with the agency director and because I was neglecting the intensity of his need to be understood and cared for when a separation brought about the feeling of being abandoned. I interpreted this to mean that I was like an unreliable mother who only pretended to care for him, a most painful experience against which he could protect himself by changing it, making me into an unreliable son and enacting his father's demands in his relation with me. To be an angry father scolding an unreliable son was preferable to feeling like an abandoned son relating to an unreliable mother.

He said that he had felt that the director was like an unreliable, unloving son and that it was true that he had been treating both the director and me in ways that reminded him of what he hated in his father. And then he added that he did not feel as fearful as he had in the past about some forthcoming important meetings, that he felt more like an equal with his colleagues. He then remained silent. After a while, I commented that I sensed a change in his emotional disposition. He said that he was no longer angry and actually felt sad thinking of our separation for a week. I said that, insofar as it was less frightening to him to identify himself with his father in spite of his father's undesirable traits, he was also less afraid to acknowledge his wish for my concern and dedication to him without experiencing that as a sexual threat. The patient then remembered these reactions. He remained silent for a short time and said that he had felt less inhibited in having sex with his wife the previous night. The session ended shortly afterward.

This illustration of an acute countertransference reaction with its immediate internal exploration by the analyst and its utilization as part of the material to be incorporated into transference interpretation is in contrast to the next example.

CHRONIC COUNTERTRANSFERENCE REACTION

The patient extensively referred to in Chapter 9, Mr. F, suffered from a severe narcissistic personality, with a history of two marriages ending in divorce, sexual promiscuity, and an incapacity to experience an emotional investment in the same woman with whom he had a sexual relationship.

In the early part of his treatment, most noticeable for many months was Mr. F's intense defense against deepening the transference relationship, which could be understood only gradually as a defense against unconscious envy of the analyst, whom he saw as a married man able to enjoy a relationship with his wife that was both emotionally and sexually satisfying. From triumphantly regaling me with his sexual exploits, only to fall back in despair because of his incapacity to maintain a sexual relationship with a woman who mattered to him emotionally, he gradually became aware that the idea that I might have a good marital relationship filled him with a sense of inferiority and humiliation. He then began to tolerate conscious feelings of envy of me.

His childhood had not been cheerful. He had described to me a complaining, distrustful, eternally dissatisfied father who attacked his wife, a domineering, combative woman, both in public and in private, for all her shortcomings. On the basis of his childhood experiences, Mr. F was convinced that all expressions of concern for another were completely phony.

He experienced his mother as chronically and totally unreasonable, filled with strange ideas about people, illness, and nature that could not be challenged, ideas that he and his older brothers had accepted during their early childhood and then came to resent bitterly as they became aware of a different reality during their school years. Although the mother had never seen a psychiatrist, the impression Mr. F created in my mind was that she must have been near psychotic. The struggle between the parents and their now-successful son continued to this day, followed by reconciliations. What follows is a development in the middle part of his treatment.

In the third year of analysis the patient acquired a new mistress, Ms. C, an aggressive and domineering woman very unlike his previous women, who had been subservient. He stressed how very satisfactory the sexual relationship with her was; he insisted that he did not love her but was strangely attracted to her precisely because she did not defer to him as his previous women had done. The relationship with her deepened over a period of time, acquiring characteristics of sadomasochistic interactions that often made me wonder whether Ms. C. was exploiting this wealthy man financially or was herself very masochistic in tolerating his reiterations that he did not love her.

Clearly, for the first time in his life he had replicated his sadomasochistic relation with his mother. At the same time, a subtle change occurred in the transference in the direction of its emptying out—I sensed that the patient was so totally absorbed in the reality of his daily life with Ms. C that it was largely replacing his world of fantasy. I also felt that the patient was increasingly "unreal" in his behavior toward me. He became more and more "shadowy," making me think of an "as if" personality, at the same time that his conflicts with Ms. C became clearer.

Over a period of months, the content of the sessions became increasingly invaded by references to the struggles with this girlfriend, complicated involvements in her struggles with members of their families, and increasing chaos in his life situation simultaneous with the development of what impressed me as robotlike behavior in the hours. For example, in reaction to an interpretation, the patient would move backward on the couch into a half-sitting position, supporting his chin in his hand as if reflecting on what I had said. He brought in typewritten pages with dreams that he wanted to read to me; when I asked why he felt the need to bring these transcriptions rather than talking freely in the hour, he said with chagrin that he was only interested in accelerating the analytic work; with a resigned gesture, he would then proceed to relate the dreams from memory.

Interpretation of his behavior was made more difficult by the subtlety of all these developments, which may appear more clear in this description than they did in the sessions. Over a period of months, I had the feeling of carrying out an "as if" analysis, in the sense that my interpretations would become so cleverly integrated in the patient's associative material that I could no longer assess their effect. When I communicated to him that I experienced an enormous distance in our relationship, he freely acknowledged that he felt independent from me and that this must indicate that he was now much healthier than before.

His ongoing friendliness, his apparent attention to everything I was saying, and an apparently uninhibited flow of free associations only punctuated my feeling that our relationship was completely phony. I felt strangely reluctant to confront the patient with my feeling, as if it would be hopeless even to try. I sensed that he would either not understand what I was saying and think I was being paranoid or react in a helpless way, as if I were making impossible demands on him, while he was obviously a "good" patient who was improving in his understanding and in his life.

In some sessions he made me feel that the only thing he needed in order to get better was for me to inculcate him with the capacity for tender love toward Ms. C.—In short, I felt paralyzed in an emotional experience of "phoniness"—a sense of enormous emotional distance in our relationship—with the alternative of either having him experience me as "crazy" if I persisted in confronting him with the robotlike aspects of his behavior or overwhelming him with demands for authenticity that he would not be able to comprehend.

Only gradually did I realize that my sense of impotence resulted from identifying with the patient in his relation to his "crazy" mother: I was submitting to the patient (mother) as would a submissive son who was carrying out a pseudoanalysis as prescribed by mother. I thought that the patient was unconsciously identifying with the mother, pretending to be caring and treating me as a son who had to be manipulated into obedience. In my efforts to break out of this situation, I was tempted to act like an impatient, controlling mother who would pretend that she knew exactly what was going on in her child without listening to him, overpowering him and forcing him to either protest in rage or obligingly submit.

In this context, the patient gradually became aware of his inability to understand women, the relief he experienced with his girlfriend because her aggressive behavior was so obvious (unconsciously, he projected his own identification with the mother onto her), and the sense that in the context of ordinary social friendliness he could not tell what kind of personality any of the women with whom he would get involved had. He also had found out, in the midst of his violent interactions with his parents, that they still had an active sexual life—apparently the only interaction that had functioned satisfactorily over the years. He reacted with shock to the sudden awareness that his relationship with Ms. C resembled that between his parents even more than he had thought. And I suddenly understood that what had been missing throughout these months was any significant reference to his father, in contrast to the total invasion of the transference by the relationship with his mother.

I suddenly also realized that I had been absorbed by the patient's descriptions of his difficulties with women. And with some frequency, I noticed myself being distracted in the hours with this patient, thinking of other aspects of my work, and it seemed to me that I had been evading him like a frightened boy who would not dare enter into a collision course with an overpowering mother. I experienced a childhood memory of my own father's avoidance of a conflict with my mother at home by escaping into his work. In immediate continuity, I then remembered a high school rebellion that I had led against a tyrannical teacher and my intense fear of his retaliation.

On reflection for several weeks, elaborating those fantasies, I thought I was identifying with the patient as an impotent child, denying my own identity as an autonomous yet concerned fatherly image for him; I was implicitly colluding with the patient's fantasy that a self-castrating submissiveness was the only alternative to dealing with a "crazy" mother, as had his violent father. This violent father image, in turn, represented the patient's projection of his own oedipal protest onto the "reasonable father" who might be able to bring order and rescue the mother from her primitive entanglements. Remnants of my own oedipal disposition had become activated in the process, contributing to my experience of paralysis in the treatment of Mr. F. Then, a few weeks later, the following session occurred.

The patient started by saying that he had had an uncanny experience. He had proposed a major business deal to a firm connected with a foreign country, and he had become fearful that this business deal would be resented by a competitor attempting to make a similar deal with still another country. He suddenly became afraid that agents working for his competitor and that other country might try to steal information from him about the specific technology involved. Although he said that he knew this was a paranoid reaction, after leaving the office he was still afraid of the representatives of the foreign firm: He thought that two men were following him that afternoon and late into the evening. He said that he had become very anxious and was oscillating between a sense that this was exaggerated and a feeling that it might be true and he should watch out. The patient felt genuinely anxious in conveying this information to me.

At the same time, as was frequent in recent months, the patient would turn to me from time to time, smiling, as if saying, "I know this is crazy, and I know you understand that I understand." I said that I realized he was oscillating between fear and a sense that the fear was absurd, and that he was looking at me as if to reassure me that he was aware of that but perhaps also to reassure himself that I was still on his side rather than silently concluding that he was crazy. The patient immediately said that he didn't think I would think that he was crazy; he smiled at me with a reassuring expression.

I told him that I felt he was giving me a reassuring smile as if some danger had to be avoided in this situation, and the patient remarked jokingly that the only danger could be that I might be allied with the foreign country with whom his competitor was colluding. I now realized that the patient had not told me which country that was, and I mentioned that to him as a further indication of his fearfulness of me. My fantasy was that the foreign competitor was my country of origin, but I did not communicate this to the patient. He then became clearly uneasy and reluctantly commented that the thought had crossed his mind that my office might be wired and that it would be easy for me to obtain confidential information from him that I could use for my own purposes. He went on to associate about the possibility of break-ins to psychiatrists' offices and linked this to the Watergate affair and to several films depicting psychiatrists involved in shady, even dangerous deals. I pointed to his effort to defend himself against a vision of me as dangerously spying on him by projecting his enemies as foreign agents rather than regarding me as a foreign agent operating against him.

The patient, again smiling and somewhat ironically, thought that, rather than being dangerous, I might need more protection for myself and recalled an incident in which someone he considered (realistically) to be a psychotic woman had appeared in my waiting room attempting to enter the office before he did. On that occasion, he had become intensely fearful that she might reappear later in the session with a gun and in attempting to shoot me would shoot him. He said, half-jokingly, "That woman might reappear any day and stab you in the back." I said that I wondered whether he was trying to make a joke out of a fantasy that otherwise might be very frightening to him—namely, that I might stab him in the back by betraying his technical innovations to a competitor.

As I was saying this, I had two contradictory feelings: that I was on the right path in interpreting his ostensible friendliness as a defense against an underlying paranoid relationship in the transference, and, at the same time, that I experienced myself as forcefully invading the patient with interpretations beyond his capacity for immediate awareness, brainwashing him, as it were, or enacting a paranoid mother. For several fleeting moments, I felt really paranoid in interpreting a primitive persecutive fantasy to this smiling, relaxed patient. But then I felt that my fantasy reflected my fear of asserting myself as a father who could transcend this madness and transform what seemed a violent interpretation into a reasonable one.

The patient suddenly appeared very tense. He said that he had just had the image of himself stabbing his mother. He then remained silent but looked extremely tense. He then said that he was very upset and that he would never do such a thing. I told him that I thought he was trying to reassure himself and me that he would never stab his mother, afraid that his wishes to stab her might be the same thing as actually stabbing her. I also wondered whether his fear and his wish to stab his mother might be connected with his fear of my stabbing him in the back: I interpreted his projecting his own rage onto me. I felt that such murderous rage also contained the disqualification of the reasonable father. I had the fantasy that I was in the role of a reasonable third person, but then I thought this might be too far beyond the patient's present experience. I said that I wouldn't be surprised if his immediate response included some effort to transform this into a humorous situation in order to take the edge off the frightening feeling we were exploring.

The patient then said that he wasn't surprised by my comments but that he had been thinking very seriously of how enraged he had become at his mother in their last extended telephone conversation, and he proceeded to talk with great emotion about an aspect of her discourse that seemed to him totally crazy and that he felt impotent to defuse. I said that I wondered whether he had been putting his sense of impotence in dealing with a crazy mother to me while himself enacting the role of the crazy mother in the session by conveying to me his crazy behavior, telling me that he knew it was crazy and yet enacting it in his watchful turning around to observe me, while I, attempting to show him the serious aspects of what was going on beyond his friendly smile and comment, easily might have been derailed by these very niceties or appeared to be crazy by pointing to the madness going on in fantasy in this room, namely, the danger that I might stab him as an impotent, enraged boy would stab a crazy, dominant mother. A lengthy silence followed. The patient said it was true that he tried to keep things on an even keel with me, and in fact that had been his usual behavior with all women, except now with Ms. C he realized how enraged he was at all women. And that was the end of the session.

What I did not bring up was the patient's identification with the mother in the absence of the oedipal father. My countertransference reaction—my enactment of an identification with a weak father and my awareness of a dissociated image of a violent father—was still too strong to permit me to introduce this new perspective. Yet my thinking had become freer, and I was no longer enmeshed in a pseudofriendly, robotlike relationship in the transference.

Now a new theme emerged in the treatment: a condensation of his fear of aggressive, frustrating, dominating, and manipulative women, on the one hand, and of doing better than his hen-pecked, distant, and aloof father (and a related despair about being able to compete with me as an idealized version of an unavailable father model), on the other, now began to pervade the hours.

COUNTERTRANSFERENCE DIAGNOSIS AND MANAGEMENT

Comparison of the cases of Mr. A and Mr. F illustrates the changing role of countertransference analysis as we shift from less to more severe psychopathology. Although with Mr. A I did not refer to my own countertransference disposition (in the sense of what might have motivated my failure to tell the patient about the suggested schedule change after the separation), obviously, in that example there was an aspect of my disposition toward the patient that influenced my neglect as well as the intensity of my momentary countertransference reaction following the patient's scolding me for interrupting his train of thought.

In the case of Mr. F, I believe that his contribution to the chronic countertransference disposition toward him that I experienced over the course of several months was of overriding importance and that, in my countertransference, more than reflecting any specific aspect of my past, I reacted under the impact of a general concern about the "as if" quality of the relationship. I experienced, I believe, the combination of a general and relatively normal narcissistic response—to long-standing failure in the task and a superego-determined guilt reaction about not helping him, all of which fed into the sense of frustration, impotence, and confusion that the patient had experienced in the relationship with his mother and was projecting onto me.

Similarly, Mr. A's communication by means of the content of his free associations was clearly dominant in the sessions; the nonverbal aspects of his behavior and my countertransference disposition were of lesser importance in determining the overall integration of my understanding and my interpretation of the transference than in the case of Mr. F. The latter's nonverbal behavior in the hours and my countertransference illustrated the need to integrate the patient's communication of his subjective experience, my observation of his behavior in the therapeutic interaction, and the countertransference into one formulation.

I see my countertransference with Mr. F as illustrating the chronicity of countertransference reaction to some patients who present severe character pathology. The robotlike quality of his reactions in the hour, my sense of unreality and impotence, and the underlying projective identification in the transference—the enactment of the relationship between a crazy mother and a pseudosubmissive son—represented the patient's contribution to my countertransference. My identification with one aspect of my own father reflected my contribution, although the patient's own incapacity to identify with a strong and generous father also played a part. The patient's verbal communication centered on his relations with women in present reality; his nonverbal communication and my emotional reaction centered on his mother transference. My sense of impotence, of being caught between phony friendliness and violence, went beyond the effect of his projective identification. Leon Grinberg's (1993) concept of projective counteridentification has a place here, as does the complementarity of the deeper layer of the patient's oedipal problems and what the chronic challenge in the transference evoked in my own countertransference potential.

The problem, in the case of chronic countertransference reactions with patients presenting severe psychopathology, is that its very slowly developing, diffuse, "invasive" nature may infiltrate the entire psychoanalytic process to an extent that interferes with its immediate analysis and may require consistent work outside as well as during the sessions in order to understand it and transform it into an interpretation.

Lucia Tower (1956) has suggested that some chronic countertransference reactions can be understood only retrospectively, after the analyst has shifted to a different emotional position. From this viewpoint, the older assumption that preoccupation with a patient outside the sessions indicates some problem in the analyst needs to be modified. Such preoccupation may sometimes derive simply from lack of understanding due to lack of experience or the unusual difficulty of the case, but, most frequently, it derives from the development of chronic countertransference reactions in cases of severe psychopathology.

I have found chronic countertransference reactions to be particularly frequent in the treatment of patients with severe narcissistic personalities, patients with regressive sadomasochistic transferences, patients who express a very primitive type of hatred in unconscious efforts to destroy the very communication with the analyst (the syndrome that Bion [1958] described as including pseudostupidity, curiosity, and arrogance), and patients with "as if" characteristics and psychopathic transferences. Patients with severe paranoid regressions and transference psychosis also may bring about chronic countertransference reactions, as may patients whose acting out takes objectively dangerous forms such as the risk of suicide, homicide, or active persecution of the analyst (for example, in the form of threats of lawsuits). In all these cases, very primitive internalized object relations and sometimes truly psychotic nuclei become dominant in the transference and apparently defy the ordinary efforts of the analyst to resolve these regressions interpretively.

I would like to point to some particular aspects of countertransference management that are helpful under conditions of chronic countertransference development. First, I have found it very useful to try to imagine how a "normal" patient would react to a "normal" analyst under the condition in which an interpretation has been given that the patient has been unable to accept or to understand, or that he immediately incorporates into a psychotic system or distorts in ways that interfere with further work. Second, what would a normal interaction between a patient, daring to depend on the psychoanalyst as a trustworthy person who is attempting to help the patient without being omniscient or omnipotent, and the analyst be like? Such an internal confrontation within the analyst between an imagined potentially normal interaction with a patient and the present transference-countertransference bind will help clarify what is abnormal or strange in the content of the patient's subjective experience, in his behavior, and in the countertransference itself and how these three elements might be understood in their mutual relations.

From a purely cognitive viewpoint, what I have just outlined may appear obvious or trivial; in practice, however, under the impact of chronic countertransference developments, it is much more difficult to reconstitute that theoretical frame of normality, and it may be much easier for an "outsider" to do so than for the analyst caught up in this situation. Therefore, collegial consultation may be helpful at any point during an analyst's career.

There are some emotional attitudes of the analyst that may become important in the treatment of patients with severe psychopathology and that may provide an important counterbalance to the risk of developing chronic countertransference reactions. It is of course crucial for the analyst to tolerate the conscious experience of powerful countertransference reactions, contain this reaction, and utilize it for self-exploration as well as for diagnosing the total transference situation (Winnicott 1949). He must also have the courage to interpret a situation when a chronic stalemate tends to induce in him a sense of futility and hopelessness, an attitude of passivity that can easily be rationalized as patiently waiting for the situation to resolve itself. Obviously, I am not suggesting that the analyst bombard the patient with interpretations but that he adopt a psychological attitude of "vehemence" when the analyst sees a situation clearly and yet feels afraid to share this understanding with the patient. This is an attitude involving cognitive clarity and contained emotional concern and courage.

Usually, a not yet fully diagnosed expression of omnipotence or omnipotent control dominates the patient's transference at such times. The probing of unconscious transference meanings in the here and now may require fearlessness regarding the possibility that the patient may experience the interpretation as a "violent" invasion, as Piera Aulagnier (1981) has described it in psychotic patients. The projective identification of the patient's omnipotence may be the mechanism involved, and the paralysis of the analyst as the patient experiences all his interventions as an attack is the consequence.

Under such conditions the analyst's interventions may range from tentative suggestions or hesitant questions to direct statements to the extreme of expressing a strong conviction. With the safeguards mentioned, this may reflect a therapeutic "impatience" in every session and a willingness and disposition to work, matched with as much patience as is necessary over an extended period of time. This combination of analytic impatience in the short run and patience in the long run is the opposite of an unconscious effort on the analyst's part to avoid a particularly difficult or painful transference-countertransference bind by withdrawing from the transference situation and maintaining a level of friendliness and relaxation that avoids facing the aggression in primitive transferences and the enactment of omnipotent control. There are times when relaxed friendliness becomes indifference and a vehement statement an expression of concern; the analyst's capacity to shift from one to the other is an indicator of his internal freedom to interpret. An analyst's strong conviction is compatible with both technical neutrality and an objective, concerned relation with the patient.

It is important that in treating patients with regressive transferences the analyst tolerate the development of scenarios in which a countertransference is fully explored by letting it resolve into a narrative, that is, a temporal sequence of events that transform the scenario of an enacted object relation into a story that illuminates the meaning of the scenario. For example, the analyst's sexual fantasies about a patient may develop into a countertransference narrative of a sexual relationship with the patient and its presumed beginning and final destruction in light of what the analyst knows about the patient and himself. The tolerance of such scenarios, evolving naturally out of chronic countertransference dispositions, may facilitate analysis of subtle aspects of the transference that are linked to these countertransference developments and highlight aspects of the transference to which the analyst was previously blind. Such tolerance may also open the road to the self-analytic function of the analyst that may recover unconscious aspects of his countertransference predisposition.

Denis Carpy (1989) has noted the usefulness of the process by which the analyst attempts to tolerate the countertransference while still giving evidence in his behavior that this process is incomplete and requires gradual working through. He points to what he considers the "inevitable partial acting out of the countertransference which allows the patient to see that the analyst is being affected by what is projected, is struggling to tolerate it, and, if the analysis is to be effective, is managing sufficiently to maintain his analytic stance without grossly acting out." I believe that this is a valid observation about one function of the countertransference in treating severely regressed patients, and I think it is no coincidence that the clinical illustration Carpy provides is of psychoanalytic psychotherapy. Pick (1985) made a related observation in discussing the process of working through the countertransference.

Gregory Hamilton (1990) has suggested that the analyst, in returning to the patient his own projective identification in a transformed and tolerable way, includes the projection onto the patient of the analyst's containing function itself. In other words, the analyst projects an aspect of his self-representation as part of the interpretive resolution of the patient's projective identification. I propose to amplify this point: An interpretation that includes the utilization of countertransference elements implies an effort to contact the normal aspect of the patient's self, trusting that this aspect, if it were freed from constraint by the dominant pathological object relation in the transference, would be able to identify with the analyst's self-representation, the analyst's experience in containing and elaborating the conflict related to the dominant object relation in the transference projected onto him. In other words, communication of the countertransference work in the context of its integration into the transference interpretation not only returns to the patient his own projective identification in a more tolerable form but adds a new component: the analyst's struggle with understanding and working through the corresponding conflict.

Successful tolerance, understanding, and interpretive integration of the countertransference may have a liberating effect on both the analyst and the patient; or, if the analyst's liberating experience does not correspond to one in the patient, this may become a clear indication that there are other aspects of the transference that stand between the interpretation and the patient's capacity to absorb it and that have to be examined.

One often hears that with sicker patients, what counts is the "real" relationship, not the interpretation. Psychoanalytic work with borderline patients strengthens my conviction that although there are many ways of supporting a patient's ego functioning, the specific effects of transference interpretation, particularly when it incorporates the countertransference, facilitates the development of a "real" relationship in the sense that it identifies whatever capacity the patient has for self-observation with the analyst's integrative function. This is the best guarantee of a patient's developing capacity to establish—at least temporarily, at first—a normal relationship as a consequence of this systematic analysis of the transference.

Chapter 11 Omnipotence in

the Transference and in the

Countertransference

Omnipotence was first described by Freud (1913, 1921) as a characteristic of the magic thinking of primitive cultures and of infantile thinking. He linked it to the state of primary narcissism and the hallucinatory gratification of desire under conditions of frustration. This
primitive mode of thinking might then reappear as omnipotence in
psychopathology, particularly in obsessive thinking. Later theorists of
both ego-psychological and object-theoretical thinking described omnipotence as a defensive operation in the psychoses, one aspect of the
permanence of magical thinking under conditions of loss of reality
testing.

Edith Jacobson (1967, 1971a), for example, described the omnipotent implications of psychotic identifications, in which refusion of
self-representations and object representations under conditions of
idealized or ecstatic states re-creates an omnipotence of thought that
serves an important defensive function together with denial of reality,

Published in *Omnipotent Fantasies and the Vulnerable Self,* edited by C. S. Ellman
and J. Reppen. Northvale, N.J.: Jason Aronson (1997), 79–99.

thus preserving an idealized state as a defense against severe depression and even schizophrenic fragmentation.

Melanie Klein's (1946) description of primitive defenses and object relations that are linked to the early struggles between the life and death instincts included omnipotence of thought as an early defensive operation. This defense, she proposed, was related to the defense against envy by means of an omnipotent fantasy of fusion of self and object that denied separation and dependence and included an omnipotent control of the object by means of projective identification. Herbert Rosenfeld's (1964, 1971) development of Klein's thinking stressed the behavioral aspects of omnipotent control as a major defensive operation in narcissistic personalities, thus shifting the emphasis from omnipotence of thought to omnipotent control as a crucial clinical manifestation of narcissistic pathology.

Winnicott (1960a, 1960b), describing the original undifferentiated structure of baby and mother, focused on the baby's sense of omnipotence when all his needs are met, in contrast to the sense of impingement when frustration of his desires faces him with the limits of his control of reality, and leads to the establishment of a transitional object on the road from primitive omnipotence to the acknowledgment of frustration and dependency.

As psychoanalytic exploration of severe character pathology, the borderline conditions, and the psychoses evolved in the hands of a broad spectrum of psychoanalytic theoreticians and clinicians (Jacobson 1967; Mahler and Furer 1968; Searles 1965; Rosenfeld 1987), the observations of the defensive functions of delusional grandiosity and omnipotence in schizophrenic, manic-depressive, and paranoid psychosis were expanded by the awareness of the importance of omnipotent control in the psychoanalytic treatment of the borderline conditions and pathological narcissism (O. Kernberg 1975).

Omnipotence therefore is at once a primitive fantasy, a mechanism of defense, and a pathological psychic structure. All three of these are present in many clinical situations.

I propose that omnipotence as an early fantasy constitutes one aspect of the "all good" fused or undifferentiated self-object representation, related to what Freud (1930) originally described as the "oceanic feeling" and potentially reactivated as an early defensive operation whenever a regressive idealized fusional state emerges as a defense against the threat of frustration, trauma, pain, and aggression. The original function of omnipotence as fantasy and defense is replicated during the stage of separation-individuation (Mahler et al. 1975) in the fantasy of reunion of the "good self" and the "ideal object," the basis of both actual, secure dependency on a good object and a satisfactory relation of the ego to the early ego ideal. The pathological transformation of this development under conditions of manic and hypomanic states reflects the regressive refusion of these ideal relations. The pathological structure of omnipotence may be observed in the entire spectrum of borderline personality organization and acquire importance, in particular, in the defensive functions of the pathological grandiose self (Kernberg 1984). Omnipotence is involved in a denial of all negative, split-off, and projected aspects of the self, in denial of dependency on other objects, and in fantasied undisturbed self-gratification.

What I have described is the defensive utilization of early omnipotent fantasies in libidinal internalized object relations. A parallel process may be described in the development of aggressive object relations, in which omnipotence evolves out of intense frustration, trauma, and pain as activators of aggressive affect and early defensive operations for dealing with it that include omnipotence and omnipotent control (O. Kernberg 1992a). In contrast to the function of omnipotence in the libidinal segment—to assure an illusional pleasure and grandiosity—control of the object of aggressive affect becomes central, and omnipotent fantasies are now transformed into the defensive operation of omnipotent control.

Under pathological conditions, the aggressive drive dominates the early development of the psychic apparatus so powerfully that it leads to the psychopathological structures that we observe in psychosis, borderline personality organization, the severe types of perversion, and some psychosomatic disorders. This dominance of aggression has its roots in the excessive activation of aggressive affects.

If we examine the progressive manifestations of the psychopathology of aggression, it becomes evident that a major transformation of the dominant aggressive affect causes this sequence to evolve. At the most primitive level of experience, the aggressive reaction centers around rage, and, in the clinical situation, aggression at any level of development eventually leads to primitive rageful affect states in the transference. The crystallization of an external bad object, that is, the separation of self- and object representations in the sector of aggression, transforms rage into hatred (and the intimately related affect of envy). It is here where omnipotence emerges in the form of an effort at omnipotent control of the bad object.

I have suggested in earlier work (O. Kernberg 1984) that projective identification may have an important early developmental function in fostering separation in the segment of primitive persecutory "all bad" states, reflecting an effort to attribute the aggression to an external source, to maintain a purified idealized self- and object representation as a core self-experience, and to protect the ideal segment of the self from the feared attack from the bad object. Clinically, projective identification—that is, the attribution to the object of an intolerable internal impulse, the maintenance of empathy with that dangerous, projected impulse, an unconscious tendency to induce the corresponding impulse in the object, and the need to control the object under the effect of the projected impulse—practically goes hand in hand with efforts at omnipotent control. We might also say that omnipotent control combines the fantasy of omnipotence with the aspect of control implied in the mechanism of projective identification. In short, omnipotent control evolves together with the psychopathology of hatred.

At higher levels of development, sadistic enjoyment of power replaces primitive hatred. At this stage, the wish is no longer to destroy the object but to make it suffer, or, in less primitive ways, to maintain it under one's control. Here omnipotent control becomes a powerful defense involved with the expression of sadistic power and the maintenance of power as an essential precondition for the individual's psychological security. At a still more advanced stage of development, the internalization of sadistic or sadistically perceived objects as part of the oedipal level of superego structures internalizes the conflict in the form of sadistic superego pressures and secondary characterological identifications with the sadistic superego typical of obsessive-compulsive personalities. Here the defensive operation of omnipotent control is transformed into the unconscious omnipotent fantasies of obsessive conditions.

In describing the typical constellation of primitive defensive mechanisms centering around splitting that characterizes borderline personality organization (O. Kernberg 1975), I mentioned omnipotence and omnipotent control together with projective identification, primitive idealization, devaluation, denial, and splitting as characteristic defensive operations. From what I have described so far, the mutual relations between omnipotence and omnipotent control, on one hand, and all these other defensive operations, on the other, may become more apparent. To begin, omnipotent fantasies, omnipotence as a defense in the libidinal sector, and omnipotent control in the aggressive sector aim at protecting the splitting of idealized and persecutory segments of psychic experience. In the case of narcissistic personalities, omnipotence and omnipotent control protect the patient from dreaded separation, dependency, and envy, maintaining the idealized concept of the pathologic grandiose self.

Projective identification and omnipotent control are indissolubly linked and reinforce each other under conditions of intense, primitive hatred, for example, in patients who have experienced severe physical or sexual abuse. Omnipotence goes hand in hand with the operation of denial in manic and hypomanic conditions, and it is the counterpart of the devaluation of significant others in schizoid, narcissistic, and hypomanic states. Primitive idealization of the self and omnipotence also are intimately linked. Thus, omnipotence and omnipotent control are essentially primitive defensive operations that are typically part of severe character pathology and psychosis.

CLINICAL ILLUSTRATION

The clinical vignette that follows illustrates omnipotence and omnipotent control. It presents a session from the psychotherapy of a patient presenting borderline personality organization and a narcissistic personality functioning on an overt borderline level. It took place in the midst of an extended period of sadomasochistic acting out in the transference.

The patient was a college student in her early twenties. I already knew that she had experienced her mother as withholding love and interest from all her children in order to encourage rivalry among them. The patient started the session by asking me why I was not able to see her later in the same day because this particular hour was very inconvenient. I told her that I had received her request from my secretary and had left a message to tell her that I would not be able to schedule a later session that day because of other commitments. The patient angrily interrupted to say that she had mentioned some time ago that she wanted to see me later that day, if possible, and that I obviously had given preference to other patients regarding her hour. I replied that I realized she was angry because she felt that I was giving preference to other patients and neglecting her. She ignored this statement and repeated her demand for another time. When I said that she was having her session even as we were speaking, she ignored that effort to focus on the here and now and repeated what she had already said. I commented that her demand for additional time—with the affirmation that this hour would be lost anyway—indicated her wish to punish me for not doing what she wanted and also to destroy her own opportunity to experience me as somebody available to help her understand what was going on now. But the patient persisted in her demand that I accede to her request. I tried saying again that what I considered most important at this point was her perception of me as uninterested and neglectful and her effort to transform me, by force, if necessary, into a good therapist again by giving her an extra session.

My interventions had no observable effect—her rage continued to mount, and every time I tried to say something she interrupted me. Finally I fell silent. After she furiously repeated her various accusations, I intervened with the remark that she was repeating herself and asked what the function of that could be. Now she fell silent. After a few minutes, I asked if the venomous look on her face and her silence were serving the same purpose as her accusations: namely, to maintain an intensely adversarial atmosphere that would preclude looking further into what was stimulating this rage.

The patient said contemptuously that if I liked, I could go on saying whatever nonsense came to my mind. I said that her accusations against me reminded me of the way she had described her mother attacking her in her childhood, leaving the patient to experience herself as the helpless victim of that assault; I suggested that enacting this role of mother in relating to me gave her a sense of strength and power, and that seemed more important to me than her efforts to obtain an additional session later that day. (This interpretation was not a new one; we had been exploring her tendency to enact relations with mother as torturer and herself as victim, with frequent role reversals in the transference, throughout this entire period of her treatment.)

After some minutes of silence, the patient said that she was aware of all that but that I had provoked this situation. I said that, if she really had been unable to come at this time, I would have evaluated whether we could find a better time to meet, but she had engineered the situation in a way that precluded such a solution. I also reminded her how often we had seen that she was an expert in provoking situations in which she would then feel that I had mistreated her. The patient replied that in any case, she could still listen to what I was saying while she was angry, and I wondered aloud whether this meant that she really was experiencing what I was saying as thoughts that changed her view about herself or whether she was now experiencing me as a powerful mother and herself as the naughty little girl who had to make amends. She said that she didn't feel she had to make any amends, and the hour ended shortly afterward.

DISCUSSION

The activation of omnipotence as a defensive operation in the transference usually takes the form of omnipotent control. The uncovering of unconscious omnipotence as part of an obsessive personality structure, in schizoid personalities and other "higher-level" personality disorders, poses much less of a technical problem than dealing with the enactment of omnipotent control in borderline and narcissistic personalities that usually occurs with the simultaneous activation of several primitive defensive operations. The activation of advanced defensive operations accompanying omnipotent control in obsessive personalities is less of a problem than the dominance of primitive defensive operations because, in neurotic personality organization, intellectualization, rationalization, and reaction-formations usually present together with omnipotent control and are less conducive to acting out of the transference. Omnipotent fantasies and enactment in psychotic conditions are the most difficult to approach with a psychoanalytic perspective.

For practical purposes, then, the management of omnipotent control in severe personality disorders represents the clinical situation we have to deal with most frequently. The main problem is how to maintain a position of technical neutrality without being manipulated into a rigidity that lends itself to an enactment of projective counteridentification—that is, a countertransference identification with the same tendency toward exerting omnipotent control that the patient is trying to avoid recognizing in himself. The therapist's masochistic compliance with the patient's pressure and demands may temporarily appear to improve the therapeutic relationship and reduce the expression of overt aggression in the transference, but it does so at the cost of driving the relevant conflict underground or leading to the splitting-off of the negative transference from a protective idealization of the therapist, related to the acting out of omnipotent control in the transference. Thus, for example, if I had agreed to the patient's demand that I give her an additional appointment late that evening, she might have relaxed immediately and shifted into telling me about new developments in her daily life, but then the underlying identification with her sadistic mother would no longer have been emotionally available for analytic work.

In my experience with severe personality disorders, it is practically unavoidable that the therapist will be forced to reassess and reassure the boundaries of the psychotherapeutic relationship in response to the expression of omnipotent control in the transference. In other words, he will need to reaffirm the overall treatment frame. And if acting out in the transference seems potentially dangerous, he will have to set limits to protect the patient and the space in which they work together from destructive aggression. Such limit-setting also protects the therapist from countertransference acting out and provides space for his countertransference analysis as a preliminary step to continued transference interpretation.

I refrained from mentioning countertransference developments in the clinical example that I gave because, being alert to many previous experiences in which the patient's demands were not met, I knew that limits on acting out in the sessions could be established.

I have found that the most difficult cases in management of omnipotent control are severely traumatized borderline patients who enact a victim-victimizer dyad in the therapeutic interaction, with an intensity and rapidity of role reversals that creates maximal risk for intense countertransference developments and countertransference acting out, which may contribute to vicious cycles of transference acting out.

The combination of intense hatred, omnipotent control, and projective identification in the transference with the need to establish and maintain firm boundaries in the treatment situation in order to continue an analytic approach will often make it almost impossible, in the short run, to differentiate the therapist's firmness, technical neutrality, and holding and containing patterns from acting out of omnipotent control in a projective counteridentification—that is, in the countertransference. The difficulty in clarifying this situation may feed into the therapist's masochistic potential and lead to a dangerous, guilt-motivated submission to the patient's acting out, eventually followed by an internal or actual rejection of the patient. If, however, the therapist can tolerate this ambiguity while maintaining an ongoing analysis of transference and countertransference outside as well as during the sessions, it is usually possible to clarify the patient's transference. At the same time, the analyst's capacity to absorb the aggression without reacting with counteraggression, abandonment of the patient, or masochistic surrender is facilitated. The therapist's consistency and firmness, in turn, will permit the patient gradually to realize that his aggression is not as dangerous and intolerable as he feared. In identifying with the observing function of his therapist, the patient may thus develop the potential for accepting and elaborating his aggression. The result will reduce the splitting that separates idealized and persecutory internalized object relations and lead to the integration of self- and object representations, the tolerance of ambivalence, and the deepening and maturing of internalized and actual object relations.

Chapter 12 The Risk of Suicide in Severe Personality Disorders: Differential Diagnosis and Treatment

In all cases of severe personality disorder the presence of suicidal ideation, suicidal intention, a history of such ideation and intention, and, of course, the nature and severity of any actual suicidal attempts is routinely investigated. For a patient who is not currently depressed and shows no evidence of suicidal ideation, intention, or behavior, the history of past suicidal ideation or action becomes part of the psychiatric record but requires no immediate intervention. When, however, a patient clearly presents a history of recent suicidal intention, desire, or behavior, the acute risk of a further attempt constitutes the highest priority for therapeutic intervention. The nature of these interventions is determined by the differentiation of truly suicidal from parasuicidal behavior, characterized by self-inflicted lesions such as cutting, burning, or excoriating the skin or by tearing out hair or nails. Discreet self-cutting is sometimes extensive yet carefully geared to avoid vascular damage. Severe self-laceration that

---

A previous version of this chapter was published in the *Journal of Personality Disorders* 15(3) (2001):195–208.

threatens arterial bleeding or lesions of major veins represents severely suicidal behavior.

Chronic parasuicidal behavior without actual suicidal intention, fantasy, or behavior is usually part of a severe personality disorder that requires long-term psychotherapeutic intervention. Whether psychopharmacological treatment should be part of such a strategy depends on whether supportive or psychoanalytic psychotherapy is offered and whether the parasuicidal behavior forms part of a broad pattern of severe self-defeating behavior, which requires particularly skilled setting up of initial treatment contracts and structuring of the therapeutic setting (Yeomans et al. 1992).

Affective disorders are commonly associated with personality disorders. If the patient is truly suicidal, and the clinician believes that there may be some suicidal risk in the near future, a pressing question is whether this suicidal intention is part of an effort to escape from the intolerable feelings and thoughts characteristic of depression or part of a depressive disorder requiring treatment in its own right. Patients whose planned suicide is not part of a depressive disorder represent cases of "suicide as a way of life," a condition reflecting the destructive and self-destructive characterological patterns typical of severe personality disorders and in particular the borderline personality disorder, the infantile or histrionic personality disorder, the syndrome of malignant narcissism, and antisocial personality disorder proper. Even when they fail to meet clinical criteria for depression, such cases of suicide as a way of life may be at risk for suicide on a characterological basis and require a specialized psychotherapeutic approach.

If the patient's suicidal intention or behavior is judged to represent an acute risk and is found to be part of a depressive illness, the question still needs to be raised: Is the suicidal intention commensurate with the severity of the depression, or is it clearly not warranted by the degree of the patient's depressive reaction, as is the case in severe personality disorders in which characterologically based suicidal behavior coincides with the presence of multiple neurotic symptoms? A significant suicidal risk may also be present in patients with less severe personality disorders, in particular those with a depressive-masochistic personality disorder. Here suicidal behavior usually corresponds to a severe characterological depression in a patient with good ego identity, a basically advanced or repression-based defensive organization, and excellent reality testing—in contrast to the typical presence of identity diffusion and prevalence of primitive defensive operations in patients with borderline personality organization.

When a suicidal risk coincides with bona fide depression that is not part of a major affective disorder, the safest therapeutic approach is a combination of psychopharmacological treatment for the depression and a psychotherapeutic approach to the patient's characterological problems (Koenigsberg et al. 2000). Such patients usually require a minimum of two sessions per week in an outpatient or ambulatory treatment arrangement with psychopharmacological treatment that usually starts with an SSRI medication at optimal dosage and is continued long enough to differentiate the psychopharmacological effects from the placebo effect that may evolve as part of the transference developments in the psychotherapeutic relationship.

If the first SSRI medication is not effective, another may be attempted and then, if the depression persists, a tricyclic antidepressant. As an alternative, an MAO inhibitor may become the treatment of choice, although this would obviously require the patient's assured compliance and responsible behavior with regard to dietary restrictions and concomitant medications. The patient's general capacity to comply in a reliable way with the therapist's recommendations, and the therapist's realistic conviction that the patient will not use these medications (in particular, the non-SSRI antidepressive medications) for suicidal purposes, will determine whether such a psychopharmacological approach is wise.

Patients with a history of having accumulated prescribed medication for suicidal purposes probably cannot be safely treated as outpatients with a combined psychopharmacological and psychotherapeutic approach if their suicidal tendencies seem relatively strong and the depression significant. Caution is particularly necessary in medicating patients with a history of antisocial behavior or irresponsible behavior toward previous treatment attempts, those with significant schizoid aloofness, paranoid distancing, general impulsivity, lack of concern for self, and a history of drug or alcohol abuse or dependency and those with a life situation characterized by loneliness and isolation, recent social failure or severe loss, or chronic self-defeating, self-mutilating, or parasuicidal behavior. A combination of several of these features may predict great difficulties for such patients in establishing an honest and dependent relationship with a therapist they experience as helpful. Patients with severe narcissistic pathology and a history of negative therapeutic reactions, for whom suicidal behavior has become a "way of life" and who present with characterological depression, may be at high risk of suicidal behavior as a response to the concerned and help-oriented attitude of the therapist.

When in doubt, it is preferable to hospitalize these patients rather than to treat them on an outpatient basis. Hospitalization is also indicated when the acute suicidal risk is part of a major affective illness, a bona fide major depression, or a depression inserted into a psychotic illness; in such instances, the suicidal risk should always be considered very high. This group includes patients with major depression, patients with schizoaffective illness, and also some chronic schizophrenic patients with a history of bizarre suicide attempts evolving within a constellation of delusional thinking that often cannot be quickly diagnosed. All these patients need to be hospitalized even though their suicidal tendencies may appear not to be acute or extreme; the very presence of suicidal ideation or intention in the context of psychotic conditions represents a high risk for suicide and an indication for hospital treatment.

From the criteria for differential therapeutic approaches to acutely suicidal patients mentioned so far, it is evident that the diagnostic evaluation of patients who present a potentially acute suicide risk requires several precise questions:

1. Is the patient depressed?
2. If so, is this a major depression or a characterological depression?
3. Does the patient suffer from a major affective disorder, particularly a major depression, a schizoaffective disorder, a schizophrenic illness, or a currently not clearly diagnosable psychotic illness?
4. Is the patient able and willing to communicate honestly about himself as well as his explicit attitude toward the therapist, and is he reliable regarding his information?
5. Does the patient show a degree of intoxication, drug involvement, or particular characterological features that would make the response to the previous question negative?

These questions imply a careful mental status examination and, of course, a good knowledge of the differential diagnosis of major depression from characterological depression. They imply a careful evaluation of the psychic symptoms of the depression, including the neurovegetative symptoms that may be present, the relation between the depressive reaction and current, objective environmental triggers, and the patient's dominant personality structure, superego functioning (honesty and responsibility), and aggressive and self-aggressive potential.

In the current sociocultural environment in the United States and its health delivery system, it is not uncommon to overdiagnose major affective disorders. This is attributable in part to the influence of patients who have learned the diagnostic language and DSM-IV criteria and are motivated to be admitted to a hospital setting or who expect some secondary gain from their therapeutic contacts. At the same time, there are patients with "double depression"—that is, a bona fide major affective disorder combined with a chronic characterological depression; in such patients, the differential diagnosis of the depressive illness may become very difficult in an acute situation. Under these conditions, it is preferable to diagnose a major affective illness and treat it accordingly, until the situation is demonstrated to be otherwise.

Another common problem is the tendency to underestimate the severity of the patient's acute depression or suicidal risk because of the histrionic features of his presentation. Histrionic features may be part of any severe personality disorder and may mask the severity of the depression and the suicidal risk. Again, when in doubt, it is preferable to hospitalize the patient, and then, combining the nurses' careful observations during the following days with repeated mental status examinations, to arrive at a definite diagnosis.

"SUICIDE AS A WAY OF LIFE"

Patients with severe personality disorders who present with acute or chronic suicidal or parasuicidal behavior without a bona fide depression are the cases we have designated as presenting "suicide as way of life." Very often suicidal or parasuicidal behavior is an expression of rage attacks or temper tantrums when the patient feels frustrated in the context of a relationship that creates intense emotional turmoil. Here suicidal behavior may express rage against others and against the self in a rather undifferentiated, impulsive way. This pattern is seen most frequently in women with borderline personality disorder or histrionic personality disorder. In men, such rageful suicidal behavior often coincides with severely narcissistic or antisocial features and requires the differential diagnosis of histrionic personality disorder, narcissistic personality disorder with antisocial features, the syndrome of malignant narcissism, or antisocial personality disorder proper. Women also present these conditions and, more frequently than men, present with severely masochistic features that include chronic self-defeating behavior together with parasuicidal or suicidal behavior.

All of these cases, in turn, must be differentiated from a second type of nondepressive chronic suicidal or parasuicidal behavior—namely, suicide as an expression of triumph over the surrounding world, a coldly prepared act of revenge or defeat of someone who is in charge of the patient, with whom the patient is involved in chronic conflictual ways. This may be one manifestation of a severe negative therapeutic reaction (O. Kernberg 1993d)—that is, a worsening of symptoms or self-experience when the patient feels that the therapist has been particularly helpful or concerned. Patients with a narcissistic personality disorder or the syndrome of malignant narcissism are prone to negative therapeutic reactions, which can take the form of a suicidal plan, carefully prepared over the course of days or weeks, with an outcome that is usually very severe and, at times, lethal. Such suicidal behavior may be among the most difficult conditions for the therapist to tolerate and treat.

All of these are patients who tend to receive antidepressive medication, in spite of not being depressed, and often accumulate such medication for suicidal purposes. Although the risk of harm is reduced with antidepressive SSRI medication, I believe that these patients should not be treated with psychopharmacological approaches or mood stabilizers.

TRANSFERENCE-FOCUSED PSYCHOTHERAPY

Over the past fifteen years, the Personality Disorders Institute of the Department of Psychiatry at Cornell University Medical College and the Westchester Division of the New York Hospital has developed a treatment approach to patients with chronic characterological suicidal behavior without depression that, as detailed in Chapter 7, we call "transference-focused psychotherapy" (TFP). This approach has been successful in many cases, dramatically so in a significant number. The clinical findings are currently being subjected to an empirically controlled research effort and have been published in book form (Clarkin, Yeomans, and Kernberg 1999). The relevant aspects of this approach, described in detail in Chapter 7, are summarized in what follows.

To begin with, a careful diagnostic evaluation of the patient is essential. Except for the strictly defined antisocial personality disorders, which are usually unresponsive to any psychotherapeutic approaches, all severe personality disorders are candidates for treatment with TFP. The prognosis varies with the type of personality disorder, in general being optimal for the borderline, histrionic, schizoid, and paranoid personality disorders and more guarded for the narcissistic personality disorder (especially with antisocial behavior), the syndrome of malignant narcissism, and the schizotypal personality disorder.

General prognostic indicators for TFP across all personality disorders include the quality of the patient's object relations; the more chronically isolated he is, the worse the prognosis. And the more severe his antisocial features, the worse the prognosis. Other prognostic features include the patient's intelligence (patients with intelligence below borderline levels do not respond well to TFC) and the secondary gain of illness (the prognosis is worse if the patient has been able to gratify passive-dependent and even parasitic wishes by abuse of his assumed incapacity for work, with massive mobilization of social resources for the handicapped).

This method requires two sessions per week of forty-five or fifty minutes each. In rare instances three sessions may be indicated for a while. A frequency of more than three sessions has a regressive impact, encouraging the tendency of many patients with severe personality disorders to convert therapy into a substitute for real life.

The overall strategy of TFP consists in the therapeutic facilitation of the activation in the transference of the primitive, pathogenic, split-off, internalized object relations characteristic of patients with borderline personality organization. This is characterized by the development of extremely persecutory or aggressively loaded object relations in the transference, alternating with extremely idealized ones. The objectives are gradually to increase the patient's tolerance for and understanding of the implications of these split-off internalized object relations in the transference, to resolve the corresponding identity diffusion, and thus to facilitate the integration of the patient's identity. In practical terms, this strategy implies that each of these primitive object relations—a relation between a self-representation and an object representation under the impact of a primitive affect disposition—is played out in the transference, with alternating role distributions. The gradual clarification, confrontation, and interpretation of the object relations activated in the transference constitute the major treatment techniques. In the process, the patient's tolerance for these internalized split-off representations of self and significant others gradually increases. He may now begin to understand the severe split between his idealized and persecutory relationships as a protection against the contamination of the idealized relationships. In ego-psychological terms, the patient is helped to achieve object constancy; in Kleinian terms, the therapeutic effort is to help the patient work through the paranoid-schizoid position and achieve the depressive position.

A three-step approach is followed: (1) the diagnostic description of a particular internalized object relation in the transference; (2) the diagnostic elaboration of the corresponding self- and object representation in the transference and of their alternative projection and enactment in the transference (and countertransference); and (3) the interpretative integration of the mutually split-off self- and object representations, leading to an integrated sense of self and of significant others, which resolves the identify diffusion that characterizes severe personality disorders. The techniques utilized in carrying out this strategy—namely, clarification, confrontation, interpretation in the here and now, in the context of systematic transference analysis, and an objectively concerned but technically neutral approach to these transferences—form the essence of TFP.

To these strategies and techniques we have to add some particular tactics that apply with patients presenting characterologically anchored suicidal tendencies. The first is the preliminary development of a treatment contract that includes features common to all patients regarding meeting times, financial arrangements, protocol for vacations and cancellations and for potential involvement of third parties, and so on; the instruction to communicate his thoughts, feelings, and perceptions freely in the therapy hours; and the therapist's responsibility to share information that might help the patient increase his knowledge of self. For suicidal patients, additional arrangements must be specified that assure the patient's survival, and patient and therapist must reach an understanding regarding the management of whatever suicidal behavior may emerge (Yeomans et al. 1992).

The treatment contract limits therapeutic contacts to the treatment hours, thus permitting the therapist to maintain an interpretive, technically neutral stance and discouraging the patient from deriving secondary gain from the symptom. Concretely, the patient is encouraged to communicate all suicidal fantasies, desires, and intentions in the therapy hours and to commit himself to refraining from any action on these desires between the hours. The understanding is that, should the patient consider himself incapable of controlling his suicidal behavior, he would go to an emergency service of a psychiatric hospital to be examined, and, if necessary, hospitalized until he is considered safe by the hospital staff.

In other words, the patient's responsibility consists in either controlling his suicidal behavior and reserving its discussion to the treatment hours or, if he is unable to do that, to assume the responsibility himself to be evaluated at an emergency service. The patient is discouraged from attempting to contact the therapist outside the treatment hours, in order to avoid secondary gain from the symptom and to keep the therapeutic communications within the context of the sessions.

Often the expression of suicidal threats to family members or others promotes powerful secondary gain that feeds into the patient's suicidal symptomatology. The therapist may have to meet with the entire family to explain the treatment arrangements and to liberate them explicitly from responsibility for the patient's survival. It needs to be stressed, once again, that, should the therapist be concerned about the patient's reliability as protector of his own survival between the sessions, it is preferable to hospitalize the patient until a definite diagnosis is achieved and his capacity for responsible participation in the treatment is reliably assessed. In practice, the suicidal behavior of these patients cannot be predicted and cannot be controlled by any external measures, not even hospitalization. Only the patient's cooperation and the elimination of secondary gain can prevent the suicide of a patient whose suicidal tendencies are anchored in his character structure.

In order to carry out the treatment effectively, the therapist must assure himself of his physical, legal, and psychological security by explaining to the family the rationale for making the patient responsible for *his* own safety. He must make it very clear to the patient and his relatives why long-term hospitalization does not seem indicated under the circumstances and what makes him recommend outpatient treatment in spite of the ongoing, uncontrollable risk of suicidal behavior. The therapist also needs to spell out these arrangements in his records, for his own legal protection. It is essential that the therapist achieve a therapeutic frame and conditions for the treatment that permit him to remain calm under conditions of explicit or implicit suicidal threats from the patient or pressures from his family members.

An essential aspect of this treatment approach is that the therapist interpret the transference implications of the treatment conditions for suicide control from the very start of the treatment, in light of his knowledge of the patient's present personality structure and history and the potential meaning he may be assigning to the therapist's intervention—as an act of invasive control, hostile dominance, or arbitrary restriction. The therapist then attempts to link this interpretation with the more general transference interpretations that may be warranted at that time. In short, an essential tactic of this treatment approach is the combination of structuring the treatment, setting limits on the patient's suicidal behavior, and immediate interpretation of the transference implications of this limit-setting, until such transference implications can be fully explored and resolved.

The underlying theoretical assumption is that, regardless of the particular psychodynamic issues activated in each case, a common feature of chronic suicidal or parasuicidal behavior is the implicit activation within the patient's mind of a sadistic, murderous object representation and the complementary activation of a defeated, mistreated, threatened self-representation. The relation between these representations of self and object is marked by intense hatred and played out in the patient's relationship with his own body. In other words, chronic suicidal and parasuicidal behavior reflect a somatization of an intrapsychic conflict. The limit-setting that is part of the treatment arrangements and the interpretative approach to the corresponding implications for the therapeutic relationship transform this somatized internalized object relation into a transference-activated internalized object relation that permits the suicidal conflict to be approached directly.

The patient's temptation to suicidal behavior is thus transformed into a potentially hateful relation between one aspect of the patient's self and one aspect of his projected object representation, attributed to the therapist. This transformation may dramatically reduce long-standing suicidal behavior. While the transference rapidly becomes a dominantly negative one, the containment, interpretive working through, and gradual resolution of that primitive transference may resolve the suicidal behavior.

ADDITIONAL AND ALTERNATIVE TREATMENT APPROACHES

Additional tactics include those indicated for all patients with severe personality disorders: the focus in each session on the material that is affectively dominant in the patient's experience; the consideration of a specific set of high-priority issues that have to be taken up regardless of transference developments; and the treatment of such typical complications as deceptiveness, paranoid regressions, and severe acting out. In the TFP approach to the treatment contract, the patient may refuse to accept the conditions laid out by the therapist. If so, it is helpful to discuss this very refusal as a manifestation of the patient's self-destructive tendencies and to explore them with the patient as part of the diagnostic process. Such exploration may lead to the conclusion that this treatment approach is not possible and that an alternative treatment is indicated. In general, a patient's refusal to accept the conditions for TFP may shift the therapeutic aims to supportive management of the patient. In supportive psychotherapy, secondary gain may be tolerated to some extent, and the family may be engaged to provide some control of the patient without overextending their commitment to the care of the patient's illness. In this context, a long-term therapeutic arrangement may be set up in which periods of brief hospitalization alternate with more or less extended periods of outpatient functioning. Under these conditions, a more adaptive compromise between impulsive and defensive configurations might be attempted without touching the underlying psychodynamics of the patient's pathology (Rockland 1992).

Another alternative treatment for patients who reject the conditions of TFP may be a cognitive-behavioral approach, in particular dialectic behavior therapy (DBT), a treatment modality specifically geared to reducing suicidal and parasuicidal behavior in borderline patients by means of a combination of validation and skills training (Linehan et al. 1993). This approach, however, also requires a treatment contract, and patients may refuse this contract as well.

In my experience, psychopharmacological approaches are usually not satisfactory for patients who present severely impulsive suicidal behavior without significant depressive symptoms. For patients who refuse all responsibilities commensurate with an adequate treatment contract, however, such a treatment approach—in particular, some combination of anxiolytic, antidepressive, and mood-stabilizing medication—may be helpful. This approach, however, requires assurance of the patient's strict adherence to prescribed use of the medication. In any case, the patient should not be medicated with several drugs for an extended period of time without any clear indication of the beneficial effects expected from such medication. There are growing difficulties in differentiating the side effects of such medication from placebo response and secondary neurotic symptoms, and the risk of misuse of such medication for suicidal attempts and secondary addictive behavior persists.

For patients who present a severe personality disorder with a severe characterological depression that reinforces and is reinforced by suicidal tendencies, the combination of a psychotherapeutic and a psychopharmacological approach creates some different problems. Given that the therapist is simultaneously evaluating transference and the psychopharmacological effects of medication, a more supportive stance is indicated during the early treatment, with some limited availability of the therapist outside the treatment sessions, to monitor the patient's depression and his capacity to refrain from suicidal behavior. During this phase of the treatment, concerns about the patient's object relations other than those with the therapist may be dominant, and the focus on the transference implications of suicidal behavior may have to wait until the depression has lifted or until it is clear that a negative therapeutic reaction is maintaining the depression. At this point the treatment may shift into consistent transference analysis, like that of patients without depression, while the psychopharmacological approach is maintained. In these cases it is usually possible, by means of careful evaluation of symptomatic changes in the context of transference analysis, to diagnose the extent to which antidepressive medication is really effective and the extent to which transference developments are maintaining, increasing, or decreasing the depressive affect. If antidepressive psychopharmacological treatment, rigorously carried out, is not effective, it may be discontinued altogether, and the treatment can continue on a purely psychotherapeutic basis, along the lines of TFP as outlined above.

If the sessions begin to be dominated by issues that would lead the therapist to consider hospitalization—that is, dishonest communication, lack of concern for self, or severe secondary gain that cannot be controlled—the patient may be asked whether he is able and willing to participate in TFP or whether hospitalization or a shift to a supportive approach is indicated.

Clinical evidence suggests that some patients in long-term supportive psychotherapy supplemented by MAO inhibitors may be helped by this combination of treatments. In our experience, long-term supportive psychotherapy with severe personality disorders as well as long-term DBT therapy geared to resolving suicidal and parasuicidal behavior are effective in many cases but do not resolve the basic personality structure of these patients.

An important implication of the recommended contract-setting approach in TFP is that the secondary gain of the characterological illness (not only of the suicidal behavior per se) needs to be controlled, either by including limit-setting in the initial contract-setting or by developing new aspects of the therapeutic contract as part of the evolving psychotherapeutic relationship. Thus, for example, in the case of patients with chronic suicidal or parasuicidal behavior that has significantly interfered with their capacity to work, to study, or to maintain ordinary social relationships, a careful reevaluation of these capacities is essential, as is the insistence that the patient normalize his work situation and social life; active engagement with others may highlight the patient's characterological difficulties and facilitate the analysis of the relation between transference developments and life difficulties.

Analysis of the transference implications of the therapist's control of the patient's suicidal behavior usually is rapidly enriched and complicated by the individualized dynamics of these patients. The therapist's alertness to the development of such specific meanings of the suicidal behavior is an essential aspect of his interpretive work. Thus, for example, some patients may respond to the limits being set on their suicidal behavior by chronic pouting, derogatory behavior, or provocative silence in the hours, expressing, among other meanings, a general destructiveness of their time, thus undermining the therapist's availability as a helpful person. All this may be interpreted, in turn, as an expression of the patient's unconscious submission to a sadistic internalized object that does not permit him to receive anything good from the therapist.

A patient's ongoing derogatory, hostile behavior in the hours, with attacks on the therapist expressed outside the hours as well, may reflect identification with a sadistic parental object, while the patient projects the attacked, mistreated self-representation onto the therapist. At times, dramatic splitting of the transference may take place, in which apparently friendly behavior in the sessions masks severely self-destructive behaviors between sessions, representing dissociated equivalencies of the negative transference whose expression is suppressed in the presence of the therapist.

The therapist's countertransference may become an important indicator of what the patient is projecting onto him, and countertransference analysis becomes an essential aspect of transference analysis in these cases. The therapist's "holding" function includes his tolerance of being the butt of the patient's aggression without withdrawing from the patient, letting himself become discouraged or depressed, vengefully abandoning the patient internally, or counterattacking him in any way in the hours. The therapist's tolerance of aggression, without a masochistic submission to the aggressive aspects of the patient's transference, may become an important experience for the patient, who, while projecting his defeated self onto the therapist, may gradually become assured of the therapist's survival and of his own survival as a good object in spite of his frightening aggression.

Maintenance of a firm frame for the treatment sessions—protecting the therapist, the patient, and their surroundings from any physical damage or aggression—is a precondition for the therapist's sense of security, essential for carrying out the complex functions of transference analysis. In particular, with patients who have been severely abused physically or sexually or who have been chronic witnesses of such abuse, the replication of these abusive experiences and memories in the transference may provoke enactments in which the patient manages to become the victim of the therapist's assumed aggression, and the therapist may become the victim of the patient's replay of that abuse with role reversal.

The therapist's ability to separate the part of himself that is emotionally reacting to the transference from the part of his mind in which he analyzes the total transference-countertransference situation (that is, in which he remains in his role as an "excluded third party") is an essential element of this treatment approach, in addition, of course, to the therapist's general knowledge and experience in transference analysis.

Chapter 13 A Technical Approach to Eating Disorders in Patients with Borderline Personality Organization

Most patients with severe eating disorders suffer from significant character pathology. Although the focus of our borderline psychotherapy research project at the Westchester Division of the New York Hospital–Cornell Medical Center is not on eating disorders per se, we believe that the experience gained in the psychodynamic treatment of borderline patients has relevance for treating patients with these disorders. In addition, the availability of a cognitive-behavioral inpatient service specializing in the treatment of eating-disorder patients has provided us with the opportunity to compare and relate the experiences of these patients. Finally, my own clinical experience in the psychoanalytic and psychotherapeutic treatment of such patients has permitted me to study some of the dominant dynamic features described in the literature regarding this pathology.

Published in the *Annual of Psychoanalysis,* edited by J. A. Winer. Hillsdale, N.J.: Analytic Press, 1995, 23:33–48.

DIAGNOSTIC ASSESSMENT

The two principal eating disorders, anorexia nervosa and bulimia nervosa, occur mostly in females. Anorexia nervosa is characterized by a reduction of at
least 15 percent of normal body weight and the patient's active refusal to achieve
normal weight; these patients are afraid of gaining weight or becoming fat; they
present significant disturbances in their body image and primary or secondary
amenorrhea. Bulimia nervosa is signaled by binge eating and efforts to control
weight by vomiting, use of laxatives, dieting, or exercise. Characteristically,
these patients have heightened concern with body weight and shape. Because
90 to 95 percent of these cases present in females, there is a tendency to neglect
the possibility of this diagnosis in some male patients with severe personality
disorders.

In our experience, the type and severity of the personality disorder are the
most important factors determining the overall prognosis for the broad range
of treatments attempted for patients with severe eating disorders. Although depression is a prevalent symptom in these patients, it is important to differentiate major affective disorders from characterological depression and the degree of severity of the depression from the affective type of personality disorder.
The major affective types of personality disorders include, from least to most
severe, the depressive-masochistic, the cyclothymic, the sadomasochistic, primitive self-mutilating syndromes, and the hypomanic. This group represents one
dimension of a spectrum of severity of personality disorders.

The second dimension is the hysterical-histrionic-borderline personality
disorder. The hysterical personality proper represents the healthiest (neurotic)
pole of the continuum, the borderline personality disorder proper the most severe; the histrionic or infantile personality is intermediate in severity.

The third dimension is that of the narcissistic personality disorders, which
range, as we saw in Chapter 3, from the narcissistic personality proper to the
narcissistic personality with overt borderline features to the syndrome of malignant narcissism and finally the antisocial personality disorder. The more severe
types of pathology on this continuum, particularly the last two, have a reserved
prognosis for psychotherapeutic treatment.

The final dimension is the obsessive-compulsive personality disorder; these
patients, at a severe level, shift into hypochondriacal, schizoid, and paranoid
personality disorders, and, at the most severe extreme, the relatively rare cases
of chronic anorexia nervosa with an underlying psychotic structure and schizophrenic episodes. In general, however, it is important to make the differential

diagnosis between an eating disorder proper and the severe anorexia of major depression and some delusional schizophrenic patients. The most common personality disorders found in patients with eating disorders are the hysterical, the histrionic or infantile, the borderline, and the narcissistic personality disorders, as well as characterological depression.

In general, patients with the higher-level personality disorders or with neurotic personality organization (the hysterical, the depressive-masochistic, and the obsessive-compulsive) have a much better prognosis and offer fewer treatment complications than those with borderline personality organization. I should add that, by including personality disorders not spelled out in DSM-III-R or DSM-IV, I am pointing to clinical syndromes well known to the psychoanalyst that have not yet found their way into our official classification system.

In each patient with an eating disorder it is important to evaluate not only the predominant character pathology but the presence or absence of identity integration, the dominant defensive structures, the quality of object relations, and, in particular, the presence or absence of antisocial features. As always, the quality of object relations and antisocial features is prognostically fundamental across the entire spectrum of personality disorders.

The first question in treating a patient with a significant eating disorder is whether the treatment can be carried out on an outpatient basis or whether a preliminary period of hospitalization is required to stabilize the patient or increase motivation sufficiently for outpatient treatment to proceed. In general, with a weight loss of 30 percent or more, not uncommon in anorexia nervosa, initial hospitalization to bring the weight back to normal is indicated. In bulimic patients, only those with sufficiently severe electrolyte imbalance, severe depression, or drug addiction may require hospitalization.

Another diagnostic issue is whether psychoanalytic psychotherapy or psychoanalysis, in contrast to a supportive type of therapy, is indicated. Patients with neurotic personality organization have an indication for psychoanalysis proper, whereas for most patients with borderline personality organization psychoanalytic psychotherapy is the treatment of choice (O. Kernberg 1984). In addition, prognosis for psychoanalytic psychotherapy will depend on the patient's ability to accept the kind of treatment contract that is a precondition for such treatment. Patients with multiple, chronic, severe acting out patterns, antisocial behavior, lack of motivation for treatment, remarkable lack of capacity for introspection, significant secondary gain of illness, and a well-documented history of negative therapeutic reactions with experienced psychotherapists may require either a preparatory period of long-term hospitalization or supportive psychotherapy, perhaps combined with cognitive-behavioral models of treatment. There is evidence from controlled studies that cognitive-behavioral treatment of bulimic patients with milder neurotic personality disorders may be helpful (Hoffman and Halmi 1993).

Some patients, in spite of presenting themselves (or having been brought by the family) for outpatient treatment, require hospitalization. These include anorectic patients with severe weight loss and those who present hypotension, bradycardia, amenorrhea, hypothermia, anemia, growth failure, lanugo, or osteoporosis. At times, not only the patient but the entire family may deny the obvious severity of the condition, despite the patient's diabetes mellitus, severe depression, or history of "double depression." Finally, in some cases the possibility of an underlying schizophrenic illness may indicate a diagnostic hospitalization. At times, hospitalization may serve the purpose of confronting an entire family with their denial of the patient's severe illness. A well-documented failure of outpatient treatments over an extended period of time may also justify a diagnostic hospitalization.

INITIAL TREATMENT STRATEGY

In the psychoanalytic psychotherapy of eating-disorder patients with borderline personality organization, the patient's potential for severe acting out makes it indispensable to set up an initial treatment contract (O. Kernberg et al. 1989). Less severe personality disorders, with relatively intact ego strength, anxiety tolerance, impulse control, and ability to maintain responsibility for daily life, may not require such particular treatment arrangements.

For the patient with borderline personality organization, once the diagnostic study has been completed and the indication for psychoanalytic psychotherapy established, we evaluate which aspects of the patient's eating disorder create dangers for her survival and the survival of the treatment in the short run. That includes all anorectic patients who are demonstrably incapable of maintaining their weight within 15 percent of normal weight and bulimic patients whose frequency of vomiting (usually ten to fifteen times a day) threatens electrolyte imbalance.

For anorectic patients, we define the optimal weight that the patient must maintain in order for outpatient psychotherapy to proceed, with the understanding that, should the patient be unable to maintain that weight, hospitalization would be indicated until the optimal weight is restored and outpatient psychotherapy may continue. If the patient is hospitalized in the same service where the psychotherapist works, psychotherapy can take place on an inpatient basis, but otherwise psychotherapy is interrupted until normal weight conditions are restored. A regular system of control by which the anorectic patient has to come to the hospital once a week to be weighed by a special nurse is advisable. The idea is to avoid the patient's temptation to tamper with her actual weight. The patient is told that anything below the agreed-on weight would trigger hospitalization in order for psychotherapy to continue. Naturally, if the patient has a significant weight loss and the first task is to restore normal weight, hospitalization would be the first step in the treatment.

In our experience, several months' inpatient treatment based on a cognitive-behavioral model is usually effective in restoring the patient's weight and providing a reeducative experience that gives the patient objective knowledge of a healthier pattern of eating after discharge from the hospital. If psychoanalytic psychotherapy starts concomitantly with hospitalization, it does not include the discussion of food or weight control. The psychotherapist makes it clear to the patient that he will not be involved in the behavioral management of the hospital program but establishes as his natural expectation the need for her to be maintained at normal weight. Sometimes cognitive-behavioral reeducation is carried out on an outpatient basis while psychodynamic psychotherapy begins; in such cases, it is helpful to maintain open communication among the staff involved, so that the psychological issues that emerge in the cognitive-behavioral treatment can be explored in the psychotherapy sessions.

It is important to provide the patient with a full rationale for the condition that she maintain the optimal weight in order to be treated on an outpatient basis. The same principle applies in the treatment of patients with severe characterologically suicidal tendencies, where the initial contract requires them to either commit themselves to controlling their suicidal behavior or enter a hospital if they cannot do so. The patient thus takes responsibility for her survival and for not damaging her body further in order to give psychotherapy time to evolve. Such instructions, we have repeatedly found, can be very effective *if there is simultaneous discussion of the underlying dynamics as these emerge in the transference situation.* In patients with severe anorexia, the therapist first explains why it is important that they accept the conditions for the treatment he established (because they are considered essential for the patient's survival). This limit-setting is followed immediately by the analysis in the transference of the intense rage and resentment the patient usually experiences in response to this interference with what is an egosyntonic, well-rationalized eating disturbance.

One anorectic patient, following the setting-up of such a treatment contract, immediately accused the therapist of the same invasive, controlling, sadistic behavior that she experienced from her mother. The therapist, while maintaining the structure established by the treatment contract, gradually elaborated this view of her as a replica of the patient's mother. The therapist pointed out that naturally the patient could not avoid intense hatred of such a terrible mother, who now appeared to be duplicated in the person of the therapist, and that one manifestation of this rage was the patient's effort to destroy by starvation her own body, perceived as the property of the mother and the therapist rather than of the patient. In other words, the therapist interpreted the transference meaning of the anorexia once the contract was in place, with the result that the patient's rage gradually became focused on the therapist while the need for hospitalization because of weight loss gradually disappeared.

A patient with borderline personality organization, a double depression, and severe bulimia vomited ten to twelve times a day and had significant parotid gland swelling and significant erosion of her teeth. As a precondition for treatment I established that she be under the consistent control of a gastroenterologist specializing in eating disorders who would inform me if and when he thought her physical condition warranted additional medical treatment or hospitalization. The patient experienced that demand as humiliating and perceived me as enjoying "parading her" before the medical profession as a distasteful person out of control; this brought us directly to similar experiences in her past of punishment by means of public exposure by both parents.

In short, the establishment of a treatment contract that controls any behavior that is life-threatening (and that, by implication, threatens the treatment as well), combined with an immediate focus on manifestations of the controlled behavior in the transference, represents the first step in the psychoanalytic psychotherapy of these patients. When acute danger does not exist—for example, in milder eating disorders, in which the patient maintains a relatively normal weight or is moderately obese and the eating disorder does not manifest electrolyte imbalance—there is no need for such a contract.

A special case is presented by patients who suffer from severe exogenous obesity and consult for treatment of this condition. Again, if the personality disorder is at a neurotic level, the treatment indication may be psychoanalysis, but for most patients with borderline personality organization it is more likely to be psychoanalytic psychotherapy. For these cases, I do not set up a contract controlling the eating disturbance because it is not acutely life-threatening. I am concerned, however, with analyzing the magical assumption that treatment will resolve the symptom without the long-term, painful, but indispensable regime of dieting. This is an instance of differentiating treatment goals from life goals: The treatment may help the patient mobilize the energy to carry out a radical change in eating habits but will not by itself ensure that such a change will take place.

Another major principle derived from our experience with patients with borderline personality organization applies in particular to patients with multiple symptoms, such as the combination of an eating disorder, suicidal or parasuicidal behavior, antisocial features (particularly kleptomania, which often goes hand in hand with bulimic patients' efforts to hoard food), alcohol and drug abuse, and a generally turbulent nature of life. Such chaotic conditions may interfere with the therapist's consistent concentration on dominant issues in the transference and may seduce him into combining an interpretive approach with supportive measures or environmental interventions. This danger may be avoided by establishing certain automatic priorities for intervention in order to protect the psychotherapeutic frame. First, as mentioned above, when there is a danger to the patient's survival or to third parties threatened by the patient (including the therapist), our response is to spell out the terms of the treatment that protect the treatment frame: limit-setting and interpretation of the behavior controlled by limit-setting as it influences the transference.

The second priority is the acute threat of disrupting the treatment (the dropping out that is so frequent in the psychotherapy of patients with severe personality disorders). Now, the indication is to interpret as rapidly as possible and in as much depth as possible the risk of the potential disruption of the treatment and all the meanings attached to it. At times, the risk of treatment interruption emerges in the therapist's fantasy without concrete evidence in the patient's communication. It is important that the therapist, while expressing concern about the possibility of a premature end of the treatment, maintain a position of technical neutrality—that is, pointing to the danger that the patient might take such a step and the reasons for it without appearing unduly eager to keep her in treatment. At all times, the patient should need the therapist more than the therapist needs the patient; if that basic equilibrium is threatened, the therapist should recognize and work through countertransference contributions before interpreting the danger of treatment disruption to the patient.

The third priority is the therapist's consistent sense of deceptiveness in the patient's communications. Because psychoanalytic psychotherapy is based on the assumption of honest communication between patient and therapist, consistent deceptiveness has high priority for interpretation, which usually leads to the unmasking of a psychopathic transference. Psychopathic transferences are characterized by the patient's basic assumption that the treatment consists of mutual manipulation and exploitation of the two persons in the relationship; the transference implications of such a fantasy enactment should be fully elaborated. The effect of such working through is to transform psychopathic into paranoid transferences, which may then be explored in more leisurely fashion.

The fourth priority is severe acting out, both inside and outside the session, such as bingeing and vomiting or weight loss; we interpret these behaviors in light of the current transference meanings.

The fifth priority consists of chronic narcissistic resistances in patients with narcissistic personality disorder. The problem here is the time required to work through these resistances; indeed, the therapist may often despair of the apparent lack of change in the hours. However, when life outside the sessions shows steady improvement for the patient (which he attributes to himself), the therapist may confidently continue to elaborate the narcissistic transferences.

It would be easy to misinterpret all these priorities as an artificial rigidification of a psychoanalytic approach. In practice, they help the therapist deal with situations that initially appear to be chaotic in multisymptomatic patients with severe personality disorders, and they protect the treatment frame, which then permits analysis of the transference in an atmosphere of safety.

DOMINANT DYNAMICS IN PATIENTS WITH SEVERE EATING DISORDERS

The dominant feature in all eating disorders is a relentless, sadistic assault on the patient's body, an attack symbolically representing four major issues.

First is a general attack on pleasure. In the simplest terms, the pleasure of eating, incorporating something good and transforming it into a symbolically as well as physically good object for survival and enjoyment of the body and the self, is fundamentally attacked. This dynamic is related to the primary inhibition of the capacity for sensual enjoyment and sexual pleasure in some severe borderline patients, related to an early, severe aggressive infiltration of all physical as well as psychological interactions in the mother-infant situation.

Second, an attack on the mother is connected to this attack on pleasure. In the dynamics of all anorectic borderline patients there are either profound conflicts involving separation-individuation or earlier conflicts involving a pathological enmeshment related to a struggle against a threatening, aggressive symbiosis with a devouring mother. The dominance of a sadomasochistic relation with the mother may play itself out in several ways. As Hilde Bruch (1973, 1985) has pointed out, many patients have a long history of surface submission to the mother while harboring a deep and growing resentment of the mother's invasiveness or her narcissistic exploitation of the child. Eventually, the anorectic patient's effort at starvation represents a masochistic form of rebellion against the mother and the assertion of autonomy under the cover of self-destruction. The situation is usually more complex, however. Chasseguet-Smirgel (personal communication) has convincingly pointed to the anorectic patient's hatred of her body as a derivative of the hatred of the mother and to her attempt to destroy her body as if it belonged to or represented the mother.

By the same token, behind the self-destructiveness of the anorectic behavior the patient appears to be divided. The transference reveals her identification with a primitive, sadistic maternal figure that has the qualities of a grandiose and destructive omnipotence, related to the pathology of malignant narcissism. Another part of the patient's self, located in her body, is simultaneously designated as the helpless victim of this sadistic, destructive maternal image. In fact, in the psychoanalytic psychotherapy of patients with severe anorexia nervosa, one frequently finds the patient alternately identifying in the transference with a grandiose, quasi-psychotic maternal introject while attacking the therapist as an equivalent of the patient's body, and experiencing herself as the victim of such a relentless, invasive assault from the therapist, perceived as the sadistic mother.

The third major dynamic is the attack on the patient's femininity, derived from several developmental stages: first there is an attack on the mother from a very early, preoedipal level, including first the mother of the experience of symbiosis and then the mother of separation-individuation. These dynamics differ from the submission to and rebellion against the mother of the advanced oedipal stage of development (in contrast to the archaic oedipal situation) and the regressive, destructive anality expressed in the wish to destroy all differentiated relationships highlighted by Chasseguet-Smirgel (1984). Boris (1984a, 1984b) has stressed the patient's projection of her own oral needs onto the mother and onto the analyst in the sense that others who want the patient to eat thus signal their unfulfilled needs, not the patient's. The patient thus protects herself against envy and resentment of the mother who is needed for food and love but whose good qualities she envies because of her teasingly withholding what the baby needs from her.

The anorectic patient's ongoing struggle against the mother often reflects not only intrapsychic distortion of early experience but the effects of actual, severely traumatic experiences, in particular the combination of the mother's actual invasiveness and her narcissistic callousness regarding the infant and child used as an extension of herself.

One of our most severely anorectic patients, an aspiring musician, was taken out of the hospital by her mother against staff advice so that the patient could perform at a concert at a time when the patient was near-cachectic. The bulimic patient with the double depression to whom I referred above had to be hospitalized at one point because of a major depression with severe suicidal tendencies. She managed to manipulate her mother into taking her out of the hospital against medical advice at a time when the staff and I felt that she was at acute suicidal risk. This patient had fantasies reaching an almost delusional quality that her mother wanted to poison her; she demonstrated her identification with the mother by manipulatively leaving the hospital when there was acute danger to her survival.

In bulimic patients, one frequently finds secondary defenses against conflicts relating to separation-individuation involving the use of bingeing to deny their dependency on significant others or to express their rage at fantasied or real abandonment. The greedy incorporation of food perceived as forcibly extracted from the mother then leads to the spoiling of that ingested food, which becomes a poison and must be expelled; as Chasseguet-Smirgel (1984) has pointed out, the simultaneous transformation of such food into excrement symbolizes the aggressive deterioration of internalized object relations.

But attacks on femininity also originate at an oedipal level, and it is in the relatively less severely disturbed patients that such advanced oedipal dynamics dominate. Here, bingeing and vomiting, devaluing feminine physical appearance, and radical efforts by severely anorectic patients to prevent full feminine development to occur reflect the fear and rejection of identification with the sexual mother and the oedipal couple. Paulina Kernberg (personal communication) has referred to the "Peter Pan" syndrome of anorectic adolescents who unconsciously attempt to maintain themselves as latency-age children, without specific gender identification. This attack on femininity broadens into the fourth issue, an attack on heterosexuality. The envy and hatred of the mother are displaced onto the father, with the consequence of intensified penis envy and a resentment of men, who are perceived as aggressive and exploitive. Whereas severely anorectic patients in general present pervasive sexual inhibition that obscures the unconscious conflicts in their relations with men, sado-masochistic sexual relations with men are quite common in women with bulimia; equally often, periods of binge eating and vomiting may alternate with periods of sadomasochistic interactions with men, when the eating disturbance recedes temporarily. Profound prohibitions against infantile sexuality are reactivated in early adolescence, provoking a regression to a preoedipal relation to the mother and to the anorectic defense against sexual maturation.

Additional dynamics have been suggested in recent years, pointing to the importance of cultural factors, the role of trauma, and the earliest relation of the infant to the mother's body. Several authors have attempted to relate the increase of eating disorders in advanced Western cultures to the effects of cultural pressures in the sense of unrealistic overemphasis on the autonomy of women in contrast to their need for validation via interpersonal relationships, pointing to unconscious conflicts between their identification with maternity, mothering, and dependency, on one hand, and the rejection of traditional female roles in a paternalist culture, on the other (Morris, Cooper, and Cooper 1989; Boskind-Lodahl 1976). Eating disorders have been included in the broad spectrum of psychopathology related to early trauma and sexual and physical abuse, together with borderline personality disorders, affective disorders, dissociative disorders, post-traumatic stress disorders, antisocial disorders, suicidality, and somatization disorders (Marziali 1992; Paris 1994a). Meltzer (Meltzer and Williams 1988), pointing to the splitting between early idealization of the surface of the mother's body and the projection of aggression into the interior of the mother's body, suggests that the infant's excessive aggression in the early mother-infant relation may lead to unconscious fantasies of a destroyed maternal body that precludes normal identification with the mother and, by means of the projective fantasy of the mother's retaliation, to the infant's introjective fears of the destroyed interior of her own body and to fear and hatred of her body.

A CLINICAL ILLUSTRATION

With regard to the dynamics of eating disorders, I have mentioned the concerted attack on pleasure, on the mother, on femininity, and on heterosexuality. In this set of dynamics, there is always an aggressor and a victim in the sense that what appears to be the patient's relation with herself reflects, at a deeper level, the relation between internalized representations of significant others and the self. The gradual transformation of these intrapsychic relations, masked by the symptoms of the eating disorder and expressed as major transference paradigms, is the central task during extended periods of the psychoanalytic treatment of these patients.

A scientist in her early thirties, treated with standard psychoanalysis four times per week, presented a borderline personality organization, an infantile personality with hysterical features, characterological depression, bulimia, and moderate obesity. She also abused drugs and had phobic fears of driving on highways and bridges. Her relationships with men were clearly masochistic in that she was interested only in men who were unavailable and unconsciously ruined opportunities with those who were potentially available. In the transference, there were long stretches during which she presented oedipal material, fears and wishes of being seduced by me that gradually shifted into wishes to seduce me as a father figure, with a parallel uncovering of dissociated unconscious guilt about this seductiveness, expressed in self-defeating patterns in her relationships with other men in her life. In fact, her oedipal conflicts were manifested not in a dynamic equilibrium involving unconscious, repressed positive oedipal longings and related guilt feelings, but in mutually dissociated or split-off acting out of unconscious guilt about good relations with men outside the sessions, simultaneous with direct expression of sexual seductiveness and fears of being rejected in the analytic situation itself.

In the third year of her analysis, a new theme emerged that gradually took over significant periods in the transference. For the first time in her life, the patient developed a homosexual attraction to a woman who worked in the same laboratory in which she did; she found this woman extremely attractive and, at the same time, a potentially serious professional rival. Her sexual feelings toward her colleague increased together with intense fear that she was trying to steal the patient's ideas in order to advance her own career. The patient seemed to become increasingly paranoid about this woman and attributed unusual powers to her (that she wanted to destroy the patient by ruining her work, producing mischief in the laboratory in many ways). At a certain point, I became confused about what in all this was reality and what was fantasy. My patient then began to suspect that I was taking the side of her colleague and was a potential enemy of hers. A severe regression in the transference developed; the patient experienced me as an enemy who was trying to destroy her confidence in herself, to such an extent that the other woman and I became practically identical.

At that stage of the treatment, her bulimic symptoms, which had been relatively minor and had not emerged as important issues earlier in the transference, now became more severe. I considered recommending a consultation with an internist but I was reluctant to suggest this to the patient in the midst of the chaotic transference situation. It was only now that I recalled very early memories in which the patient had perceived her mother as both intensively protective and yet invasive—controlling the patient and reading her mind. It became apparent that the patient had always felt that her body, her movements, her speech, her intentions, could not be trusted because they might really represent her mother's intentions. The patient had lived with the conviction that her mother could not tolerate her independence or autonomy during her childhood years. The fear of driving on highways or over bridges now became clarified as fear of being taken over by the mother, who would punish her with death for attempting to escape from the mother by racing away from home on highways or over bridges.

We were now able to explore how she was repeating her relationship with mother in her relationship with me, experiencing me as an invasive mother who was assaulting her simultaneously in the sessions and at her workplace, while at other times, without being aware of it, she was identifying with this invasive mother in attempting to prevent me from contributing to her understanding and from thinking clearly. I suggested that the terrible confusion about whether her rival was indeed creating a "gaslight" situation at work or whether my patient only fantasized this development was part of a pattern that also evolved in the hours. While she felt controlled and inhibited by me, at times I felt controlled and inhibited by the combination of the patient's consistent distortion of what I was saying (interpreting it as an attack), her confused narrative about what was going on in the laboratory, and her experience of my efforts to clarify that confusion as an invasive, sadistic effort at thought control.

The patient also realized that she was binge eating in order to replace her now-dangerous dependency on me, while her vomiting permitted her not only to free herself from the mother's poisonous food but to avoid awareness that in her obesity she had become like her mother. The search for a dependent relationship with the mother displaced onto the greedy incorporation of food, the vomiting as an effort to get rid of the mother's poison as well as of the patient's identification with her, the projection of the mother onto me while enacting the mother's invasive behavior in her confusing disassembling of my interpretations—all seemed to be complementary facets of the same conflictual relationship with a primitive, invasive, and sadistic mother.

Gradually, the patient became able to think more clearly about what was going on at work, and her communications in the sessions also became clearer. These developments permitted us to discover that the patient's rival was indeed actively attempting to undermine her work, a fact confirmed by evidence from other co-workers, and that the patient's intense attraction to the woman she had intuitively perceived as a potential enemy reflected her masochistic submission to the mother. The binge eating and vomiting disappeared as her internal submission to and conflictual identification with the mother were worked through in the transference.

In later stages of her analysis, it became apparent that the internal, unconscious submission to the mother from whom she felt she could not differentiate herself also represented the acting out of oedipal guilt, the split-off counterpart to her conscious oedipal fantasies and wishes in the transference. The patient now became more inhibited in the expression of her sexual fantasies relating to me and consciously more fearful in her sexual involvement with men. Her unconscious, self-defeating behavior with men changed to a sexual inhibition that reflected her oedipal guilt more directly and could be worked through at that point. In the advanced stages of her treatment, she was able to establish a satisfactory relationship with a man whom she eventually married and with whom the relationship has remained very satisfactory over the years.

In this case, binge eating spontaneously evolved as a major aspect of the transference relationship and thus facilitated the resolution of this symptom. In many cases, however, the dominant symptom—for example, severe anorexia—may be stubbornly split off from spontaneous communication in the transference, and obsessive concerns with "right" and "wrong" foods may occupy much time in the sessions in spite of efforts to analyze the unconscious dynamics of these obsessive concerns. Under these circumstances, the patient's very insistence on talking about food while the analyst is exploring the transference relationship may facilitate the analysis of her denial of the conflicts in the transference by focusing on the symptom.

Regarding the unconscious conflicts of patients with eating disorders, one might say that all of these patients treat themselves badly, and the defensive split between their image of their body and their self-concept masks the collusion of the self with the destructive internalized object representation. The analysis of the collusion of the healthy part of the self with such an internal enemy, a hostile introject seducing the patient to treat her body as not belonging to the self, is the counterpart of the patient's attack on the analyst when the analyst threatens that collusion. Here object relations theory and ego psychology converge in the analysis of a conflict between impulse and defense that involves a conflictually internalized object relation, while, at the same time, in her unconscious collusion with the internal enemy, the patient is denying her responsibility for herself and ultimately for the attacks on herself carried out in the name of a sadistic internalized object.

Finally, at such crucial points in the treatment, when the patient is able to assume full responsibility for herself while still being aware of the identification processes involved in her previous collusion, it is time for the analyst to explore with the patient the nature of the early treatment contract and the reasons the therapist had to impose conditions in order to keep the patient alive and to preserve time for the analysis of her unconscious conflicts. At such moments, an implicit split in the therapist's relation with the patient is also resolved, namely, that between the therapist protecting the frame of the treatment by measures that the patient usually experiences as invasive control and the fact that these measures essentially reflect the analyst's concern for the patient's survival and for the success of the treatment. This analytic resolution of parameters of technique may help consolidate the patient's full autonomy, while permitting her to realize fully that autonomy and mature dependency are not mutually contradictory.

Chapter 14 The Management of Affect Storms in the Psychoanalytic Psychotherapy of Borderline Patients

CLINICAL MANIFESTATIONS

The following discussion is based on experience treating borderline patients with the psychoanalytic psychotherapy referred to as transference-focused therapy (TFP) that we have developed at the Personality Disorders Institute of the Cornell University Medical College (Clarkin, Yeomans, and Kernberg 1999). The management of affect storms in the sessions of patients with borderline personality organization and severe regression in the transference presents us with two apparently opposite and yet complementary situations. The first is one in which an open, observable affect storm explodes in the psychotherapeutic setting, usually with an intensely aggressive and demanding quality but also, at times, with what on the surface appears to be a sexualized assault on the therapist, the invasiveness of which reveals the condensation of sexual and aggressive elements. The patient,

An earlier version of this chapter was published in the *Journal of the American Psychoanalytic Association* 51(2)(2003):517–544.

under the influence of such an intense affective experience, is driven to action. Capacities for reflectiveness, cognitive understanding, and verbal communication of internal states in general are practically eliminated. Thus the therapist must depend mainly on observation of nonverbal communication and countertransference in order to assess and diagnose the nature of the object relation whose activation is giving rise to the storm of affect.

The explosive behavior of some severely ill patients takes the form of repetitive, consistent enactment of affect outbursts. Here, the patient's verbal communications, session after session, are punctuated by intense affects that momentarily dominate the picture, only to shift rapidly into a different kind of affective explosion. Under these circumstances, a chronically chaotic situation is enacted that may convey the impression that the patient experiences the therapist's every statement as traumatic; the patient's readiness to feel traumatized is consistently, monotonously enacted, session after session.

The second situation, namely, long periods during which the patient's rigid, repetitive behavior, along with a paucity of affective expression—in fact, a deadly monotony—permeates the session, seems almost the opposite of the first. The effect on the interaction between patient and therapist during such periods can be as powerful and threatening as that of overt "storms." The therapist can feel bored to the point of despair, rage, or indifference or can at least recognize that an impasse has been reached. On realizing that the significant information is coming from these countertransference reactions and the patient's nonverbal communication, the therapist can attempt to analyze and interpret the nature of the scenario that is being enacted via the patient's behavior. This regularly leads to the striking emergence of the violent affect that the rigid monotony had masked, a violent affect often felt first in the countertransference and then rapidly materializing in the therapeutic interaction, once that countertransference is utilized as material for interpretation of the nature of the transference.

Affect storms and extreme defenses against them are far from ubiquitous in the treatment of borderline personality disorders. In the psychotherapy of most borderline patients, as in the psychoanalytic treatment of neurotic patients, we can generally rely on their verbal description of subjective states, their free associations being the most important channel of communication. Over time, carefully pursuing the ever-changing nature of these patients' communications, we discover the affectively dominant themes in the patient's discourse—the derivatives of unconscious conflicts in the interplay among defensive operations, impulse derivatives, and compromise formations—and are usually able to diagnose the gradual emergence and consolidation of dominant infantile object relations in the transference.

Naturally, in all cases, nonverbal communication and countertransference are important channels of communication, but they convey dramatically more meaning than does the content of verbal communication by patients with severely regressed transference developments (O. Kernberg 1984, 1992a). What is, however, typical of borderline patients in general is that long-term evaluation of the course of free associations alone fails to yield a clear picture of the dominant unconscious conflict in the transference. These patients' communication is fragmented, and the dissociation (splitting), with fragmentation of their world of object relations, presents itself as rapid sequences of verbalized fantasies and modes of relating themselves to the therapist that change from moment to moment. This kaleidoscopic behavior is based on the activation in the transference of shifting unconscious object relations, activated with rapid "exchanges" between enactments of self- and object representations, while the reciprocal representations of object or self are projected onto the therapist. Or, primitive dissociation, or splitting, manifests itself as a dissociation between verbal communication, nonverbal communication, and countertransference, determining a confusing experience for the therapist even when there seems to be a certain continuity of the verbal material of free association. Primitive dissociation, therefore, may take the form of dissociated or fragmented verbal communication or of dissociation among the various channels of communication in the transference.

We have learned from experience that the optimal way to explore the patient's material analytically is to attempt to diagnose the transference developments moment to moment (Clarkin, Yeomans, and Kernberg 1999). The therapist has to take a very active role in such rapid diagnosis and interpretive interventions, paying close attention simultaneously to all three channels of communication (verbal, nonverbal, and countertransference) and describing (to himself) in a metaphorical way the dominant object relation activated in the transference. This permits the therapist gradually to assess which pair of opposite internalized object relations is serving the function of defense and which represents the corresponding impulse configuration in the transference at any given moment. Analysis of the rapidly emerging and shifting transference dispositions gradually reveals a typically rather small repertoire of dominant object relations in the transference. These can gradually be sorted out into object relations dyads with defensive functions and those with impulsive functions.

These functions may be rapidly interchanged while the dominance of the same pair of object relations dyads remains stable.

For example, the patient may in rapid succession attack the therapist, complain bitterly about how she is being treated, furiously criticize the therapist's behavior, and cry silently, as if bitterly disappointed and depressed about being rejected and unfairly accused or mistreated. What appear at first to be chaotic shifts in the relationship turn out to be the systematic alternation of the relation between a persecutory, scolding, and derogatory object and a rejected, depressed, and impotent self, the roles being rapidly assigned and reassigned to the patient and the therapist. The role reversals repeat the same relations again and again. Meanwhile another object relation may be enacted with the same pattern of role reversal, representing another aspect of the transference, completely dissociated from the first. For example, a sexualized form of transference may emerge, the therapist being accused of prurient interest as his only investment in the treatment, while at the next moment the patient may become unmistakably seductive. Here two sets of mutually split object relations dyads are dominant in the transference and may become impulsive or defensive in relation to each other. The relation of these dyads to each other needs to be worked through gradually.

The interpretive spelling out of the unconscious meanings in the here and now of each internal object relation activated in the transference, with the gradual sorting out of self- from object representations and the dominant affect linking them, permits the therapist to achieve the strategic goal of eventually integrating mutually split-off, idealized, and persecutory internalized object relations. This cannot be done during severe affect storms.

SOME THEORETICAL FORMULATIONS

Several authors have dealt with the theoretical implications of these clinical phenomena. The approach developed at the Personality Disorders Institute, already implicit in what has been said so far, assumes that in the transference, primitive, dissociated, internalized object relations have been activated—split along the lines of idealized and persecutory relations that, in our view, need to be clarified, confronted, and interpreted in terms of their self-representation, object representation, and affective dominance. This approach consists of, first, sorting out the dominant object relation in the transference, then diagnosing the self- and object representations and their reciprocal enactment or projection in the transference in both the idealized and the persecutory segments, and, finally, achieving integration of these mutually dissociated transferences through interpretation. The successful carrying out of these three major strategic steps over time leads to the integration of the patient's self and of his internal world of object representations, to the consequent resolution of the syndrome of identity diffusion, and to the establishment of a normal ego identity. This development also brings about the mutual toning down and maturation of the patient's affects, with a concomitant increase in cognitive control, the capacity for self-reflection, impulse control, and anxiety tolerance and the development of sublimatory potential.

The consistent attention to transference and countertransference developments, the implicit split of the therapist into one part that is included in the transference-countertransference bind and one part that remains as the "excluded other" carrying out the analytic task and, symbolically, thus consolidating the triangular oedipal relationship over time and resolving the regressive dyadic enactments, complements this technical approach. This approach is essentially analytic in terms of the management of the transference by interpretation alone, the maintenance or analytic reestablishment of technical neutrality as needed, and a maximal focus on the analysis of the transference rather than a supportive management of it.

This approach, I believe, is commensurate with the major currents of object relations theories and reflects an integration of aspects of Kleinian, British Independent, and ego-psychology approaches (Kernberg 2001). Several other potentially alternative but, in my view, really complementary theoretical formulations that appear to me to be commensurate with the overall approach outlined above include the following.

Ignacio Matte-Blanco's Theory of Bi-logical Functioning

Matte-Blanco (1975, 1988) has stated that "the system Unconscious treats the converse of any relation as identical with the relation. In other words, it treats asymmetrical relations as if they were symmetrical." For example, in the relation "John is the father of Paul," it treats the converse relation, "Paul is the son of John," as if "Paul is the father of John," that is, as symmetrical. This principle of symmetry is complemented by the principle of generalization. In simple terms, the dynamic unconscious, Matte-Blanco suggests, treats a part or segment or individual member of a larger set as equivalent to the larger set, and that in turn is equivalent to whatever still larger set it may belong to. As a consequence, particular subsets of the general set that are markedly disparate may be treated as equivalent because of the equivalence following the principle of generalization. Thus, for example, if a dark room represents the absence of the needed mother, an infant's primitive fantasy transforms darkness into a bad mother, a general principle of which a black object, the black pupils of the eye of a stranger, and a black dog may all be disparate subsets considered as equivalent, and induce terror by signifying a bad, frustrating mother.

The fusional experience that accompanies primitive rage as well as sexual excitement, the experience of the entire world as a hostile, invasive, destructive force under the dominance of primitive hatred, or the sense of transcendence or oneness with the world of the individual in love illustrates this symmetrization, which, under certain circumstances, we might say disrupts ordinary secondary process thinking. Usually, however, ordinary secondary process thinking respects asymmetry and rejects the generalization of subsets.

The mental apparatus, in Matte-Blanco's view, thus functions as a "bi-logical" system, alternating between symmetric and asymmetric thinking. The earliest affective experiences between mother and infant, in particular the peak affect states that express primitive rage and euphoria, operate under the principles of symmetry and generalization and may be considered, precisely, as the point of origin of the psychic manifestations of drives. Peak affective experiences alternate with other interactional experiences under low-level affect conditions from birth onward in which a surprisingly high degree of inborn capacity for differentiation—that is, for asymmetrical thinking—takes place. From this viewpoint, one might consider that, from birth onward, symmetrical and asymmetrical thinking operate alternately, hence the various combinations of symmetrical and asymmetrical thinking in varying developmental levels, affect activation, and regression.

The implication of this theory is that what on the surface appears to be the simple loss of the capacity for symbolic thinking and loss of cognitive control during affect storms represents the activation of symmetrical thinking reflecting the deepest unconscious layers of the mind. Hence, during intense affect storms, the focus on the nature of the logic implied in the patient's thinking may be helpful in analyzing both the nature of the primitive object relation activated at such times and the emerging unconscious fantasies apparently blurred by the very intensity of the affective situation. The understanding and interpretive explanation of the patient's experience may be significantly facilitated by the therapist's tolerance and utilization of partial symmetrization of his own affective experience in the countertransference and in communicating his interpretations.

Kleinian and Generally British Contributions

An alternative theoretical view, again, I believe, commensurate with our approach, is the Kleinian analysis of the dominance of primitive defensive operations, projective identification in particular, during transference regressions. The result of projective identification is to induce in the therapist the affective experience that the patient cannot contain in his own mental functioning while in the grip of powerful affects (Klein 1946, 1957). The therapist's function of transforming the patient's projected "beta elements" into "alpha elements" is carried out by providing, by means of interpretation, an "apparatus for thinking" for the patient (Bion 1967, 1970). Thus the therapist facilitates the patient's reintrojection of the previously not tolerated and projected psychic experience.

The contemporary Kleinian focus on the "total transference situation" (Spillius 1988) is compatible with our focus on interpretation of verbal content, nonverbal behavior, and countertransference in an integrative formulation guided by the analysis of the dominant, primitive internalized object relations of the patient that are activated in the transference (Clarkin, Yeomans, and Kernberg 1999). Our focus on the unconscious in the "here and now," before attempting any genetic reconstruction, is commensurate with a contemporary Kleinian approach and also with Joseph and Anne-Marie Sandler's (Sandler and Sandler 1998a) stress on the analysis of the "present unconscious" as a precondition for the analytic elaboration of the unconscious template reflecting the "past unconscious."

Another theoretical approach, again compatible with our approach to the treatment of affect storms in borderline patients, is that of both Kleinian and British Independent schools regarding what several authors have described as the imprisonment of a traumatized self within a sadistic object (Kohon 1986; Rosenfeld 1987; Spillius 1988). This formulation proposes the equally threatening alternative in the patient's unconscious fantasy of a complete, defensive isolation of the self, with total unavailability of any object contact. Under both conditions the patient lacks a protective "skin" that would separate self from nonself and at the same time permit contacts with a human environment.

André Green's Formulations

The threat of either total, catastrophic isolation or boundary-blurring invasion overlaps, it seems to me, at least in part, with André Green's conceptualization of the identification of the patient with a "dead mother" (Green 1993b). This is an identification in which the contact with an ambivalently loved and hated—and lost—object can be maintained only by elimination of the self's mental functioning in a paralyzing emptiness. In André Green's formulation, it is the capacity for affective representation that is destroyed in this process and replaced by violent acting out or somatization. This represents, at a metapsychological level, the overwhelming dominance of the death drive in terms of a total, destructive "deobjectalization" (Green 1993b).

A related approach to affect storms, more recently developed by Green (2000), refers to the "central phobic position" of borderline patients. He proposes that there exists in these patients a central fear of the activation of a traumatic situation that forces them either to withdraw regressively from particular mental content or to anticipate its consequences defensively, so that the patient is in a constant attitude of escaping from a traumatic recognition of his psychic experience. Under these circumstances, all efforts of the therapist to help the patient acquire awareness of his psychic experience become traumatic events. Here the struggle against mental representation reflects not only the effort to avoid a specific internalized object relation but a general effort to eliminate the representation of mental conflict. Therefore, a patient's active efforts to destroy the representational expression of the conflict may reflect both a general defense against the activation of a traumatic situation and a specific unconscious identification with a dead or destructive object.

I believe that these formulations parallel our efforts to clarify the nature of the most regressive transferences of patients whose mental life is dominated by hatred, that is, by the aggressively determined object relations typical for the syndrome of malignant narcissism, where only mutual destructiveness seems to provide meaning and closeness and only a greatly reduced remnant of a libidinal investment is still available (O. Kernberg 1992a).

An Ego-Psychological Approach

Still another formulation of the nature of severe transference regressions of borderline patients has been suggested from an ego-psychological perspective by Peter Fonagy's (Fonagy 2000; Fonagy and Target 2000) hypothesis of "mentalization" and "self-reflectiveness." In essence, he proposes that, in the infant-mother relation, the normal function of mothering includes both her empathic internalization of the infant's experience and her capacity to formulate that experience to him, while still indicating her differentiated relation to his experience. Thus mother's communication includes clarification of what is going on in the infant's mind, her empathy with it, and her different reaction to his experience.

The mother of the future borderline patient is postulated to be incapable of accepting empathically the infant's communication and unable to elaborate it, thus leaving the infant alone with what becomes an unbearable, overwhelming psychic experience that cannot be mentalized adequately; or else the mother identifies herself with the infant without being able to establish an internal distance from his experience. Reflecting to the infant such a total identification with his intolerable affect state results in that state's becoming even more overwhelming, with a momentary loss of ego boundaries.

If the mother can appropriately reflect and communicate the infant's experience, the infant is permitted to internalize not only the understanding of his own experience but also the mother's reflection about it, thus fostering the infant's normal awareness of and interest in his own mental functioning and that of the other person ("mentalization"). These processes foster the development of a self-reflective integrative ego function that strengthens capacities for symbolization and containment of emotional experience. This formulation, which stresses the cognitive aspects of the structuralization of primitive internalized object relations, also seems to me eminently compatible with the object relations perspective underlying our approach.

TRANSFERENCE-FOCUSED MANAGEMENT
OF AFFECT STORMS

In initial interviews borderline patients usually show far better control of affect than they are able to maintain during effective treatment. The likelihood of periods of inordinate violence of the patient's affect, and its expression in action or countertransference, requires, however, that patient and therapist agree in advance on the conditions of the treatment that will make management of such episodes possible. These conditions must include the maintenance of a clear and stable boundary of the therapeutic setting. This boundary involves not only the fixed time and space of the psychotherapeutic relationship but also the extent to which the patient may yell, the requirement to avoid any destructive action against the therapist, his belongings, the office, and the space in which the treatment takes place, and protecting the patient from any dangerously destructive action against the self. The patient must understand that physical contact between patient and therapist is prohibited as a condition of treatment.

With these boundaries in place, it begins to be possible to carry out the diagnosis and interpretation of the dominant object relation and of the corresponding primitive defensive operation (projective identification in particular) as these become activated in the sessions. When affect storms occur, however, the patient may not be able to accept any interpretation, especially an interpretation of projective identification, because he perceives it as a traumatizing assault. Here the recommendation of John Steiner (1993) to interpret the nature of what is projected as "object centered," spelling out the patient's perception of the therapist in great detail, without either accepting that perception or rejecting it, gradually facilitates the patient's better tolerance of what he is projecting, as well as clarifying the nature of what is projected and the reasons for it, before interpretation of the projection proper "back into the patient."

Affect storms place a special strain on the therapist's tolerance of the countertransference; it is necessary both to keep one's mind open to exploring (mentally) the implications of the strong feelings aroused by the patient's behavior and to protect oneself against acting them out. The therapist has to attempt to stay in role, even when responding with corresponding intensity to the intensity of the patient's affect.

We have observed in our borderline psychotherapy research projects that some therapists whose interpretive interventions seem relevant, clear, in sufficient depth, and expressed at an appropriate tempo in moment-to-moment contact with the patient nevertheless have difficulty in their treatments because of a pronounced discrepancy between the intense affective activation in the patient and the outward serenity of the therapist. Nothing is more effective in further inflaming an affect storm than a wooden, unresponsive, or soft-spoken therapist whose behavior suggests either that he doesn't "get it" or that he is contemptuous of the patient's loss of control or terrified and paralyzed by the intensity of the patient's feelings. The therapist must be willing and able to engage the patient at an affective level that has an appropriate intensity and that recognizes and yet "contains" the affect of the patient.

This situation, in which patient and therapist are expressing themselves at the same affective level, is not infrequent in the treatment of severely disturbed patients. It may reflect Matte-Blanco's concept of a primitive level of symmetric logical functioning, in which the self's very intensity of affect determines the combination of generalization and symmetric thinking, with the result that only a related, somewhat corresponding intensity of affect on the part of the object enables communication to be maintained.

It may seem obvious to state that the therapist's affective response must be sensitive to that of the patient, particularly when the dominant affects are so extremely aggressive or invasive. The fact remains that at certain points, technical neutrality, in the sense of not taking sides regarding the issues that are in conflict in the patient, may be perfectly commensurate with an intensity of affect expression that signals the therapist's availability, responsiveness, and survival, without contamination by the patient's hatred. The enactment in the transference-countertransference bind that intense types of projective identification provoke may be functional in the sense of permitting the diagnosis of the primitive object relation being enacted.

The effective management of affect storms eventually makes it possible to interpret the dominant set of object relations from surface to depth, that is, from the defensive to the impulsive side, starting from the patient's conscious, egosyntonic experience and proceeding to the unconscious, dissociated, repressed, or projected aspects of the patient's experience and the motivations for the defenses against it. This process permits the transformation of the affect storm, with its components of action and bodily responses, into a representational experience, a linkage of affect and cognition in terms of the clarification of the relation between self- and object representation within the frame of a dominant affect (Clarkin, Yeomans, and Kernberg 1999).

The psychoanalyst whose patients can tolerate a standard psychoanalytic technique may never have to address the occasional affect storm in the manner just described. But it may be an essential application of psychoanalytic technique to patients for whom most psychoanalysts would see standard psychoanalysis as contraindicated and for whom a transference-focused psychoanalytic psychotherapy may be the treatment of choice (O. Kernberg 1999).

The deadening calmness with which some patients defend against affect is a chronic behavioral enactment that is split off from the content of verbal communication. Seemingly the opposite of an affect storm, it nevertheless evokes an intense countertransference reaction that may be understood in relation to the patient's nonverbal behavior but is much more difficult to relate to what he communicates verbally, because the therapist tends to get lulled over time into accepting the patient's monotonous behavior. The therapist's problem is not so much the containment of an intolerably intense countertransference reaction as the sense of internal paralysis or guilt about increasing loss of interest in a patient who, on the surface, seems to be "so uncommunicative."

For example, one of our patients spoke in an aggressive and derogatory tone of voice, almost never looking at the therapist, while talking about various subjects apparently unrelated to this chronic aggressive demeanor. Another patient used to slouch on a couch, sipping from a water bottle, almost conveying the impression of a sleepy baby expecting to be soothed and comforted into total sleep, while filling the hours with trivial contents. The first patient reported chronic experiences of hostile reactions by other people toward her, which she interpreted as directed against everybody having her racial characteristics. The second patient would exasperate health personnel because of her effective way of extracting supplies and support for her totally passive, indolent, and parasitic lifestyle. The task in both cases, obviously, was finding a way to bring into consciousness an aspect of the therapeutic interaction that was totally dissociated from the verbal communication and yet central in the transference and in the patient's life experience outside the sessions.

The indication is for a clear, noncritical focus on what is going on in the session, raising the patients' interest in their nonverbal behavior and gradually facilitating the explanation of its transferential function. Such an approach tends to evoke strong denial, or the patient may simply ignore the therapist's comments, smile indulgently, and maintain the behavior that has been highlighted. The patient may be accustomed to receiving similar confrontations from others in less friendly ways and is prepared to neutralize them. It may be helpful to analyze the patient's view of the motivation of those others; this information provides a preview of how the patient is going to experience the therapist's confrontations. The therapist's persistence in analyzing what is going on in the session eventually transforms the monotony of behavior into a storm of affect. This represents a moment of truth, in which the violent reaction reflects the object relation against which the monotonous behavior had been a defense. At such points, the therapist may interpret that underlying object relation in what John Steiner (1993) has proposed as an "object centered" way. "Object centered" interventions facilitate an immediate analysis of the total object relation, for example, in the statement "Because you perceive me as having such hostile and derogatory ways of treating you, it is natural that your own reaction to me at this point should be like that of an enraged child scolded by a cold and cruel father."

In these situations, Winnicott's (1958) concept of "holding" and Bion's (1970) concept of "containing" are useful ways to conceptualize the therapist's capacity to integrate, in his interpretive interventions, a combined understanding of the patient's behavior and his own countertransference, without enacting the countertransference. Having said that, it needs to be added that partial enactments of countertransference responses are almost unavoidable under the trying circumstances created by repeated affect storms or the deadening patterns of defenses against them. Such partial enactment or even acting out of the countertransference does not, in my view, represent a serious danger to the treatment or a significant distortion of technical neutrality.

To the contrary, if the therapist feels comfortable with his overall approach to the patient and can honestly acknowledge, without excessive guilt or defensiveness, having lost control over his affect expression at a certain point, this may convey to the patient that affect storms are not that dangerous, that some mild loss of control is only human and doesn't preclude a return to an objective and concerned treatment relationship. At times, the therapist's expression of outrage at something outrageous communicated with a provocative calmness by the patient may be an appropriate way of maintaining contact. These patients may require, as part of the analysis of the underlying dynamics, an affectively intense investment on the part of the therapist in pointing, moment by moment, to the hidden violence behind the deadening monotony. Observed from the outside, it is as if a totally phlegmatic and controlled patient were in treatment with a hysterical or even violent therapist. The therapist himself may feel uneasy in a role that he may experience as "supportive" (because of the intense activity required) or even controlling or manipulative. The therapist, however, may have good reasons to reassure himself that his intensity is not in the service of controlling the patient's actions or of "moving" the patient in any particular direction but rather is designed to clarify what is going on by accentuating the emotional exploration of a development in the session at that moment. The therapist works, to use Bion's words, "without memory nor desire" in exploring in depth the hidden violence in the present interaction (manifest in his reading of the patient's behavior and in the countertransference). The therapist's manifest affective investment may be an important way in which he asserts his standing on the side of life and of investment in object relations, as opposed to deadly "de-objectalization." Insofar as the therapist is not pushing or encouraging or demanding in his response to the patient but is verbalizing his perception of the present interaction, this is still an "exploratory" and not a "supportive" approach.

At points during intense affect storms, whether spontaneous or following the confrontation of deadening dissociative behavior patterns in the hours, the patient may not be able to listen at all to the therapist. It is as if the patient's intolerance for developing representational expression of his own affects now includes efforts to destroy the therapist's representational expression of the patient's affective experience. In other words, the patient's destructive impulses may take the path of efforts to destroy the therapist's capacity for cognitive functioning.

The therapist has to differentiate incapacity to listen at the height of affect storms from the chronic dismissing of everything the therapist says as an expression of the "syndrome of arrogance" described by Bion (1957, 1970). As part of this syndrome, a combination of pseudostupidity, curiosity (regarding the therapist), and arrogance reflects the dominance of primitive hatred in the transference, together with the patient's incapacity to tolerate the awareness of his own hatred. Acting out totally replaces the ordinary subjective awareness of affective experience. There are still other patients whose chronic dismissal of what comes from the therapist is part of narcissistic resistances in the transference that need to be resolved with the usual interpretive approaches to the intolerance of a dependent relation to the therapist (see Chapters 3 and 8).

Returning to the problem of affect storms, there are times when the therapist has to wait until the intensity of the affect storm subsides before making an interpretive comment; at other times, it may be helpful simply to ask the patient if he believes that he would be able to tolerate a comment from the therapist at that point. I find it helpful, at times, to tell the patient that I have thoughts on my mind that I am hesitant to spell out, because I do not know whether the patient might react to them with such vehement anger that he would have difficulty understanding what I am trying to say. If the patient then tells me, ragefully, that he does not want to hear anything from me, I may remain silent for the moment and only later interpret what the reasons might be for the patient's intolerance of any communication from me.

Under such circumstances, it is helpful if the therapist first ascertains whether his intervention already includes the elaboration of the countertransference disposition that is part of the material included in his planned intervention. If the therapist experiences himself as controlled by the countertransference, this is an indication for waiting and internal elaboration before intervening. It is also extremely important that the therapist feel safe in his intervention, because to be afraid of the patient is to send a powerful message that cannot but increase fear in the patient; at such times, the patient's rage is a defense against his fear of his own aggression. The therapist's physical, psychological, professional, and legal safety are indispensable preconditions for work with very regressed patients, and the therapist must take whatever measures are necessary to assure that safety; this is a precondition for effective concern for the safety of the patient.

One important complication in the psychodynamic psychotherapy of borderline patients is the danger of the "spilling over" of severe affect storms from the sessions into the patient's life outside the sessions. For example, one patient developed an intensely erotic attachment to the therapist and felt that if the therapist were not to leave his wife and all other emotional commitments and dedicate himself solely to the patient, her life would no longer be worth living. This intense erotic transference contained, as may seem obvious, significantly preoedipal elements, the desperate claim of a baby to have the exclusive attention of her mother. On the surface, however, it took the form of a "falling in love" that became so disturbing to the patient that she expressed to her husband her despair about the therapist's failure to respond to her love. This of course threatened her marriage as well as the treatment.

Under such circumstances, it may become important to set limits on the patient's behavior outside the hours or even to intervene directly in the patient's life, with a clear understanding that this means a significant move away from technical neutrality, requiring its interpretive reinstatement later on (Clarkin, Yeomans and Kernberg 1999). These, fortunately, are rare complications when general concern is taken to maintain clear treatment boundaries. If, however, the therapist ignores or does not systematically interpret acting out of the transference, major "spilling over" into the patient's external life becomes much more likely. For example, one patient lingered on in the therapist's waiting room over a period of hours. Because this acting out in the transference was not addressed in the sessions, the patient ended up practically sleeping in the waiting room all day long, creating serious complications both for the patient and for the therapist's professional practice.

SOME PARTICULAR COMPLICATIONS
OF SEVERE AFFECT STORMS

Some patients learn to use affect storms to frighten family members and the therapist, eventually controlling the therapist by instilling fearful avoidance of dealing with particular issues. Some inexperienced therapists may remain paralyzed by fear of losing both the patient and the supervisor's favorable opinion if they confront the patient with the intimidating behavior. Therapists of difficult borderline patients need the support of their supervisors and their peers so as not to be judged negatively if the patient disrupts the treatment, and they need to be helped to face this situation by evaluating all the paranoid fantasies that the patient may induce in the therapist's mind.

Patients "spoiled" by a lifetime of success in intimidating others may threaten to injure the therapist or objects in the therapist's office, to declare vehemently an intention to end the treatment because of rage at the therapist, or to threaten lawsuits. The therapist must maintain the boundaries of the treatment and so structure the situation as to be able to maintain control without being provoked into a "counterprovocative" mode, threatening the patient with certain action unless the patient "behaves." The situation is best handled by means of a calm statement that reclarifies the conditions under which the treatment can be maintained, perhaps a comment indicating that the therapist would be sad if the treatment had to be interrupted because the patient was not willing or able to maintain these conditions, followed by interpretation of the unconscious functions of the patient's behavior.

A therapist may be taken aback by the extent to which certain outrageous behavior patterns are second nature to the patient. If the therapist feels that the therapeutic relationship has not developed sufficiently for an effective exploration of this behavior and postpones addressing it for too long, the therapist may cease to expect any different behavior from the patient. Chronically self-destructive behavior patterns that express severe regression, such as staying away from work, avoiding interactions with significant others, or rationalizing an isolated, vegetative, or parasitic lifestyle may remain so egosyntonic that, when the therapist finally raises questions about them, the patient may react with intense indignation. The implicit threat of violence or of abandoning the treatment when the patient's lifestyle is being questioned, or a consistently dismissive reaction to the therapist's efforts to examine this issue, may induce in the therapist an internal state of passively giving up.

Probably there are thousands of borderline patients who have managed to lead empty lifestyles in order to obtain medical disability support, becoming dependent on more fortunate family members or on endless welfare support, or ending up with a life restricted to obtaining pleasure from food, drugs, or alcohol or simply from sleeping and watching television. Often these patients turn out to be highly intelligent, well-educated people whose early traumatic experiences and severe pathology of object relations in adolescence are followed by a gradual extinction of all investments in intimate encounters, sexual life, work, and other interests. When eating remains as almost their only pleasure in life such patients reach middle age morbidly obese, physically neglected, welfare-"contained." They enter psychoanalytic psychotherapy with the typical "deadening" transference that replicates their destruction of object relations in ordinary life. The therapist is faced with the dissociation between verbal content and nonverbal manifestations in the hours plus the corresponding countertransference activation mentioned above. Psychodynamically, the unconscious identification with a sadistic object whose love is assured only by the patient's self-destructive submission to it may now become manifest in attacks on the therapist and treatment, the patient projecting an unrealistic demanding self onto the therapist. The identification with a "dead mother" described by André Green (1993b) may be a specialized instance of this development.

In these cases, the activation of primitive affect storms in the hours may be the first sign of psychological life for many years. These are extremely difficult cases; the prognostic indicators for change include, in addition to at least normal intelligence, the absence of antisocial behavior and the possibility of reducing secondary gain via an active work situation that, eventually, will provide more gratification than that obtained from a parasitic social support system. If the patient has been able to maintain some semblance of object relations and a stable work situation or professional engagement, the prognosis is much better.

Some patients test the limits of the therapist's tolerance in ways that are difficult to control without the therapist's feeling inappropriately punitive. Examples include patients who neglect themselves physically, smell bad, and make the therapist's waiting area and office space unpleasant for others; patients whose erotic seductiveness takes primitive forms such as arriving without underwear and exposing themselves in the hours in subtle enough ways that the therapist is concerned about whether confronting this behavior may be experienced by the patient as an erotic seduction or an attack; patients whose aggressive behavior takes the form of chronically insulting not only the therapist but his office personnel, with potentially damaging door-slamming and throwing of objects in the therapist's office space. Obviously, these are not behaviors that are expected from patients in standard psychoanalytic treatment. Senior therapists often refuse to treat such patients. Junior therapists, in turn, may lack the experience to deal effectively with such extreme and yet, at times, subtly disguised behaviors.

Unless the therapist explicitly informs the patient of what he can and cannot tolerate, it may not be possible to analyze the patient's motivation for behavior that makes the therapist uncomfortable. When the patient's behavior exceeds limits that have not been clearly spelled out in advance, it is helpful for the therapist to be direct and matter-of-fact in specifying the behavior he cannot accept, without any interpretive effort at that point. It may be neither possible nor necessary to justify, on the basis of therapeutic principles, why some specific behaviors need to be limited. For example, a patient may start taking books from the therapist's bookshelf and examining them without having asked the therapist's permission. Such mild yet maddening presumptions of intimacy and entitlement cannot be addressed as long as doing so will restrict the therapist's technical neutrality. If the therapist returns to such behaviors at a later point, when their transference implications have become available for interpretive work, and technical neutrality is thus restored, these situations can be resolved very satisfactorily. What is important is that the therapist feel comfortable within the treatment structure and able to maintain it in the long run without experiencing himself as unduly restricted.

There are patients who express an unconscious tendency to burn all the bridges behind them—and before them—through a subtle, unobtrusively alienating behavior in the hours. It can take the form of repetitive dismissal of whatever comes from the therapist or of a chronic lack of concern for themselves expressed by consistently missing sessions, coming late, or declaring the wish to end the treatment as part of minor tantrums. In the long run the therapist may be tempted to agree with the patient that the treatment is useless and be relieved at the prospect of ending the attempt. This, on the surface, does not represent an affect storm in the ordinary sense but a gradual erosion of the therapist's emotional involvement and commitment to the patient, and eventually it requires only a relatively minor acting out on the part of the patient to provoke the therapist into colluding with ending the treatment. The diagnosis of such a condition in the course of its development is equivalent to diagnosing the chronic countertransference distortions that may occur also with much less severely ill patients and without the serious consequences they have here. It is important to transform such a slippery road into an active exploration. Insofar as it is the destructiveness of the patient that is insidiously producing deterioration of the therapeutic relationship, an active clarification and confrontation of that situation unmasks the violence of the destructive impulses unconsciously expressed by the patient. This unmasking may initially feel to the therapist like violent behavior on his own part, a countertransference reaction that requires analysis.

Some of these patients may evoke in the therapist the emotional conviction that they are less than real or less than human or that ordinary responses of concern for themselves and their lives cannot be expected of them. Eventually the therapist may realize that his hopeful expectations for the treatment have begun to erode. I am talking about hopefulness in the sense of a conviction that, if the patient made a real effort, he would be able to achieve a life situation much more satisfactory than the one in which he is presently paralyzed. The loss of this hope or expectation represents a serious countertransference problem, complicating and threatening the psychotherapy in a basic way.

There are patients who appear to utilize the passage of time to destroy themselves and the treatment in unobtrusive ways. By wasting time in the sessions they implicitly deny the value and the transitory nature of life itself. A general attitude that may be helpful to the therapist is to combine a long-range patience in working through the same issues again and again with a clear sense of impatience in each session, interpreting again and again the patient's efforts to eliminate the significance of each concrete encounter with the therapist. Yielding to the temptation of the opposite behavior—that is, endless patience (actually mere passivity) in each session, while a chronic impatience accumulates in the therapist and disposes him to a sudden, impatient rejection of the patient, determined by an outburst of negative countertransference—is a major danger in such cases.

A tendency of some patients toward a masochistic exploitation of the therapeutic situation may be uncannily linked to the development of perversity in the transference. I am referring to patients who use the fact that they are in a psychotherapeutic treatment as a defense against the anxiety caused by their deteriorating life situation. It is as if, as long as they are in therapy and can harbor the unconscious fantasy that now the therapist carries the responsibility for their life, they may abandon realistic anxiety or depression about the destructiveness of their situation. Other patients implicitly challenge the therapist to change their life situation, with an unconscious and sometimes conscious sense of triumph over the therapist's inability to effect change in their circumstances. Unconscious envy of the therapist, particularly prominent in severe narcissistic pathology, may express itself in this way; such patients may unconsciously arrange for the treatment to harm them by choosing a therapist whose location requires inordinate travel time or costs too much or who cannot schedule sessions that do not interfere with vital aspects of personal life or work. The linkage of this complication with the syndrome of perversity consists in the implicit recruitment of the love, concern, and dedication implied in the therapist's work in the service of self-directed and other-directed aggression (O. Kernberg 1992a).

There are patients who develop chronic affect storms in the sessions as a vicarious living-out of conflicts that usually are under control in their ordinary life. Here a particular use of the treatment as "secondary gain" is an expression of a more general tendency of some borderline patients to replace life with the treatment interaction. This development becomes obvious over a period of time in which interpretations seem not to bring about any change in the material of the sessions and, at the same time, the patient's withdrawal from all other life situations, the emptiness and immobility he evinces outside the sessions, express a sharp contrast with what is going on in the treatment. This secondary gain needs to be interpreted consistently, and its destructive effects on the patient's life and on the treatment must be gradually clarified and interpreted.

The destructive and self-destructive impulses of some patients are so powerful that the unconscious pleasure in destroying the treatment overshadows any concern these patients may have for improving their life situation and psychological functioning. It is as if the triumph over the therapist's efforts to help were the only unconscious source of pleasure remaining in the patient's life. At times, setting a realistic time limit to a treatment in which such a "recruitment of love at the service of aggression" has taken place may present the last opportunity for the patient within this treatment frame. This situation may be considered a particular case of the development of perversity within the transference and usually presents in patients with severe narcissistic pathology, particularly the syndrome of malignant narcissism (O. Kernberg 1992a).

I referred above to patients who, instead of either severe affect storms or monotonous deadening of the hour, present a chronic, agitated, traumatophilic, histrionic, or chaotic affect display both in the transference and outside the therapeutic setting. The diagnosis of the dominant object relation throughout that apparent chaos is essential if one is to interpret and modify this pattern. In these cases, one must carefully evaluate whether such a chronic affective pattern masks an undiagnosed secondary gain, such as the destructive undermining of intimate relationships or of potentially satisfactory work situations.

When antisocial behaviors complicate the situation further, such behaviors require early attention, because they signal most clearly the destructive attempts directed at the patient's object relations. Irresponsibility toward the management of money and unconscious or conscious eroding of the support system that permits the treatment to be carried out are alarm signals that the treatment is under attack. Because such behaviors are often intimately woven into the patient's chaotic life system they may initially be neglected.

The interpretation of behaviors that reduce active therapeutic time has to take precedence over everything else. The patient may attempt to seduce the therapist with life crises that would seem to be extremely urgent, while simultaneously underusing the therapeutic space and thus denying the therapist sufficient time to examine the crisis. Irresponsible exploitation of relatives who are supporting the patient's treatment and acting out the negative transference by undermining the therapist in the eyes of those whom the patient needs for the treatment to be maintained are other manifestations of perversity, in the sense that the therapist's technical neutrality and respect for the patient are exploited in the service of expressing unbridled aggression toward him and destruction of the therapeutic relationship.

Quite frequently, a severe transferential acting out and an apparently unrelated, urgent life situation occur simultaneously in the session. The therapist is faced with an apparently impossible dilemma: Focusing on the life crisis prompts the patient to triumphantly insist that the therapist's efforts to understand the crisis do not help at all. If, on the other hand, the therapist focuses on what is going on in the transference, the patient indignantly complains that the therapist is "narcissistically" concentrating on what refers to himself, while neglecting the urgent situation the patient is facing. Patients who use such "double-edged affect storms" with some frequency manage to create extremely chaotic treatment situations in which the therapist finds it difficult to orient himself.

There are several approaches that may help under such conditions: first, to decide, session by session, what seems most urgent. If the crisis in the patient's external life indeed has a dangerous quality of urgency, it should be explored fully while keeping in mind that the patient may well undermine any attempt at collaboration with the therapist. If such a "blockage" occurs, one should revert to the analysis of the transference situation as an impediment to helping the patient understand what is going on outside the sessions. Second, in some cases, particularly if it is a relatively early manifestation of this pattern and the therapist is as yet uncertain how to deal with it in an integrated way, it may be helpful to suggest a temporary increase in the frequency of sessions in order to have more time to deal with the emotional crisis in the patient's life and with its transference implications. The risk, of course, is of inadvertently encouraging the patient to use affect storms to extract more time from the therapist. This eventually will have to be explored.

To begin with, however, the additional time may enable the therapist to become clearly aware of the defensive nature of the double-edged affect storms and to convey this awareness to the patient. Gradually an emphasis on the analysis of the transference can be developed as a precondition for permitting the patient to utilize what he may be receiving in the treatment and to understand why he is not able to utilize it in his daily life. Given the standard frequency of two psychotherapeutic sessions per week in our research project, an increase to three sessions per week for a limited period of time seemed reasonable for such patients and could be reduced once the situation was under control. A three-session-per-week schedule might seem helpful over an extended period of time, but a very careful analysis may reveal that coming to the sessions is acquiring the secondary gain of escaping from the tasks of the patient's life situation. In our experience, a frequency of two sessions per week is the very minimum in which transference-focused psychotherapy can be carried out. Three sessions per week may be optimal for many cases, but four sessions per week, in our experience, do not increase the progression of the treatment. To the contrary, four or more sessions per week tend to increase the secondary gain of "treatment replacing life" for these severely regressed patients.

Patients with unlimited financial means present a special problem in the sense that the absence of the usual necessity to weigh cost against benefit decreases the motivation of patient and therapist to examine the meaning of a gradual increase in the frequency of psychotherapy sessions. The patient and the therapist experience the additional sessions as indispensable because any discussion of restoring the original frequency generates intense anxiety in the patient. Yet a careful analysis of the material usually reveals an unconscious destruction of what the patient is receiving from the therapist as the driving force in increasing the number of sessions. The analysis of the patient's unconscious destruction of what he receives may make it possible to revert to a more reasonable schedule that prevents the treatment from replacing life.

A CLINICAL CASE ILLUSTRATION

The patient was a twenty-eight-year-old woman with a borderline personality organization and a narcissistic personality, functioning on an overt borderline level. Her main difficulties were chronic suicidal behavior, inability to maintain a work situation in spite of having obtained two master's degrees in the biological sciences, and lack of gratifying, stable sexual or love relationships. Her chaotic relations with men would evolve into severely sadomasochistic interactions with eventual rupture of the relationship. She had drifted from one subordinate job to another and experienced severe affect storms and chronic fights with her family members, leading to such isolation from them that at one point she almost became a "street person."

The sessions with her had been marked by intense affect storms and by the patient's rejecting practically everything I said, distorting my statements into attacks aimed at her. She had expressed endless complaints about my coldness, indifference, invasiveness, and cruelty and given endless descriptions of the warm, friendly, understanding, and spiritually lifting quality of previous therapies in which she had engaged. It was she herself, of course, who let me know that most of these therapeutic encounters were of brief duration, except with one psychotherapist who practically adopted her and blurred the boundaries between therapy and personal friendship. The treatment with me was in its second year, the longest she had remained in a treatment situation, and in the context of this treatment she had been able to take up and maintain a job commensurate with her knowledge and experience, for the first time in her life. The suicide attempts had stopped, her impulsive and chaotic relations with men had decreased, and the relationship with her family had become less stormy, although it is not an exaggeration to say that "all hell would break loose" in most sessions with me.

To summarize the outstanding dynamics of her case: her mother was a chronically alcohol-dependent person who eventually developed an organic brain syndrome secondary to alcohol dependency. During the later years of the patient's childhood and adolescence the mother remained in bed, in a semicomatose state. The father, a respected college professor, tried to "discipline" the patient, his youngest daughter, who, in contrast to her older siblings, evolved as a major source of concern for him because of her severe behavioral disturbance from early adolescence onward. He tried to interfere with the patient's chaotic sexual life, and she experienced him as both intrusive and jealous of her relations with other men.

Starting early in the transference, she alternated between times of violent and complaining behavior and a haughty grandiosity and pseudostupidity that seemed to reflect closely Bion's description of the syndrome of arrogance. At other times, a subdued, complaining, yet subtly erotically seductive behavior prevailed. In this phase she presented herself in minimal acceptable clothing and engaged in clearly exhibitionist behavior. Early interpretations had focused on her fear that only a caring father could protect her from the empty indifference of the relationship with the mother but that such a concerned father would invariably become sexually seductive and exploit her. There was no history of sexual abuse reported by this patient, and it was not difficult to interpret her fear that any concern of mine for her would seem a sexual exploitiveness as a projection onto me of her own wishes to seduce the father, the only alternative to the catastrophic unavailability of the mother.

In simple terms, either I was perceived as intrusive, invasive, and potentially sexually seductive or as cold, indifferent, and lethargic. In recent months, this behavior shifted into ever more powerful rage attacks. She accused me violently of not listening, of distorting what she said, of imprisoning her in this treatment. She seemed totally impervious to all my interpretations. She attempted to throw objects at me and managed to damage minor objects in the room; on a few occasions, I had to forcefully warn her that any further damage to any object in the room or a physical attack on me would mean the immediate end of the session. She learned exactly what her limits were and often would stand in front of me, shaking her hands and yelling at me.

The present session started exactly with such a development of intense rage and yelling. I pointed out to her that she had left the last session talking with me calmly about a problem at work, and I gave indications that my helping her to sort out her emotional reaction to a subordinate at work had helped her decide how to handle the situation. Because of that, I went on, I wondered whether she now had to create a scene and attempt to provoke me into a rage because of her own experience of hatred and violence as an expression of profound guilt about the implications of having moments of good relations with me. After this comment of mine the patient got much worse, accusing me even further of total ignorance, distortion, lack of memory of what had happened in the last session, and focusing only on her relationship with me, rather than on the terrible problems she had to face at work every day.

My next comment was that she was feeling much worse after I pointed out that she maintained a fighting situation because she could not stand the memory of good moments in her work with me. I wondered whether now she felt that I was trying to make her feel guilty because of her treating me in this way after the good relation that had evolved in the last session. The patient interrupted me several times, and in apparently repeating what I said, completely distorted my words.

At that point I grew impatient, and in a strong voice told her that she was talking sheer nonsense and that she knew it perfectly well. I illustrated, point by point, in what way she had just distorted everything that I had just said, interrupting her as loudly as she would interrupt me while I was trying to say this. Retrospectively, this acting out of my countertransference was probably motivated only in part by her rage attacks, to which I had already become quite well-adjusted, and reflected in part an impatience and irritability of mine having to do with unrelated administrative problems that had emerged on that particular day. In any case, I thought, as soon as I had finished talking, that I had enacted the hateful, persecutory object that she had unconsciously projected onto me. I had reacted as the victim of a sadistic, overwhelming, invasive, hateful object, becoming myself such an object in turn, attempting to reproject the victim role onto her.

While I was thinking along these lines, the patient, to my big surprise, responded in a totally natural voice, and in a thoughtful way, that I couldn't tolerate her affect storms: Wasn't the treatment geared to permit her to express herself freely in the hours? After a little while, recovering from my shock, I said:

"I am impressed by the fact that you can only talk to me in a normal way if I talk to you as loudly and harshly as you talked to me before. I wonder whether this is a confirmation that you can't tolerate it if I talk to you in a thoughtful, calm way as if talking to an adult, rational woman. Or maybe," I went on, "only when I yell at you can you really believe that I care. When I calmly try to help you understand what is going on, you experience that as indifference or phoniness." Now the patient remained silent, and after a few minutes started to cry. She then said that I did not know how much she was suffering. I wondered whether perhaps the only way in which she felt able to let me know how much she was suffering was to attempt to provoke me with hateful behavior, so that I could experience the sense of impotence and paralysis that she had mentioned she experienced at times at work. Shortly after this exchange the hour ended.

One may interpret this situation as the effect of projective identification of a primitive, hatred-dominated, persecutory object and the partial acting out in the countertransference of this projected object by the process of projective counteridentification. In other words, the relation between a sadistic object and its victim, possibly a very primitive layer of experience reflecting the deeply dissociated hatred of an unavailable mother or the relation with a "doped" mother who could only be aroused by violence, had been enacted now. But the reversal of this relation, which might have been expected as the consequence of my countertransferential acting out, did not occur, and, to the contrary, the patient was able to register for the first time in this session my communication to her. This clinical vignette illustrates the complexity, challenges, and risks involved in the diagnosis and management of affect storms.

At the end, in successful treatments, affects are translated into a relation between self-representations and object representations. The result of integrative interpretation of primitive transferences is resolution of identity diffusion and the integration of the internal world of objects. The overall objective of retransforming somatization and acting out into a full emotional experience will coincide with what in Kleinian terms is the depressive position and in traditional ego-psychological terms the consolidation of ego identity. In Peter Fonagy's terms, patients achieve the capacity for mentalization and self-reflectiveness, and in André Green's terms the capacity of preconscious functioning with fantasy, daydreams and dreaming, and the full capacity for symbolic representation. In the process, we expect patients who are able to benefit from this treatment to be able to resume a satisfactory love life, intimacy and friendship, creativity and effectiveness in work, and the finding of their own ways of satisfaction and creativity in other areas of their life.

References

Abraham, K. (1919). A particular form of neurotic resistance against the psycho-analytic method. In: *Selected Papers on Psychonalysis*. New York: Brunner/ Mazel, 1979, pp. 303–311.

———. (1920). Manifestations of the female castration complex. In: *Selected Papers on Psycho-Analysis*. London: Hogarth Press, 1927, pp. 338–369.

———. (1921–1925). Psycho-analytical studies on character formation. In: *Selected Papers on Psycho-Analysis*. London: Hogarth Press, 1927, pp. 370–417.

Akhtar, S. (1989). Narcissistic personality disorder: Descriptive features and differential diagnosis. In: *Narcissistic Personality Disorder: Psychiatric Clinics of North America*. Otto F. Kernberg, ed. Philadelphia: W. B. Saunders, pp. 505–530.

———. (1992). *Broken Structures*. Northvale, N.J.: Jason Aronson.

Akhtar, S., and Thompson, J. A., Jr. (1982). Overview: Narcissistic personality disorder. *American Journal of Psychiatry* 139:12–20.

Alexandris, A., and Vaslamatzis, G. (1993). *Countertransference: Theory, Technique, Teaching*. London: Karnac Books.

American Psychiatric Association. (1968). *Diagnostic and Statistical Manual of Mental Disorders: DSM-II*. Washington, D.C.: American Psychiatric Association.

———. (1980). *Diagnostic and Statistical Manual of Mental Disorders: DSM-III*. Washington, D.C.: American Psychiatric Association.

————. (1987). *Diagnostic and Statistical Manual of Mental Disorders (Third Edition, Revised): DSM-III-R.* Washington, D.C.: American Psychiatric Association.

————. (1994). *Diagnostic and Statistical Manual of Mental Disorders: DSM-IV.* Washington, D.C.: American Psychiatric Association.

Aulagnier, P. (1981). *La Violence de L'Interpretation.* Paris: Presses Universitaires de France.

Bach, S. (1977a). On the narcissistic state of consciousness. *International Journal of Psychoanalysis* 58:209–233.

————. (1977b). On narcissistic fantasies. *International Review of Psychoanalysis* 4:281–293.

Bataille, G. (1957). *L'Erotisme.* Paris: Minuit.

Benjamin, L. S. (1992). An interpersonal approach to the diagnosis of borderline personality disorder. In: *Borderline Personality Disorder.* John F. Clarkin et al., eds. New York: Guilford Press, pp. 161–198.

————. (1993). *Interpersonal Diagnosis and Treatment of Personality Disorders.* New York: Guilford Press.

Bion, W. R. (1957). On arrogance. In: *Second Thoughts: Selected Papers on Psychoanalysis.* New York: Basic Books, 1968, pp. 86–92.

————. (1958). On arrogance. *International Journal of Psychoanalysis* 39:144–146.

————. (1961). *Experiences in Groups.* New York: Basic Books.

————. (1967). Notes on memory and desire. *Psychoanalysis Forum* 2:272–273, 279–280.

————. (1968). *Second Thoughts: Selected Papers on Psychoanalysis.* New York: Basic Books.

————. (1970). *Attention and Interpretation.* London: Heinemann.

Blum, H. P., ed. (1985). *Defense and Resistance: Historical Perspective and Current Concepts.* New York: International Universities Press.

Boris, H. N. (1984a). On the treatment of anorexia nervosa. *International Journal of Psychoanalysis* 65:435–442.

————. (1984b). The problem of anorexia nervosa. *International Journal of Psychoanalysis* 65:315–322.

Boskind-Lodahl, M. (1976). Cinderella's stepsisters: A feminist perspective on anorexia nervosa and bulimia. *Signs* 2:342–356.

Bruch, H. (1973). *Eating Disorders.* New York: Basic Books.

————. (1985). Four decades of eating disorders. In: *Handbook of Psychotherapy for Anorexia and Bulimia.* D. M. Garner and P. E. Garkinkel, eds. New York: Guilford Press.

Bursten, B. (1989). The relationship between narcissistic and antisocial personalities. *Psychiatric Clinics of North America* 12(3):571–584.

Cahn, R. (1996). Psychotherapies des névroses et des psychoses. In: *Psychanalyse,* by A. de Mijolla and S. de Mijolla-Mellor. Paris: Presses Universitaires de France.

Carpy, D. (1989). Tolerating the countertransference: A mutative process. *International Journal of Psychoanalysis* 70:287–294.

Chasseguet-Smirgel, J. (1984). *Creativity and Perversion.* New York: W. W. Norton.

————. (1989). The bright face of narcissism and its shadowy depths: A few reflections. *Psychiatric Clinics of North America* 12(3):709–722.

Clarkin, J. F., P. A. Foelsch, K. N. Levy, J. W. Hull, J. C. Delaney, and O. F. Kernberg. (2001). The development of a psychodynamic treatment for patients with borderline personality disorder: A preliminary study of behavioral changes. *Journal of Personality Disorders* 15(6):487–495.

Clarkin, J. F., J. W. Hull, F. Yeomans, T. Kakuma, and J. Cantor. (1994). Antisocial traits as modifiers of treatment response in borderline patients. *Journal of Psychotherapy Practice and Research* 3:307–143.

Clarkin, J. F., H. Koenigsberg, F. Yeomans, M. Selzer, O. F. Kernberg, and P. Kernberg. (1992). Psychodynamic psychotherapy of the borderline patient. In: *Borderline Personality Disorder.* John F. Clarkin, E. Marziali, and H. Munroe-Blum, eds. New York: Guilford Press, pp. 268–287.

Clarkin, J. F., F. Yeomans, and O. F. Kernberg. (1998). *Treatment of Borderline Personality.* New York: Wiley.

———. (1999). *Psychotherapy for the Borderline Personality.* New York: Wiley.

Cleckley, H. (1941). *The Mask of Sanity.* St. Louis: Mosby.

Cloninger, C. R., et al. (1993). A psychobiological model of temperament and character. *Archives of General Psychiatry* 50:975–990.

Cooper, A. M. (1989). Narcissism and masochism: The narcissistic-masochistic character. *Psychiatric Clinics of North America* 12(3):541–552.

Costa, P. T., and T. A. Widiger. (1994). Introduction to *Personality Disorders and the Five-Factor Model of Personality.* P. T. Costa and T. Widiger, eds. Washington, D.C.: American Psychological Association, pp. 1–10.

Depue, R. A. (1996). A neurobiological framework for the structure of personality and emotion: Implications for personality disorders. In: *Major Theories of Personality Disorders.* J. F. Clarkin and M. F. Lenzenweger, eds. New York: Guilford Press, pp. 347–383.

deVagvar, M. L., et al. (1994). Impulsivity and serotonin in borderline personality disorder. In: *Biological and Neurobehavioral Studies of Borderline Personality Disorder.* K. R. Silk, ed. Washington, D.C.: American Psychiatric Press, pp. 23–40.

Dicks, H. V. (1967). *Marital Tension.* New York: Basic Books.

Ellis, H. (1898). Auto-eroticism: A psychological study. *Alienist and Neurologist* 19:260–299.

Erikson, E. (1956a). The problem of ego identity. In *Identity and the Life Cycle.* New York: International Universities Press, 1959, pp. 104–164.

———. (1956b). The problem of ego identity. *Journal of the American Psychoanalytic Association* 4:56–121.

Etchegoyen, R. H. (1991). *Fundamentals of Psychoanalytic Technique.* New York: Karnac Books.

Ezriel, H. (1950). A psychoanalytic approach to the treatment of patients in groups. *Journal of Mental Science* 96:774–779.

Fairbairn, W. (1954). *An Object Relations Theory of the Personality.* New York: Basic Books.

Fenichel, O. (1945). *The Psychoanalytic Theory of Neurosis.* New York: W. W. Norton.

Fonagy, P. (2000). The development of representation. Paper presented at the Lindauer Psychotherapiewochen, April 15, 1999.

Fonagy, P., and Target, M. (2000). Playing with reality III: The persistence of dual psychic reality in borderline patients. Paper presented to the Borderline Symposium, the Munich Institute of the German Psychoanalytical Association, April 2000.

Foulkes, S. H., and E. J. Anthony. (1957). *Group Psychotherapy: The Psychoanalytic Approach*. Baltimore: Penguin Books.

Fraiberg, A. (1983). Pathological defenses in infancy. *Psychoanalytic Quarterly* 60:612–635.

Freud, S. (1905). Three essays on the theory of sexuality. *S.E.* 7:125–245. London: Hogarth Press, 1953.

———. (1908). Character and anal eroticism. *S.E.* 9:167–175. London: Hogarth Press, 1953.

———. (1913). Totem and taboo. *S.E.* 13:1–164. London: Hogarth Press, 1955.

———. (1914). On narcissism. *S.E.* 14:67–102. London: Hogarth Press, 1957.

———. (1915). Instincts and their vicissitudes. *S.E.* 14:109–140. London: Hogarth Press, 1957.

———. (1916). Some character-types met with in psycho-analytic work. *S.E.* 14:309–333. London: Hogarth Press, 1957.

———. (1919). "A child is being beaten": A contribution to the study of the origin of sexual perversions. *S.E.* 17:175–204. London: Hogarth Press, 1955.

———. (1921). Group psychology. *S.E.* 18:67–143. London: Hogarth Press, 1955.

———. (1927). Fetishism. *S.E.* 21:147–158. London: Hogarth Press, 1961.

———. (1930). Civilization and its discontents. *S.E.* 21:59–243. London: Hogarth Press, 1961.

———. (1931). Libidinal types. *S.E.* 21:215–220. London: Hogarth Press, 1961.

———. (1940). Splitting of the ego in the process of defense. *S.E.* 23:273–274. London: Hogarth Press, 1964.

Galenson, E. (1986). Some thoughts about infant psychopathology and aggressive development. *Internationl Review of Psychoanalysis* 13:349–354.

Gibeault, A. (1998). *A La découverte de L'arrière-Pays*. Du processus analytique en psychanalyse et en psychotherapie.

Gill, M. M. (1954). Psychoanalysis and exploratory psychotherapy. *Journal of the American Psychoanalytic Association* 2:771–797.

Goldberg, A. (1989). Self-psychology and the narcissistic personality. *Psychiatric Clinics of North America* 12(3):731.

Green, A. (1993a). *Le Travail du Négatif*. Paris: Les Editions de Minuit.

———. (1993b). *On Private Madness*. Madison, Conn.: International Universities Press.

———. (1997). *Las Chaînes d'Eros: Actualité du Sexuel*. Paris: Editions Odile Jacob.

———. (2000). La Position phobic centrale. In *La Pensée clinique*. Paris: Editions Odile Jacob.

Grinberg, L. (1993). Countertransference and the concept of projective counteridentification. In: *Countertransference: Theory, Technique, Teaching*. A. Alexandris and G. Vaslamatzis, eds. London: Karnac Books, pp. 47–65.

Grossman, W. (1986). Notes on masochism: A discussion of the history and development of a psychoanalytic concept. *Psychoanalytic Quarterly* 55:379–413.

———. (1991). Pain, aggression, fantasy, and concepts of sadomasochism. *Psychoanalytic Quarterly* 60:22–52.

Grunberger, B. (1979). *Narcissism: Psychoanalytic Essays*. New York: International Universities Press.

———. (1989). *New Essays on Narcissism*. London: Free Association Books.

Guttmacher, M. (1961). Pseudopsychopathic schizophrenia. *Archives of Criminal Psychodynamics* (Special Psychopathy Issue), pp. 502–508.

Hamilton, N. G. (1990). The containing function and the analyst's projective identification. *International Journal of Psychoanalysis* 71:445–453.

Hare, R. D. (1970). *Psychopathy: Theory and Research.* New York: Wiley.

———. (1986). Twenty years of experience with the Cleckley psychopath. In: *Unmasking the Psychopath.* William H. Reid et al., eds. New York: Norton, pp. 3–27.

———. (1991). *Manual for the Hare Psychopathy Checklist—Revised.* Toronto: Health Care Systems.

Hare, R. D., and S. Hart. (1995). Commentary on antisocial personality disorder. In Livesley, J., *The DSM-IV Personality Disorders.* New York: Guilford Press, 127–134.

Hare, R. D., and Shalling, E. (1978). *Psychopathic Behavior: Approaches to Research.* New York: Wiley.

Hare, R. D., S. Hart, and T. Harpur. (1991). Psychopathy and the DSM-IV criteria for antisocial personality disorder. *Journal of Abnormal Psychology* 100:391–398.

Heimann, P. (1950). On countertransference. *International Journal of Psychoanalysis* 31:81–84.

Henderson, D. K. (1939). *Psychopathic States.* London: Chapman and Hall.

Henderson, D. K., and R. D. Gillespie. (1969). *Textbook of Psychiatry: For Students and Practitioners,* 10th ed., rev. I. R. C. Batchelor. London: Oxford University Press.

Hoffman, L., and K. Halmi. (1993). Treatment of anorexia nervosa. In: *Current Psychiatric Therapy.* D. Dunner, ed. Philadelphia: W. B. Saunders, pp. 390–396.

Holder, A. (1970). Instinct and drive. In: *Basic Psychoanalytic Concepts of the Theory of Instincts.* H. Nagera, ed. New York: Basic Books, 3:19–22.

Horowitz, M. J. (1989). Clinical phenomenology of narcissistic pathology. *Psychiatric Clinics of North America* 12(3):531–539.

Hull, J. W., J. F. Clarkin, and T. Kakuma. (1993). Treatment response of borderline inpatients: A growth curve analysis. *Journal of Nervous and Mental Disease* 181(8): 503–508.

Israel, P. (1998). Report of the committee on psychoanalysis and allied psychotherapies of the Executive Council of the IPA.

Jacobson, E. (1953). On the psychoanalytic theory of affects. In: *Depression.* New York: International Universities Press, 1971, pp. 3–47.

———. (1964). *The Self and Object World.* New York: International Universities Press.

———. (1967). *Psychotic Conflict and Reality.* New York: International Universities Press.

———. (1971a). *Depression.* New York: International Universities Press.

———. (1971b). Acting and the urge to betray in paranoid patients. In: *Depression.* New York: International Universities Press, pp. 302–318.

———. (1971c). *Depression: Comparative Studies of Normal, Neurotic, and Psychotic Conditions.* New York: International Universities Press.

Jeammet, P. H. (1996). Psychodrame psychanalytique individuel. In: *Psychanalyse et psychotherapies.* D. Widlöcher and A. Braconnier, eds. Paris: Flammarion, pp. 33–43.

Jonas, J. M., and H. G. Pope. (1992). Axis I comorbidity of borderline personality disorder: Clinical implications. In: *Borderline Personality Disorder.* John F. Clarkin et al., eds. New York: Guilford Press, pp. 149–160.

Jones, E. (1955). The God complex. In: *Essays in Applied Psycho-Analysis*. E. Jones, ed. New York: International Universities Press, 1964, 2:244–265.

Joseph, B. (1989). *Psychic Equilibrium and Psychic Change*. London: Tavistock.

Kernberg, O. F. (1965). Notes on countertransference. *Journal of the American Psychoanalytic Association* 13:38–56.

———. (1970). Factors in the treatment of narcissistic personalities. *Journal of the American Psychoanalytic Association* 18:51–85.

———. (1974). Further contributions to the treatment of narcissistic personalities. *International Journal of Psychoanalysis* 55:215–240.

———. (1975). *Borderline Conditions and Pathological Narcissism*. New York: Jason Aronson.

———. (1976). *Object Relations Theory and Clinical Psychoanalysis*. New York: Jason Aronson.

———. (1980). *Internal World and External Reality: Object Relations Theory Applied*. New York: Jason Aronson.

———. (1984). *Severe Personality Disorders: Psycho-therapeutic Strategies*. New Haven: Yale University Press.

———. (1988). Identity, alienation, and ideology in adolescent group processes. In: *Fantasy, Myth, and Reality*. Madison, Conn.: International Universities Press, pp. 381–399.

———. (1989a). The narcissistic personality disorder and the differential diagnosis of antisocial behavior. *Psychiatric Clinics of North America* 12(3):553–570.

———. (1989b). A theoretical frame for the study of sexual perversions. In: *The Psychoanalytic Core: Festschrift in Honor of Dr. Leo Rangell*. H. P. Blum, E. M. Weinshel, and F. R. Rodman, eds. New York: International Universities Press, pp. 243–263.

———. (1989c). An ego psychology object relations theory of the structure and treatment of pathologic narcissism. *Psychiatric Clinics of North America* 12(3):723–729.

———. (1991). Sadomasochism, sexual excitement, and perversion. *Journal of the American Psychoanalytic Association* 39:333–362.

———. (1992a). *Aggression in Personality Disorders and Perversions*. New Haven: Yale University Press.

———. (1992b). Paranoiagenesis in organizations. In: *Comprehensive Textbook of Group Psychotherapy*. H. Kaplan and B. J. Sadock, eds. Baltimore: Williams and Wilkins, pp. 47–57.

———. (1993a). Acute and chronic countertransference reactions (German translation). In: *Wege zur Deutung im psychoanalytischen Prozess*. G. Junkers, ed. Bremen: Arbeitstagung der Deutschen Psychoanalytischen Vereinigung, pp. 35–57.

———. (1993b). Convergences and divergences in contemporary psychoanalytic technique. *International Journal of Psychoanalysis* 74:659–673.

———. (1993c). Psychoanalytic object relations theories. In: *Key Concepts of Psychoanalysis*. W. Mertens, ed. Munich: Klett-Cotta, 96–104. Also in: *Psychoanalysis: The Major Concepts,* B. E. Moore and B. D. Fine, eds. New Haven: Yale University Press, 1995, 450–462.

———. (1993d). The psychotherapeutic treatment of borderline patients. In: *Borderline Personality Disorder: Etiology and Treatment*. J. Paris, ed. Washington, D.C.: American Psychiatric Press, pp. 261–284.

―――. (1993e). Suicidal behavior in borderline patients: Diagnostic and psychotherapeutic considerations. *American Journal of Psychotherapy* 47(2):245–254.

―――. (1994). Aggression, trauma, hatred in the treatment of borderline patients. *Psychiatric Clinics of North America* 17(4):701–714.

―――. (1995). *Love Relations in Normality and Pathology.* New Haven: Yale University Press.

―――. (1996a). The analyst's authority in the psychoanalytic situation. *Psychoanalytic Quarterly* 65(1):137–157.

―――. (1996b). A psychoanalytic theory of personality disorders. In: *Major Theories of Personality Disorders,* J. F. Clarkin and M. F. Lenzenweger, eds. New York: Guilford Press, pp. 106–140.

―――. (1997a). The interpretation of the transference: Merton Gill's contribution. Presented at the panel "Analyzing Transference: Contemporary Responses to Merton Gill," at the annual meeting of the American Psychoanalytic Association, San Diego, California, May 16, 1997.

―――. (1997b). The nature of interpretation: Intersubjectivity and the third position. *American Journal of Psychoanalysis* 57(4): 297–312.

―――. (1999). Psychoanalysis, psychoanalytic psychotherapy, and supportive psychotherapy: Contemporary controversies. *International Journal of Psychoanalysis* 80(6):1075–1091.

―――. (2001). Recent developments in the technical approaches of English-language psychoanalytic schools. *Psychoanalytic Quarterly* 70(3):519–547.

―――. (2003). The management of affect storms in the psychoanalytic psychotherapy of borderline patients. *Journal of the American Psychoanalytic Association* 51(2):517–544.

Kernberg, O. F., E. D. Burstein, L. Coyne, A. Applebaum, L. Horwitz, and H. Voth. (1972). *Psychotherapy and Psychoanalysis: The Final Report of the Menninger Foundation's Psychotherapy Research Project.* Kansas: Menninger Foundation, vol. 36, nos. 1 and 2.

Kernberg, O. F., M. A. Selzer, H. W. Koenigsberg, A. C. Carr, and A. Appelbaum. (1989). *Psychodynamic Psychotherapy of Borderline Patients.* New York: Basic Books.

Kernberg, P. F. (1989). Narcissistic personality disorder in childhood. In *Psychiatric Clinics of North America.* New York: W. B. Saunders, pp. 671–694.

Kernberg, P. F., and A. K. Richards. (1994). Love in preadolescence as seen through children's letters. In *The Spectrum of Psychoanalysis: Essays in Honor of Martin Bergman.* A. K. Richards and A. D. Richards, eds. Madison, Conn.: International Universities Press, pp. 199–218.

Kernberg, P. F., A. S. Weiner, and K. K. Bardenstein. (2000). *Personality Disorders in Children and Adolescents.* New York: Basic Books.

Klein, M. (1940). Mourning and its relation to manic-depressive states. In: *Contributions to Psychoanalysis, 1921–1945.* London: Hogarth Press, 1948, pp. 311–338.

―――. (1946). Notes on some schizoid mechanisms. In: *Developments in Psychoanalysis.* J. Riviere, ed. London: Hogarth Press, 1952, pp. 292–320.

―――. (1952). The origins of transference. In: *Envy and Gratitude.* New York: Basic Books, 1957, pp. 48–56.

―――. (1957). *Envy and Gratitude.* New York: Basic Books.

Koenigsberg, H. W., O. F. Kernberg, M. H. Stone, A. Appelbaum, F. E. Yeomans, and D. Diamond. (2000). *Borderline Patients: Extending the Limits of Treatability.* New York: Basic Books.

Kohon, G. (1986). *The British School of Psychoanalysis: The Independent Tradition.* London: Free Association Books.

Kohut, H. (1968). The psychoanalytic treatment of narcissistic personality disorders. *Psychoanalytic Study of the Child* 23:86–113.

———. (1971). *The Analysis of the Self.* New York: International Universities Press.

———. (1972). Thoughts on narcissism and narcissistic rage. *Psychoanalytic Study of the Child* 27:360–400.

———. (1977). *The Restoration of the Self.* New York: International Universities Press, 1977.

———. (1979). Two analyses of Mr. Z. *International Journal of Psychoanalysis* 60:3–27.

Krause, R. (1988). Eine Taxonomie der Affekte un ihre Anwendung auf das Verständnis der frühen Störungen. *Psychotherapie und Medizinische Psychologie* 38:77–86.

Krause, R., and P. Lutolf. (1988). Facial indicators of transference processes in psychoanalytical treatment. In: *Psychoanalytic Process Research Strategies.* H. Dahl and H. Kachele, eds. Heidelberg: Springer, pp. 257–272.

Laplanche, J. (1992). *Seduction, Translation, Drives.* London: Institute of Contemporary Arts.

Liberman, D. (1983). *Lingüística, interacción comunicativa y proceso psicoanalítico.* Buenos Aires: Ediciones Kargieman.

Linehan, M. M. (1993). *Cognitive-Behavioral Treatment of Borderline Personality Disorder.* New York: Guilford Press.

Little, M. (1951). Countertransference and the patient's response to it. *International Journal of Psychoanalysis* 32:32–40.

Loewald, H. W. (1986). Transference-countertransference. *Journal of the American Psychoanalytic Association* 34:275–287.

Lussier, A. (1982). *Les Déviations du désir: Etude sur le fétichisme.* Paris: Presses Universitaires de France.

Mahler, M., and M. Furer. (1968). *On Human Symbiosis and the Vicissitudes of Individuation.* New York: International Universities Press.

Mahler, M., F. Pine, and A. Bergman. (1975). *The Psychological Birth of the Human Infant.* New York: Basic Books.

Marziali, E. (1992). The etiology of borderline personality disorder: Developmental factors. In: *Borderline Personality Disorder.* John F. Clarkin et al., eds. New York: Guilford Press, pp. 27–44.

Matte-Blanco, I. (1975). *The Unconscious as Infinite Sets.* London: Duckworth.

———. (1988). *Thinking, Feeling, and Being.* London: Routledge.

McDougall, J. (1993). Countertransference and primitive communication. In: *Countertransference: Theory, Technique, Teaching.* A. Alexandris and G. Vaslamatzis, eds. London: Karnac Books, pp. 95–133.

McGlashan, T. H., and R. K. Heinssen. (1989). Narcissistic, antisocial, and noncomorbid subgroups of borderline disorder: Are they distinct entities by long-term clinical profile? *Psychiatric Clinics of North America* 12(3):653–670.

Meltzer, D. (1977). *Sexual States of Mind.* Perthshire, Scotland: Clunie Press, pp. 132–139.

Meltzer, D., and M. H. Williams. (1988). *The Apprehension of Beauty.* Old Ballechin, Strath Toy, Scotland: Clunie Press.

Milgram, S. (1963). Behavioral study of obedience. *Journal of Abnormal and Social Psychology* 67:371–378.

Mitchell, S. A. (1988). *Relational Concepts in Psychoanalysis.* Cambridge: Harvard University Press.

Modell, A. (1976). The holding environment and the therapeutic action of psychoanalysis. *Journal of the American Psychoanalytic Association* 24:255–307.

Morris, A., T. Cooper, and P. J. Cooper. (1989). The changing shape of female fashion models. *International Journal of Eating Disorders* 8:593–596.

Näcke, P. (1899). Die sexuellen Perversitäten in der Irrenanstalt. *Psychiatrische en Neurologische Bladen* 3:122–149.

Ogden, T. H. (1993). The analytic management and interpretation of projective identification. In: *Countertransference: Theory, Technique, Teaching.* A. Alexandris and G. Vaslamatzis, eds. London: Karnac Books, pp. 21–46.

Oldham, J. M. (1994). Personality disorders. *Journal of the American Medical Association* 272:1770–1776.

Paris, J. (1994a). *Borderline Personality Disorder.* Washington, D.C.: American Psychiatric Press.

———. (1994b). Sexual abuse and dissociative processes in the etiology of borderline personality disorder. Plenary presentation of the Conference on Borderline Personality Disorder of the New York Hospital–Cornell Medical Center, Westchester Division, June 9, 1994.

Perry, J. C., and J. L. Herman. (1993). Trauma and defense in the etiology of borderline personality disorder. In: *Borderline Personality Disorder.* Joel Paris, ed. Washington, D.C.: American Psychiatric Press, pp. 123–140.

Pick, I. B. (1985). Working through in the countertransference. *International Journal of Psychoanalysis* 66:157–166.

Plakun, E. (1989). Narcissistic personality disorder: A validity study and comparison to borderline personality disorder. In: *Narcissistic Personality Disorder: Psychiatric Clinics of North America.* Otto F. Kernberg, ed. Philadelphia: W. B. Saunders, pp. 603–620.

———, ed. (1990). *New Perspectives on Narcissism.* Washington, D.C.: American Psychiatric Press.

Pulver, S. (1970). Narcissism: The term and the concept. *Journal of the American Psychoanalytic Association* 18:319–341.

Racker, H. (1957). The meaning and uses of countertransference. *Psychoanalytic Quarterly* 26:303–357.

Reich, A. (1951). On countertransference. *International Journal of Psychoanalysis* 32:25–31.

———. (1953). Narcissistic object choice in women. *Journal of the American Psychoanalytic Association* 1:22–44.

———. (1960). Pathologic forms of self-esteem regulation. *Psychoanalytic Study of the Child* 15:215–232.

Rinsley, D. B. (1989). Notes on the developmental pathogenesis of narcissistic personality disorder. *Psychiatric Clinics of North America* 12(3):695–707.

Riviere, J. A. (1936). A contribution to the analysis of the negative therapeutic reaction. *International Journal of Psychoanalysis* 17:304–320.

Rockland, L. H. (1989). *Supportive Therapy: A Psychodynamic Approach.* New York: Basic Books.

———. (1992). *Supportive Therapy for Borderline Patients: A Psychodynamic Approach.* New York: Guilford Press.

Ronningstam, E., and J. Gunderson. (1989). Descriptive studies on narcissistic personality disorder. In: *Narcissistic Personality Disorder: Psychiatric Clinics of North America.* Otto F. Kernberg, ed. Philadelphia: W. B. Saunders, pp. 585–602.

Rosenfeld, H. (1964). On the psychopathology of narcissism: A clinical approach. *International Journal of Psychoanalysis* 45:332–337.

———. (1971). A clinical approach to the psychoanalytic theory of the life and death instincts: An investigation into the aggressive aspects of narcissism. *International Journal of Psychoanalysis* 52: 169–178.

———. (1975). Negative therapeutic reaction. In: *Tactics and Techniques in Psychoanalytic Therapy,* vol. 2, *Countertransference.* P. L. Giovacchini, ed. New York: Jason Aronson, pp. 217–228.

———. (1978). Notes on the psychopathology and psychoanalytic treatment of some borderline patients. *International Journal of Psychoanalysis* 59:215–221.

———. (1987). *Impasse and Interpretation: Therapeutic and Anti-Therapeutic Factors in the Psychoanalytic Treatment of Psychotic, Borderline, and Neurotic Patients.* London: Tavistock Publications.

Sadger, J. (1908). Fragment der psychoanalyse eines homosexuellen. *Jahrbuch für Sexuelle Zwischenstufen* 9:339–424.

Sandler, J. (1976). Countertransference and role responsiveness. *International Review of Psychoanalysis* 3:43–47.

Sandler, J., and A. M. Sandler. (1987). The past unconscious, the present unconscious, and the vicissitudes of guilt. *International Journal of Psychoanalysis* 8:331–341.

———. (1998a). *Internal Objects Revisited.* London: Karnac Books.

———. (1998b). On role-responsiveness. In: *Internal Objects Revisited.* London: Karnac Books, pp. 47–56.

Scheidlinger, S., ed. (1980). *Psychoanalytic Group Dynamics.* New York: International Universities Press.

Searles, H. (1965). *Collected Papers on Schizophrenia and Related Subjects.* New York: International Universities Press.

Segal, H. (1981). Countertransference. In: *The Work of Hanna Segal.* Northvale, N.J.: Jason Aronson, pp. 81–87.

Sherwood, V. R., and C. P. Cohen. (1994). *Psychotherapy of the Quiet Borderline Patient.* Northvale, N.J.: Jason Aronson.

Spillius, E. B. (1988). *Melanie Klein Today: Developments in Theory and Practice.* London: Routledge.

Steinberg, B. J., et al. (1994). The cholinergic and noradrenergic neurotransmitter systems and affective instability in borderline personality disorder. In: *Biological and Neurobehav-*

ioral Studies of Borderline Personality Disorder. Kenneth R. Silk, ed. Washington, D.C.: American Psychiatric Press, pp. 41–62.

Steiner, J. (1987). The interplay between pathological organizations and the paranoid-schizoid position. *International Journal of Psychoanalysis* 68:69–80; also in *Melanie Klein Today,* vol. 1, *Mainly Theory,* ed. E. B. Spillius. London: Routledge, 1988, pp. 324–342.

———. (1990). Pathological organizations as obstacles to mourning: The role of unbearable guilt. *International Journal of Psychoanalysis* 71:87–94.

———. (1993). *Psychic Retreats: Pathological Organizations in Psychotic, Neurotic, and Borderline Patients.* London: Routledge.

Steiner, R. (1989). On narcissism: The Kleinian approach. *Psychiatric Clinics of North America* 12(3):741–770.

Stoller, R. J. (1975). *Perversion: The Erotic Form of Hatred.* Washington, D.C.: American Psychiatric Press.

———. (1979). *Sexual Excitement.* New York: Pantheon.

———. (1985). *Observing the Erotic Imagination.* New Haven: Yale University Press.

Stone, M. H. (1980). *The Borderline Syndromes.* New York: McGraw-Hill.

———. (1989a). Murder. *Psychiatric Clinics of North America* 12(3):643–651.

———. (1989b). Long-term follow-up of narcissistic/borderline patients. *Psychiatric Clinics of North America* 12(3):621–641.

———. (1990). *The Fate of Borderline Patients.* New York: Guilford Press.

———. (1993a). *Abnormalities of Personality.* New York: W. W. Norton.

———. (1993b). Etiology of borderline personality disorder: Psychobiological factors contributing to an underlying irritability. In: *Borderline Personality Disorder.* Joel Paris, ed. Washington, D.C.: American Psychiatric Press, pp. 87–102.

———. (1994). Characterologic subtypes of the borderline personality disorder: With a note on prognostic factors. In: *Borderline Personality Disorder: The Psychiatric Clinics of North America.* Isaiah Share, ed. Philadelphia: W. B. Saunders, pp. 773–784.

Tartakoff, H. (1966). The normal personality in our culture and the Nobel Prize complex. In: *Psychoanalysis: A General Psychology.* R. M. Lowenstein et al., eds. New York: International Universities Press, pp. 222–252.

Torgersen, A. M. (1985). Temperamental differences in infants and six-year-old children: A follow-up study of twins. In: *The Biological Basis of Personality and Behavior: Theories, Measurement, Techniques, and Development.* J. Strelau, F. H. Farley, and A. Gale, eds. Washington, D.C.: Hemisphere Publishing.

———. (1994). Genetics of personality disorder. Presented at the First European Congress on Disorders of Personality, June 16, 1994. Nijmegen, The Netherlands.

Tower, L. E. (1956). Countertransference. *Journal of the American Psychoanalytic Association* 4:224–255.

van der Kolk, B. A., et al. (1994). Trauma and the development of borderline personality disorder. In: *Borderline Personality Disorder: The Psychiatric Clinics of North America.* Isaiah Share, ed. Philadelphia: W. B. Saunders, pp. 715–730.

van der Waals, H. G. (1965). Problems of narcissism. *Bulletin of the Menninger Clinic* 29:293–322.

van Reekum, R., et al. (1994). Impulsivity in borderline personality disorder. In: *Biological and Neurobehavioral Studies of Borderline Personality Disorder.* Kenneth R. Silk, ed. Washington, D.C.: American Psychiatric Press, pp. 1–22.

Volkan, V. (1973). Transitional fantasies in the analysis of a narcissistic personality. *Journal of the American Psychoanalytic Association* 21:351–376.

———. (1976). *Primitive Internalized Object Relations.* New York: International Universities Press.

———. (1979). The "glass bubble" of the narcissistic patient. In: *Advances in Psychotherapy of the Borderline Patient.* J. Leboit and A. Capponi, eds. New York: Jason Aronson, pp. 405–431.

———. (1987). *Six Steps in the Treatment of Borderline Personality Organization.* Northvale, N.J.: Jason Aronson.

———. (1993). Countertransference reactions commonly present in the treatment of patients with borderline personality. In: *Countertransference: Theory, Technique, Teaching.* A. Alexandris and G. Vaslamatzis, eds. London: Karnac Books, pp. 147–163.

Wallerstein, R. S. (1991). Scales of psychological capacity.

———. (1995). *The Talking Cures: The Psychoanalyses and the Psychotherapies.* New Haven: Yale University Press.

Widiger, T. A., and A. J. Frances. (1994). Toward a dimensional model of the personality disorders. In: *Personality Disorders and the Five-Factor Model of Personality.* P. T. Costa and T. Widiger, eds. Washington, D.C.: American Psychological Association, pp. 19–40.

Widiger, T. A., et al. (1994). A description of the DSM-III-R and DSM-IV personality disorders with the five-factor model of personality. In: *Personality Disorders and the Five-Factor Model of Personality.* P. T. Costa and T. Widiger, eds. Washington, D.C.: American Psychological Association, pp. 41–56.

Widlöcher, D., and A. Braconnier. (1996). Traitement psychanalytique. In: *Psychanalyse et psychothérapies.* Paris: Médecine-Sciences, Flammarion.

Widlöcher, D., and Prot, V. A. (1996). *Psychanalyse et psychothérapies.* Paris: Médecine-Sciences, Flammarion.

Winnicott, D. W. (1949). Hate in the countertransference. *International Journal of Psychoanalysis* 30:69–75.

———. (1958). *Collected Papers: Through Pediatrics to Psycho-Analysis.* New York: Basic Books.

———. (1960a). Ego distortion in terms of true and false self. In: *The Maturational Processes and the Facilitating Environment.* New York: International Universities Press, 1965, pp. 140–152.

———. (1960b). The theory of the parent-infant relationship. In: *The Maturational Processes and the Facilitating Environment.* New York: International Universities Press, 1965, pp. 37–55.

Yehuda, R., et al. (1994). Peripheral catecholamine alterations in borderline personality disorder. In: *Biological and Neurobehavioral Studies of Borderline Personality Disorder.* Kenneth R. Silk, ed. Washington, D.C.: American Psychiatric Press, pp. 63–90.

Yeomans, F. E., J. Gutfreund, M. A. Selzer, J. F. Clarkin, J. W. Hull, and T. E. Smith. (1994).

Factors related to drop-outs by borderline patients: Treatment contract and therapeutic alliance. *Journal of Psychotherapy Practice and Research* 3:16–24.

Yeomans, F. E., M. A. Selzer, and J. F. Clarkin. (1992). *Treating the Borderline Patient: A Contract-Based Approach.* New York: Basic Books.

Zinoviev, A. (1984). *The Reality of Communism.* New York: Schocken.

Index

Abraham, K., 14, 47

Abuse. *See* Physical abuse; Sexual abuse

Acting out, 43, 44, 73, 103, 122–23, 125, 139–40, 153, 180, 191, 207, 208, 212, 233–34, 240, 244

Adolescents: identity diffusion in, 61–64, 67; normal identity crisis in, 61; neurotic personality organization in, 62, 64; superego in, 62–64, 75; love experiences of, 63, 74–75; psychotic personality organization in, 64–66; reality testing in, 64–66; diagnosis of narcissistic pathology in, 66–69; and school failure, 67–68; antisocial personality disorder in, 69–72, 137–38; diagnostic evaluation of character pathology in, 72–75; sexuality of, 74–75; with malig-

nant narcissism syndrome, 138–39

Affect storms: of borderline patients, 220–44; clinical manifestations of, 220–23; transference-focused psychotherapy (TFP) for, 220, 228–44; and countertransference, 222, 224, 225–26, 229–32, 237–38, 243–44; and transference, 222–24, 228–44; theoretical formulations of, 223–28; and Matte-Blanco's theory of bi-logical functioning, 224–26, 229; Green's formulations on, 226–27; Kleinian and generally British contributions on, 226; ego-psychological approach to, 227–28; complications of severe affect storms, 234–41; double-edged affect storms, 239–40; clinical case illustration of, 241–44

Primitive transferences, 26, 244
Projective counteridentification, 179, 190, 191
Projective identification, 186–88, 226, 229, 244
Prot, V. A., 98
Pseudologia fantastica, 58
Pseudo-psychopathic schizophrenia, 136
Pseudostupidity, 37, 179
Psychoanalysis: of personality disorders, 22, 23–26; biases in, 77; and sexual normality, 77–78; for perversions, 84–91; and erotic capability, 90–91; contemporary controversies in, 95–119; relation between psychoanalytic psychotherapy and, 95–99, 102–7, 115–19; objective of, 99; Gill's definition of, 100–101, 115; techniques of, 100–102, 105–7, 115; strategy in, 106, 107; tactics of, 107; indications and contraindications for, 108, 116–17, 230; critique of author's theoretical approach to, 109–10; and eating disorders, 207. *See also* Countertransference; Transference
Psychoanalytic psychotherapy: of personality disorders, 22, 23–26; and envy, 35–36, 43–44, 172, 238; and transferences dominated by hatred, 37–44; of incest victims, 39–42; for borderline personality organization, 84, 114, 120–29; for perversions, 84–91; contemporary controversies in, 95–119; relation between psychoanalysis and, 95–99, 102–7, 115–19; training in, 95–96, 112–14; definition of, 98–99; objective of, 99; free association in, 102, 123, 168, 172, 221, 222; techniques of, 102–7; relation between supportive psychotherapy and, 104–5, 106; strategy in, 106, 107; indications and contraindications for, 107–9; tactics of, 107; critique of author's theoretical approach to, 109–10; and psychopathic, narcissistic, and

paranoid transference, 130–53; for antisocial personality disorder, 135–38; for malignant narcissism syndrome, 138–39; priorities of urgency of intervention, 139–40; for sexual inhibition in patient with narcissistic personality disorder, 154–66; acute and chronic countertransference reactions, 167–83; omnipotence in transference and countertransference, 184–91; suicide risk in severe personality disorders, 192–204; eating disorders in borderline patients, 205–19; and affect storms in borderline patients, 220–44. *See also* Countertransference; Limit-setting; Technical neutrality; Transference; Transference-focused psychotherapy (TFP)
Psychoanalytic theory of personality disorders: reasons for formulation of, 3; categorical versus dimensional models in, 4–6; temperament, character, and structure of normal personality, 6–11; and affects and drives, 11–14; neurotic personality organization, 13, 14, 17; psychoanalytic model of nosology, 14–17, 22; borderline personality organization, 15, 16–17; psychotic personality organization, 15; and reality testing, 15–16; developmental, structural, and motivational continuities in, 17–23; psychoanalysis and psychoanalytic psychotherapy, 22, 23–26
Psychodrama, psychoanalytic, 111, 117
Psychodynamic psychotherapy, 120–29. *See also* Psychoanalytic psychotherapy
Psychopathic transference, 37, 43, 113, 148–51, 179, 212
Psychopharmacological approaches, 194, 197, 202–3
Psychosomatic disorders, 32
Psychotherapy. *See* Psychoanalytic psychotherapy; Psychodynamic psychotherapy; Supportive psychotherapy;